The Motherlode

100+ WOMEN WHO MADE HIP-HOP

◆ ◆ ◆

CLOVER HOPE

ILLUSTRATIONS BY RACHELLE BAKER

ABRAMS IMAGE, NEW YORK

Table of Contents

INTRODUCTION:
NICE FOR A GIRL

Roxanne Shanté believes she inspired the term "female rapper."

She swears it happened in 1985 during the New Music Seminar at New York's Marriott Marquis—site of the annual MC Battle for World Supremacy. At fifteen years old, Shanté was already a battle rap legend with a hit song, 1984's "Roxanne's Revenge," which made her the first-ever female rap star. She was favored to win. But after making it to the final round, she lost to another acclaimed rapper, Busy Bee, in what could only be described as a heist. There was a consolation prize: Everyone told her she was nice for a girl.

It was clear Shanté got robbed. Years later, one of the judges, Kurtis Blow, maker of the first hit rap record ("Christmas Rappin'"), admitted what was already an established fact in hip-hop—that he scored her low on purpose. Other judges awarded her 8s, 9s, and 10s. Blow gave her a 4, because he didn't like the optics of a girl winning a rap battle, no matter how much she outperformed her opponent.

Because of incidents like this—the possibility of a non-male champion in a rap battle—Shanté says the concept of the "female rapper" was created.

"I was just a great rapper," she said to Jezebel in 2016. "And then, they were like, 'Well, listen Shanté—we understand that you're a great rapper, but why don't you do this: Why don't you settle for being the best female rapper ever?'" She told DJ Vlad in 2018, "Before me, there was no such title as 'female rapper.' Everybody was just 'rappers' and 'MCs.'"

The words "female rapper" did appear in publications before that 1985 battle. The *Boston Globe*, in 1980, referred to the Sequence as "three female rappers," misspelling the group's name as "Sequins" in print. But Shanté's origin story is still valid. That battle marked the day she realized there were different stakes for her—expectations that made it seem like she was inferior. And this naturally shaped the course of history.

By then, hip-hop and rap were two different things: a culture and a business, respectively. Male rappers were "rappers," and women who did it, though talented, were different. They had breasts, which they could flaunt if they wanted, and therefore needed a separate title. They were entering a man's world, and to the mainstream press, their decision to even rap at all seemed astonishing and brave. The words "female rapper" often appear with the phrase "male-dominated" somewhere nearby, alluding to women being "let into" an exclusively male domain (hip-hop) as opposed to being a natural part of it.

"A growing number of women have made 'rapping,' a male-dominated music, their own language of liberation," the *Philadelphia Inquirer* reported in 1985. "Tired of being put down, female rappers are standing up and talking back," reads a New York *Daily News* story from 1991.

"It'd be nice if we were just considered rappers, not 'female rappers.' But hip-hop is male-dominated," rapper/producer Angela Zone, known as Ang 13, said to the *Chicago Tribune* in 2004.

"Female rapper" never sat well with women who thought of themselves as simply rappers who identified as women. Unfortunately, "rapper who identifies as a woman" would be too clunky to say, and "female rapper," or "woman rapper" (both of which are used in this book), is still a better version of the worst word in the world: "femcee," a combination of "female" and "emcee" (which is not used in this book). Even more offensive, somehow, than "femcee" is that British rapper Lady Sovereign was nicknamed "Feminem," as in "female Eminem," defying all reason.

After an initial rush of opportunity in the seventies, when women had to jump through hoops to get on a mic, there was the golden age of the eighties, after which female rappers began occupying token roles on labels, in a music industry that exploited and gradually segregated them over decades, setting many like Shanté up for failure. On assignment for *Vibe* in 2006, I flew to St. Louis to interview Penelope Jones, then a twenty-five-year-old rapper who'd signed to Nelly's Universal Records imprint, Fo' Reel Entertainment. Rappers, at that point, had to have at least one woman in their crew. Penelope was Nelly's artist (though, after being indicted for conspiracy to commit drug trafficking, she later got dropped from the label). St. Louis had been off the radar in rap until Nelly came around and turned the Old MacDonald song into a banger ("E.I."). Penelope

wanted to create a similar sensation. She mentioned another rapper from the city, Ebony Eyez, who had released an album under Capitol Records in 2005, then become a flash in the pan.

"I hated to see that for her, because I really thought that she would do better than she did," Penelope said. "It's scary for me, looking at what happened with her and seeing how people embrace female rappers, so that's something that's really been on my mind a lot. Female rappers don't make it as much." Trina, Eve, Missy Elliott, Remy Ma, and Shawnna had sold millions of records during an era when female rappers were prolific. But as Penelope expected, her own odds of success were low. She never released an album. Then came the infamous fourteen-year Grammy drought, a time when the number of female rappers signed to major labels hit a historic bottom (from forty in the late eighties and early nineties to three in 2010). The music industry's failure of imagination led to a near wipeout.

When Nicki Minaj found global success as a rapper, pop star, and entertainer after years without a woman rapper on the top of the charts or in mainstream conversations, she made a point of clarifying her status. "Absolutely, I do not see myself as a female rapper anymore, I'm sorry," she told MTV News in 2014. "I see myself as a rapper . . . I've worked with the greats, and I've held my own with the greats, and they respect me, so I should respect myself enough to see myself the same way they see themselves."

While her instinct was to base her fame and sales success on the same metrics as men, she knew,

"FEMALE RAPPER" NEVER SAT WELL WITH WOMEN WHO THOUGHT OF THEMSELVES AS SIMPLY RAPPERS WHO IDENTIFIED AS WOMEN.

like Shanté, that having a separate label for women—that being seen as a "female rapper"—would exclude her from being considered the *best* rapper—something rap fans love debating, even though there's no real answer.

Given how women have rejected the title, I hesitated to use "female rapper" in this book. Whenever a woman broke a record in rap, it was a milestone worth celebrating that would otherwise get lost in a profession where men claim the highest titles—in which case "female rapper" became a badge of honor. MC Lyte was the first female rapper with a gold record in 1993. Salt-N-Pepa were the first female rappers to win a Grammy Award (Queen Latifah won Best Rap Solo Performance the same year). Da Brat was the first to go platinum, when record labels believed women couldn't sell. Lauryn Hill was the first female rapper to have a No. 1 single on the *Billboard* Hot 100, in 1998, and Cardi B became the first to have three.

In 2019, more women made a case for change. Megan Thee Stallion, a rapper out of Houston, had fans across genres treating her "Hot Girl Summer" slogan like a proverb. "I am female, and I am a rapper. But I don't like the term when it's used to put you in a box," she told me in an interview for *W* magazine. "Don't call me a female rapper because you think that you're putting me in a category. 'Cause I am an artist. I just so happen to be female and I rap." That year, too, the Brew Podcast tweeted a very bogus-looking "Top 50 Rappers of All Time" list absent of any women, not even Lauryn Hill, causing widespread strife on the internet, as if the list held any authority, and ironically at a time when more women were thriving, releasing projects, and building fan bases: Nicki Minaj, Cardi B, Megan Thee Stallion, Lizzo, Saweetie, Noname, City Girls, Kash Doll, Doja Cat, et al. It'd

been more than a decade since there wasn't just one trendsetting female rapper, and so many of them controlling their image and art.

While the mainstream model of success was still largely reliant on sex appeal, there were finally more options. That year, a record seven women rappers entered the *Billboard* Hot 100 chart. With more women seamlessly breaking into rap and becoming the genre's figureheads, it was a good time to challenge the use of "female rapper" and ideas about women being separate but equal.

The Motherlode, a title taken from Yo-Yo's 1991 debut album, *Make Way for the Motherlode*, covers the rise and fall and rise of generations of female rappers, some of it explained in their own words. Some of the women are icons, others lesser known but no less pivotal to the foundation and evolution of hip-hop. Instead of writing complete biographies, I wanted to focus on each rapper's contributions, be it a song, a look, or a movement. There's also commentary from producers, directors, writers, and stylists who help tell a version of hip-hop history from the perspective of black and Latina women who cocreated it.

My last anecdote comes courtesy of Ludacris, who I spoke to in 2008 for an *XXL* cover story about his balance of being a rap star and actor. We talked about his new album and his being underrated as a rapper, and by the end of the interview, he admitted to having misconceptions of his own.

"I never judge anybody," he said. "But my stereotype and my instinct subconsciously was that . . . what does this girl, like, really know about hip-hop? And I'm sure a lot of people say that." (Yes.) He went on. "But as I have a conversation with you, I start realizing how much of a hip-hop fan you are," he said. "And I can only respect that."

He was telling me I was nice for a girl.

WHENEVER A WOMAN BROKE A RECORD IN RAP, IT WAS A MILESTONE WORTH CELEBRATING THAT WOULD OTHER-WISE GET LOST.

THE FIRST WOMEN

One of the quietest battles in hip-hop began with an unresolved question: Who was the first female rapper? There were many of them in the seventies—Sweet N' Sour ran with DJ Kool Herc, the father of hip-hop, as did an MC named Pebblee Poo. But Herc once gave the title of "first" to someone else, MC Smiley, a one-time member of Mercedes Ladies. MC Sha-Rock, a member of the Funky Four Plus One, disagreed, and so she settled the issue in writing, citing decades of confusion and what she viewed as inaccuracies: "Everybody in New York City knew not only was I the first female MC, but I also was the best female MC," she wrote in her 2010 memoir. Her book title left no further room for error: *Luminary Icon . . . : The Story of the Beginning and End of Hip Hop's First Female MC*.

Calling Sha-Rock "one of the firsts" or even "the first prominent female MC," she says, isn't enough. She was a founding member of hip-hop in the early seventies, an MC, and a B-girl—the girls who break-danced, which is one of hip-hop culture's four elements, next to deejaying, emceeing, and graffiti. "When you say 'prominent,' that's an understatement. I was more than that. I laid the foundation for every female MC that came after me," she says. "I rocked at more park jams and venues in New York City. I traveled from borough to borough and state to state bringing rhyming and MC styles to others that didn't know about what was going on in the Bronx."

Sheri Sher, of Mercedes Ladies, agrees. "I'm from the Bronx, and the only person I would say was the first is Sha-Rock."

To the women in hip-hop who were never awarded the reverence of, say, an Elvis (the "King of Rock," despite not having invented rock), being known as first is what secures their legacy. Privately and publicly, they've disputed facts, debating not just which of them came first but also secondary titles, like who was the first solo female MC, separate from being part of a crew.

In the absence of *Billboard* charts, press, and social media to validate an MC's popularity in the seventies, stories and memories later served as receipts. There was also physical evidence: event flyers, cassette tapes, and the occasional rare video to cement their place.

Pebblee Poo uses her membership in DJ Kool Herc's crew, the Herculoids, as a starting point. She remembers joining Herc's crew at around age fourteen, after an MC named Dr. Bombay took her to rhyme for Herc at Cedar Park in the Bronx. "Kool Herc is the father of hip-hop," she says, "so I am the first female hip-hop soloist."

The Kool Herc affiliation is key, since he's known as the Einstein of hip-hop. In 1967, he immigrated from Jamaica to the Bronx at age twelve, bringing his deep knowledge of sound systems with him. On August 11, 1973, his sister Cindy Campbell threw a back-to-school jam in a rec room at 1520 Sedgwick Avenue. As Herc deejayed the party, he extended the "breaks" in the records on vinyl—the points where the vocalists drop out to let the rhythm breathe—a simple innovation that was huge: He flipped the essence of disco, the popular black music at the time, into something fresh, and from there, he became the man who, thanks to a woman (his sister), gave birth to hip-hop.

The hottest DJs (Grandmaster Flash, Afrika Bambaataa) adapted Herc's style, adding twists and scratches, a technique credited to DJ Grand Wizzard Theodore. Every kid in the Bronx wanted to be an MC (they only later became known as rappers), and many of them tried. There was Coke La Rock (Kool Herc's MC, recognized as the first) and Queen Kenya, who was part of Bambaataa's Universal Zulu Nation. But Sha-Rock remembers, "Queen Kenya made announcements. She would say something like, 'Get 'em, Bam. Get 'em, Bam.' But she wasn't an MC that would kick rhymes."

The MCs who performed enough shows could be famous in the Bronx, which meant their name would appear on flyers, plastered across the borough. Their crew would perform in parks, schoolyards, community centers, at house parties, and on street blocks, as what started out as a culture evolved into a lucrative industry.

As a member of her brother's group, Master Don and the Death Committee, Pebblee Poo performed and also recorded a handful of songs with Enjoy Records, including the 1982 single "Funkbox Party, Pt. 1," where she raps, "Well, ladies, if you got a man / And he's making all the money that he can, throw ya hands in the air." (Master P sampled the "uhh!" part for the hook to "Make 'Em Say Uhh!"). Pebblee Poo followed up with her solo single "A Fly Guy" in 1985.

She has more credentials. In October 2005, she received a letter on behalf of the New York State Senate, signed by Rubén Díaz Sr., a Bronx district senator at the time. It's imprinted with an official state seal and declares her "the first woman to perform as a hip-hop soloist."

"There were no physical records, but you know where you stood," says Pebblee Poo. "And sometimes you wanna consider yourself something that you're not. But if nobody speaks up or lets you talk, then how do things get rectified?"

Debbie D has a different recollection of who was the first solo female MC. "It can't be, 'I got on the mic with Kool Herc and that makes me a soloist,'" she says. "If I go downstairs and change my tires, does that make me a mechanic?" Before Debbie D broke out as a soloist, she was part of DJ Patty Duke & the Jazzy 5 MCs, when crews were still the best way to gain notoriety. At the tail end of 1981, she toured the tristate area with Wanda Dee, a well-known beatboxer and DJ. She also appeared in the 1984 movie *Beat Street* with MC Sha-Rock and Lisa Lee as the trio Us Girls—before joining DJ Marley Marl's Juice Crew All-Stars— and stamped her solo career with a pair of records, produced by Marley Marl: "Tom, Dick and Harry" and "The Other Woman."

In 2017, Debbie D started posting throwback hip-hop event flyers on Instagram, with captions dissecting names, venues, and artwork based on her own empirical data. "Early hip hop flyers (pre 79) were made by the person sponsoring the party or drawn by hand by (graffiti) artists," one caption reads. There are plenty of flyers with her name on them, including a pink flyer, dated September 12, 1980, for a birthday party at the T-Connection in the Bronx; it's available on Cornell University's

DEBBIE D

NEVER FORGET:
She describes herself as "the first female MC to break out from a male crew and become a female soloist."

WHO SHE IS:
Debbie D (Debora Hooper) relocated from Harlem to the Webster Houses in the Bronx in 1976 and started emceeing in 1977. She later joined DJ Patty Duke & the Jazzy 5 MCs, performed shows with DJ Wanda Dee, and was also a member of DJ Marley Marl's Juice Crew.

LISTEN:
On "Tom, Dick and Harry," Debbie D raps, "First of all, it's you that makes us feel / That we're always going after / Yo' dollar bill," noting the irony of men who brag about money while they call women gold diggers.

◆ ◆ ◆

archive of more than one thousand hip-hop event flyers, spanning from 1976 to 1984. Debbie D calls herself a "flyerologist."

"Being able to point out intricate details, the only people that can actually do that are pioneers," she says. "If you didn't live during that time, you wouldn't even know half those people. These are the people I performed with in the parks and at the clubs." She says of Pebblee Poo, "She can't show me twenty flyers. She can't show me five."

These flyers not only mark the spread of hip-hop; they identify who was first to invent a culture and, in turn, who deserves recognition. Even the smallest details are sacred because the average music fan's timeline of women in rap likely begins around MC Lyte, Salt-N-Pepa, or even later—long after Debbie D's era. I asked a small sampling of friends to name the earliest female rapper they could think of, and the answers, predictably, were skewed by age. MC Lyte came up most. One (a person in their late thirties) out of ten said Roxanne Shanté, who's regarded as the first major female rap star, and two precious millennials named Queen Latifah.

In the past, Sha-Rock reached out to women who claimed to be first, including Pebblee Poo, to correct them. In February 2020, Sha-Rock broadcast herself live on Facebook to debunk the timeline Debbie D had been providing online and in interviews, including one in which Debbie D gave credit to Sha-Rock as "the most prominent and the most successful" early female MC. "For Debbie D or anybody to say she was one of the firsts, I'll never settle for that. 'Cause none of them was on the ground floor or front lines when I first started to rhyme at venues or parks," Sha-Rock says. "You'll never come across any other female MC in the winter of 1977 until the end of the summer of 1978 with authentic and un-doctored proof of their existence before Sha-Rock."

Some titles are never up for debate (there's only one Queen of Soul, and it's Aretha Franklin), and some are hedged with ambiguity (including by me, in this book)—a person "is considered" or is "credited as," because history is what a dominant group decides is fact. There are always conflicting versions when no one is keeping score, and the passage of time so easily erodes relevance. As hip-hop made platinum and gold out of an art form born from racism and poverty—and gave power to black men to run a culture they could finally call their own—the women within it battled twice as hard to even be recognized.

But for a generation of women whose cultural output exists mostly as shadows of memories, the ability to archive their history online, at least, is valuable. Debbie D documented her legacy of being first on all social media platforms—Twitter, Facebook, Instagram, SoundCloud, and YouTube—as well as her website. Her list of hip-hop matriarchs (the first women) includes herself, Pebblee Poo, Mercedes Ladies, Lisa Lee, and MC Sha-Rock. They're what she calls "the mothers of the movement." "When you look at a span of work, when you look at the record, you see the same girls," she says. "There's a reason for that. We were your most prominent girls, so we are the matriarchs in the culture."

Some early female MCs would later resent Roxanne Shanté for being recognized as the one who opened doors for other women, becoming a radio star. But anyone who was someone in hip-hop when it formed is an originator. Still, it is nice to have a title or an answer that's definitive, and Sha-Rock presents a convincing case as to why. Saying there is no answer is an unacceptable answer.

"As writers, you like to play it safe. So instead of you having the argument, you'll say, 'Sha-Rock is one of the first female MCs.' Because 'one of the firsts' is easy for y'all to say. Because you don't want the drama. And I have a problem with that," she says. "Because it takes away from the true history of female MCs, as well as my history as the first female MC in a male-dominated area. It matters because that is who you are. That is your brand. That is what you have brought to the history of women, be it hip-hop culture or rap. It matters. It matters that Nicki Minaj was reigning for this amount of years. It matters that Trina had been the reigning queen for this amount of years. It matters that Cardi B won a Grammy. Because these are women who have contributed and broke down barriers in hip-hop."

The arguments and technicalities could be written off as petty. But in their hashing out all the facts, the tension is what forms a more concrete version of history—a collection of firsts—even if these disputes go on forever and ever until the end of time.

PEBBLEE POO

NEVER FORGET:
She considers herself the "first female hip-hop soloist."

WHO SHE IS:
Pebblee Poo (Pebbles Riley), one of fourteen siblings, grew up with her grandmother in the Bronx, after her mother was murdered. By the time Pebblee Poo joined DJ Kool Herc's Herculoids, she'd been a member of the break-dancing crew Smoke-A-Trons, and a highlight of her youth was a talent show at Junior High School 22 in the Bronx, where she danced to a vinyl 45 of Stevie Wonder's "Superstition" set to 78 speed. In 1980, she joined her older brother Donel, aka Master Don, in his group, the Death Committee.

LISTEN:
Pebblee Poo released her solo single, "A Fly Guy," in 1985, after Profile Records founder Cory Robbins asked her to record a response to the Boogie Boys' "A Fly Girl."

MC SHa-ROCK

◆ ◆ ◆

NEVER FORGET:
She's considered (and considers herself to be) hip-hop's first prominent female MC.

WHO SHE IS:
MC Sha-Rock (Sharon Green) was five years old when her mother moved her and her three siblings out of their home in Wilmington, North Carolina, away from their angry, abusive father. She was eight when they left to live in the Bronx and then Harlem—where she discovered poet Nikki Giovanni and singer Betty Wright—and then back to the Bronx, in a one-bedroom apartment on Webster Avenue. She helped form the Funky Four Plus One in 1978.

LISTEN:
One of the longest rap songs ever recorded, "Rappin' and Rocking the House" is nearly sixteen minutes long (equal to the length of about five pop songs in 2020) and finds MC Sha-Rock rapping over a "funky beat": "Four of them fellas / Plus One is me."

◆ ◆ ◆

Saturday Night Live booked primarily white musical guests in its earliest seasons, with the occasional outlier. When Richard Pryor hosted in December 1975 (Season 1), poet Gil Scott-Heron performed. Three episodes later, Bill Withers sang "Ain't No Sunshine" when actor Buck Henry hosted. Appearing on *SNL*—then America's coolest late-night variety series—meant, at that point, you had juice.

On February 14, 1981, in *SNL*'s sixth season, Debbie Harry, lead singer of Blondie, hosted the show and performed an eleven-minute set, then ceded the stage to the Funky Four Plus One, a group of MCs she knew through a mutual friend, Fred Brathwaite, known as Fab 5 Freddy. (Grandmaster Flash once described Freddy as "the liaison between whites downtown and this black culture in the Bronx"; in other words, Freddy was a key connector of hip-hop to the mainstream music world.)

Harry introduced her band's additional guest act that night as "among the best street rappers in the country," and in case the use of "street rappers" didn't give it away, this was among the first nationally televised performances of rap. In the middle of the stage was MC Sha-Rock, around three months pregnant, wearing a fuchsia top and bright white fringed cowboy boots, moving in step with her four bandmates. The group performed their single "That's the Joint," while their DJ, Breakout, stayed in the cut, visible on the lower third of the screen.

Blondie guitarist Chris Stein told *Wax Poetics* in 2015 that the authorities at *SNL* had been "nervous" about the performance. "I remember trying to explain to them how scratching worked. Trying to verbalize what that is for someone who has no idea, it's really difficult," he said. (Scratching is the sound you hear because of a DJ's back-and-forth movement of a vinyl record as it's playing.)

The performance was big. Not only was rap beamed into American households via network TV, but a young black woman was at the forefront. Viewers who'd never known or seen hip-hop until then heard about it through MC Sha-Rock just as rap was gaining national momentum fast. Five and a half months after that *SNL* episode aired, Viacom launched a revolutionary TV network centered around music videos and called it MTV: Music Television. Still, it wasn't until seven years later, in 1988, that MTV debuted a hip-hop program, *Yo! MTV Raps*, with a familiar face, Fab 5 Freddy, as host. This time, his job was to act as a liaison between the world of hip-hop and a young, white, predominantly male TV demographic.

"When you have people like Jay-Z, who says in his book [*Decoded*] that when he first saw the Funky Four on *Saturday Night Live*, it was monumental," says Sha-Rock, "that means that even though they didn't know our history, and they may not have known the extent of how we came to that point, that was a monumental time for all of us."

To understand the significance of the Bronx as the birthplace of hip-hop and the genesis of crews like Funky Four Plus One, it helps to remember how combustible the borough was. A string of fires in the seventies—what author Jeff Chang described as "the fires of abandonment" in his book *Can't Stop Won't Stop: A History of the Hip-Hop Generation*—produced a sea of deserted buildings and storefronts, and a combination of poor budgeting, neglect, and bad governance made the Bronx a near-uninhabitable matrix of overlooked blocks. But gangs that were active the decade prior—Black Assassins, Savage Skulls—disbanded and regrouped as crews, some of which named themselves after neighborhoods and focused on nonbelligerent activities: dancing, deejaying, tagging (graffiti), and music, led by DJ Kool Herc.

The citywide blackout of 1977 led to a rush of "shopping sprees" during which future DJs magically "inherited" turntables and began to host jam sessions in local parks. "DJ equipment wasn't cheap, so everybody went shopping during the blackout," says original Funky Four Plus One member Guy Todd "Rahiem" Williams, who left the group to join Grandmaster Flash and the Furious Five. "When the lights came on, everybody had equipment."

The summer before Sha-Rock started at Evander Childs High School in the Bronx, a boy named JJ taught her how to break-dance. She'd never tried emceeing either but knew she could learn quickly. When DJ Breakout, and his brother Darnell, aka Brothers' Disco, held auditions to find MCs in Breakout's basement one day, Sha-Rock showed up, introduced herself, and traded rhymes with the guys in the room. She met KK Rockwell and Keith Keith that day.

The original members of Funky Four (or Funky Four Plus One, also known as Funky Four Plus One More)—Sha-Rock, KK Rockwell, Rahiem, and Keith Keith—formed in 1978 and switched lineups more than Destiny's Child. Rahiem and Sha-Rock left in 1979; MC Jazzy Jeff and L'il Rodney C then joined. Sha-Rock described the group in her book as "the hood version of Gladys Knight and the Pips." L'il Rodney C and KK Rockwell later left to form a duo, leaving Jazzy Jeff, Keith Keith, Sha-Rock (who returned to become the "Plus One" of the group), and a new member, Ikey C.

The Funky Four, in their prime, performed at popular venues like the T-Connection in the

NOT ONLY WAS RAP BEAMED INTO AMERICAN HOUSEHOLDS VIA NETWORK TV, BUT A YOUNG BLACK WOMAN WAS AT THE FOREFRONT.

Bronx, Harlem World Club, and Webster PAL. MC street battles between crews like themselves, Grandmaster Flash and the Furious Five, and the Cold Crush Brothers propelled the tradition of battling in hip-hop at a time when being part of a unit was vital. Crews were a ticket to fame and, even more so for girls, credibility. "You could not get on nobody's [sound] system in New York City because they had their own crews and they wasn't letting you on at the same time," says Sha-Rock. "You had to be down with a well-known group to play at any venue or rock in any parks."

The Funky Four signed to Enjoy Records for about three months and released their single "Rappin' and Rocking the House" in 1979 before joining Sylvia Robinson's Sugar Hill Records, where they recorded "That's the Joint." Whenever they booked gigs like *SNL*, they were building a bigger profile for hip-hop beyond the New York boroughs. They were successful enough that they began touring, and when Sha-Rock got pregnant, her bandmates worried it would kill their plans. But there were other internal problems, including division over money, as well as contract disputes with Sugar Hill (similar to almost every other act on Sugar Hill), which led to arguments and eventually separation. In all their permutations, the Funky Four is considered the first rap crew to have a female MC, which makes MC Sha-Rock hip-hop's first "First Lady" of a crew, before having women in cliques evolved into something more calculated. "Many groups that were forming were trying to get a girl to be a part of their group; so their group could have a girl that could rhyme like me," she says.

From the 1990s through the 2000s, record labels used the influence of crews and their big-name rappers to continue to market women as protégés: Lil' Kim broke in through Notorious B.I.G., Foxy Brown through LL Cool J and Jay-Z, Eve with Dr. Dre and DMX, Trina via Trick Daddy, Remy Ma with Fat Joe, Nicki Minaj through Lil Wayne. This system of control, whether people saw it that way or not, allowed men to keep power and promote women they considered worthy while keeping male approval as the key to success. More often, the women were seen as accessories.

As Funky Four Plus One dissolved, MC Sha-Rock bounced back in a trio with two of her peers, Debbie D and Lisa Lee; you can see the three of them, as a group called Us Girls, performing in the 1984 movie *Beat Street*. But that was the height of Sha-Rock's career. She recalls recording her first song without the group around 1983 or 1984: an unreleased track with the Sequence's Angie B. (she later changed her name to Angie Stone), who sang on the record, produced by Malcolm McLaren, the famed Sex Pistols manager. (Sha-Rock recorded another song, "The Circuit," with producer Mark the 45 King, in the nineties.) For the most part, the move to recorded rap swallowed up early MCs who couldn't craft hits.

"The majority of us didn't understand the transition that we had to make from being MCs rapping in the parks for free and in the clubs to actually being songwriters and recording artists," says Williams (Rahiem). "That's the reason most of the first generation of pioneers of rap didn't really have hit records and don't have a body of work as far as a musical catalog to reference."

MC Sha-Rock retired from her job as a law enforcement officer in Texas in 2019 and began planning a biopic to stamp her place as a founder and as one of the few early MCs to appear on national network television. After Funky Four Plus One, *SNL* invited another rap act to perform on the show. It was Run-D.M.C., five years later.

WANDA DEE

She Speaks

In the 1920s, Josephine Baker [drew a] road map [for] all the female [entertainers] who came after her. She created the glamour and glitz. She had her own line of makeup, the extended ponytail, the outfits, the catsuits, the banana dance. She was the woman who'd walk down the street in fishnets and a jacket, a cheetah on a leash, with her ass out. She did it all, she did it first, and she didn't get [nearly enough of] the accolades that she deserved.

When I met my husband, Eric, he was like, "Why don't you be the first glamorous female rapper?" He enlisted a hair stylist, Gerard Duré, and said, "Color her hair this color," which was honey blond, and they gave me big, curly, glamorous hair, like [the locks of] Dominique Deveraux or Diana Ross. I went to a video rental store and [collected] a stack of videotapes of all the greats: Josephine Baker, Tina Turner, Eartha Kitt, Diana Ross, Grace Jones, Sarah Vaughan, Cleo Laine, Lena Horne. Eric put together the image and the sound, and he choreographed my dances.

We put together a show and presented it at the World in 1987. We came onstage to an original

NEVER FORGET:
She appears as a DJ in the 1984 movie *Beat Street,* and a young New Edition opened one of her DJ shows in Paterson, New Jersey.

WHO SHE IS:
Wanda Dee (LaWanda Ann McFarland) grew up with five brothers and sisters in Harlem and was raised in the Bronx. She learned deejaying through hip-hop's top DJs Kool Herc and Afrika Bambaataa. Wanda performed shows with MC Debbie D before partnering with another MC, Sisco Kid. She later became a solo artist, releasing scandalous singles like "Blue Eyes" and "I Wanna See You Sweat" in the late eighties and nineties.

LISTEN:
"To the Bone," the type of high-energy song played at sweaty dance clubs, features lyrics like "touch me, crave me" and moaning on the track.

song I wrote and produced called "Use Your Hands." I had Diana Ross hair, a formfitting two-piece spandex outfit, and a white floor-length chinchilla fur coat. In the audience that night was Kadeem Hardison, MC Lyte, Kool Moe Dee, Melle Mel. The place erupted into all kinds of screams and hooting and hollering, 'cause they'd never seen a hip-hop act presented with glamour. It had a mixture of everything: Vegas style and hip-hop dancers. I threw the coat off and revealed the tight red outfit, and the crowd went off.

My husband and I co-wrote "To the Bone," and we wrote it deliberately with double

entendres, tongue-in-cheek, the way Eartha Kitt sang her songs. Sexy but fun. Women [rappers] didn't receive it well, thinking I was a slut selling records with my butt. They were used to jeans and backwards hats. *We gotta wear big hair and makeup and heels?* It was rough. I was just having fun, and while having fun with the genre, I wanted to knock down some doors. I wanted to be remembered as the woman who dared to be different and did it unapologetically.

First Ladies of Rap Crews

MC Glamorous

Not only was she a member of the Glamour Girls trio, she was also one of three women MCs in Marley Marl's Juice Crew All-Stars, alongside Roxanne Shanté and Debbie D. She later left hip-hop and converted to Islam, going by the name Chaplain Jamillah.

Baby Love

An influential B-girl, Daisy Castro was the youngest member of the Rock Steady Crew, a squad of break-dancers. She was fifteen when she rapped on their 1983 song "Hey You" and appeared as a dancer in the movie *Beat Street*.

Jha Jha

Despite her lack of extensive solo output, New York rap fans remember Jha Jha as the sole, tough-talking, female member of Cam'ron's Harlem collective, Dipset.

Magnolia Shorty

A classic New Orleans bounce artist, she signed to Cash Money Records and released one album in 1996, *Monkey on the Dick*. Magnolia died tragically in 2010 in a double homicide while sitting in a car. Drake sampled her voice on his No. 1 *Billboard* Hot 100 single "In My Feelings" in 2018.

Isis

Before changing her name to Lin Que, she ran with the X Clan, a Brooklyn-based crew that pushed black empowerment.

Hurricane G

Part of New York's Hit Squad, the Puerto Rican rapper from Brooklyn appeared on songs with Redman, Keith Murray, Xzibit, and the Cocoa Brovaz. She released two albums, along with her most memorable single, "Somebody Else," about a treacherous guy. She also acts as Sean "Puffy" Combs's hype woman on "PE 2000," the 1999 lead single from his second album, *Forever*.

Ms. Melodie

She was a member of Boogie Down Productions and was married for a time to KRS-One. "I'm Ms. Melodie and I'm a born-again rebel / The violence in rap must cease and settle," she raps on a single, "Self-Destruction," by the collective Stop the Violence Movement. She died in 2012 at age forty-three.

Storm

She joined 2Pac's group Outlawz after meeting him on a film set and appears on three songs on his two-disc album *All Eyez on Me*.

Sweet N' Sour

MCs from the seventies remember her as one of the members of DJ Kool Herc's Herculoids crew who performed with them at events across the Bronx, along with Pebblee Poo.

Ms. Roq

She signed to Aftermath Entertainment and raps with a distinct raspy flow on two tracks on Dr. Dre's *2001* album, "Let's Get High" and "Murder Ink."

Ms. Tee

Label co-founder Ronald "Slim" Williams signed this First Lady of Cash Money Records who popularized the fast-paced bounce music that defines New Orleans hip-hop.

MERCEDES LADIES

In the summer of 1979, a group of girls in the Bronx set out to assemble their own crew. This would be different from other crews in hip-hop, which were mostly filled with boys—it was their version of the Shirelles or the Supremes, stacked with a team of young women who would go around promoting parties, calling themselves Mercedes Young Ladies (later shortened to Mercedes Ladies), because the name sounded sophisticated.

For branding, the girls bought iron-on block letters for twenty cents each and affixed their group name onto T-shirts, sweatshirts, and jackets worn with fitted jeans and slicked-back hair. Their promotional gear worked. At parties, the city's most popular DJs—Grandmaster Flash, Afrika Bambaataa, Breakout—would shout out "Mercedes Young Ladies!" on the mic. Grandmaster Flash and the Furious Five stamped the girls' legacy on wax in the song "Superappin'": "I know a fly young lady would like to ride / In my Mercedes, young ladies."

Mercedes Ladies was the first prominent group of female MCs and DJs in a culture where that's now mostly nonexistent. While the 1990s, the age of Salt-N-Pepa and J.J. Fad, signaled the end of an era for female rap groups, there've been plenty of crews for men: Run-D.M.C., Beastie Boys, N.W.A, and Public Enemy. A Tribe Called Quest, Goodie Mob, Onyx, EPMD, De La Soul, and Wu-Tang Clan. Bone Thugs-N-Harmony, the Roots, Geto Boys, Naughty by Nature, the Lox, Hot Boys, Three 6 Mafia, G-Unit, Odd Future, A$AP Mob, and Migos. Just to name a few. Now try naming ten female rap groups.

Outside of famous duos and trios, the original five women of Deadly Venoms, from the nineties, are probably the largest in size, billed as a female version of Wu-Tang Clan. Wu member Inspectah Deck once told *Vibe*, "Nine sets of eyes and nine brains make a big difference in this motherfucker." But the idea of strength in numbers (in said motherfucker) hasn't applied to women in rap. While men have consolidated their solo skills into duos, trios, and Avengers-style supergroups, there've been barely enough women to simply collaborate on a rap song.

Mercedes Ladies saw themselves as a sorority of sorts: a union of female DJs, MCs, and dancers. Sheri Sher was the glue of the group. Born and raised in the Bronx, she was the daughter of a single mom with eleven kids. A nighttime post office job didn't provide enough for her mom to pay rent, so Sheri pitched in, working summer jobs to help out the family. At around age fourteen, she made new friends—Rene Pearson (aka RD Smiley), Rene's niece Deborah Carter (aka Little Bit), and Tracey Peterkin (aka Tracey Tee)—at Evander Childs High School in the Bronx.

When school let out for the summer, the girls would attend free block fairs around Boston Road, a haven for black and Latinx teens in need of entertainment. They would watch and listen to DJ Grandmaster Flash, the L Brothers, and DJ Kool Herc perform as a form of catharsis, their own voices drowned out by adult-sized speakers powered by streetlights.

"It took me away from having to take on adult responsibilities, thinking about where we were gonna live next. It took me away from everything, and then once I started rapping, it made me have a voice," says Sheri Sher. "When I went home, I just wanted to cry. But when you on that mic, you make that hard situation seem enjoyable. People wanted to see you, and you felt seen."

Her group mate Evelyn Codrington (aka Eve-a-Def) grew up in the Bronx, on Daly Avenue. Evelyn says her mother had "a nervous breakdown" the day she gave birth to her. When Evelyn was sixteen, she met Sheri through a mutual friend, Zina Major, and they began the process of forming a crew, initially as a way to promote parties. "Before the Mercedes Ladies actually started rapping and deejaying, they were actually a girl empowerment crew," Debbie D said in an interview with AllHipHop.

Mercedes Ladies booked gigs through their manager, Trevor, a party promoter so famous he didn't have a last name (at least not one any of the members can recall) and who also managed the L Brothers. Sheri, Tracey, RD Smiley, Zina Zee, and Eve-a-Def had their first meeting with Trevor at a rehearsal space on Freeman Street in the East Bronx, where the girls sorted out their roles, and they met their newest member, D'Bora Meyers (aka Baby D). She first saw Grandmaster Flash perform at a park and remembers telling her boyfriend, Poochie, "I'm gonna be just like him." When Poochie and his friend laughed, proving them wrong became something of a playground challenge.

The first Mercedes Ladies show was a big affair at 63 Park, a schoolyard on Boston Road in the Bronx that doubled as an informal event space.

"One thing about the Bronx, you had to be a who's who of rap, which was mostly male. If you wasn't part of Grandmaster Flash or Bambaataa, you was not expecting to get on the mic," says Sheri

Sher. "You had to be dope. We could not get on that mic and sound like garbage. We came with our A game." Few rap groups that were formed in the seventies, regardless of gender, survived past that era. But those that managed to earn eternal reverence, like Cold Crush Brothers and Grandmaster Flash and the Furious Five, did so through a process of oral tradition in which men passed down the stories of other respected men. This left girl groups like Mercedes Ladies feeling shut out, even if unintentionally.

Explanations for why female rap duos and groups became obsolete range from jealousy to pettiness. But the assumption that women can't get along as a unit ignores the fact that every era of rap has boosted very few women, let alone entire groups, or that most groups tend to crumble over tension and egos. After an era of affluence, members of the Wu-Tang Clan lost contact with each other and engaged in epic public clashes over the years before reuniting. Raekwon summarized it best in an interview with Hot 97's Miss Info in 2007: "One minute, you my brother, one minute we doing business," he said. "And that's the problem."

"You don't see female rap groups anymore," says Sheri Sher. "You get one female rapper who comes out, and within two or three years, she'll have all these hit songs. Then they bring another one to throw at her to make her feel threatened. And then it's a war, and it's: Who takes the throne now?"

In the early 1980s, Mercedes Ladies recorded two notable songs: a rap version of the Pointer Sisters' classic "Yes We Can Can" for Russell Simmons (which he later re-gifted to his artist, R&B singer Alyson Williams, as her first single for Profile Records in 1986) and "Don's Groove," a collaboration with an MC named Donald Dee in 1984. They disbanded soon after.

"

WHEN I WENT HOME, I JUST WANTED TO CRY. BUT WHEN YOU ON THAT MIC, YOU MAKE THAT HARD SITUATION SEEM ENJOYABLE.

"

DEBBIE HARRY

THE FIRST RAP SONG TO CLAIM THE NO. 1 SPOT ON THE *BILLBOARD* HOT 100 SINGLES CHART WASN'T "RAPPER'S DELIGHT" OR ANYTHING BY A BLACK ARTIST. It was Vanilla Ice's "Ice, Ice Baby," released in 1990. A year later, Marky Mark and the Funky Bunch's "Good Vibrations," led by future Calvin Klein underwear model (and actor) Mark Wahlberg, became the second No. 1 rap song. Those musicians were also white. And, no, this wasn't an aberration. White acts were taking black music to the white masses, igniting a trend, which continued for decades, beginning with "Rapture."

Released in 1981, punk rock band Blondie's single "Rapture" featured a rap verse performed by Debbie Harry and became the first song with a rap verse (a technicality) to top the Hot 100. The song, while rocketing hip-hop to an audience beyond its Bronx roots, made Harry the Big Bang to centuries of white girls rapping with "blaccents."

After Sugarhill Gang's "Rapper's Delight" was released in 1979, rap songs earned airplay throughout much of the

eighties, but "Rapture" exposed a generation of white audiences to a genre initially considered ephemeral. A scene in an episode of the Netflix docuseries *Hip-Hop Evolution* shows everyone from Rodney Dangerfield (on

his 1983 comedy album *Rappin' Rodney*) to actor-filmmaker Mel Brooks trying on rap for kicks.

"Rapture" itself is a spell, with bells that appear out of nowhere, a beat worthy of a Shaft strut, and Debbie Harry's soothing falsetto floating through the first half. Midway through, she breaks the spell with a some-what-on-beat rap verse that name-checks Fab 5 Freddy and DJ Grandmaster Flash. KRS-One made the song more sublimely hip-hop when he sampled Harry's melody for his 1997 single "Step Into a World (Rapture's Delight)."

When MTV launched on August 1, 1981, the network entered the music-video era with the Buggles' prescient "Video Killed the Radio Star," also airing videos by the Who, Rod Stewart, and Pat Benatar. In MTV's first twenty-four hours, Blondie's "Rapture" was the sole piece of rap on the network, and Run-D.M.C.'s "Rock Box" was the first *all*-rap video ever played on MTV—a full three years later. Although hip-hop fans rebuked MTV for ignoring rap videos (surprise: rappers routinely fought to get their videos played on the network), this was just the begin-ning of a trend of mainstream institutions excluding the genre.

In March 1991, *Billboard* started using sales-based analytics compiled by Nielsen SoundScan, which was more efficient than the old-school method of phoning record-store managers. It also showed how much white people were investing in rap. The *New Republic* reported that year, "Although rap is still proportionally more popular among blacks, its primary audience is white and lives in the suburbs."

The *Billboard* charts have been historically biased and confusing when it comes to categorizing black music—*Billboard* once had a chart called Hot Black Singles, which wasn't a dating service. Despite the fact that she made bona fide pop songs, they classi-fied Rihanna as R&B. After rapper Lil Nas X debuted on the country chart in 2019 for his single "Old Town Road," *Billboard* removed the song, claiming it didn't qualify as country.

What the Hot 100 has done is magnify the blind spots in the music industry. As of 2019, only four women had a No. 1 rap song on the Hot 100 as a solo artist: Lauryn Hill ("Doo Wop [That Thing]," Iggy Azalea ("Fancy"), Cardi B, and Lizzo ("Truth Hurts"). Only in 2018 did Cardi B make his-tory as the first female rapper to have two No. 1 songs on the chart ("Bodak Yellow" and "I Like It"), then the first to have three after her collaboration with Maroon 5, "Girls Like You," went No. 1.

The success of "Rapture" had repercussions. More people listened to rap, only to sweep it away from its origins. "How many people heard rap for the first time through that record without understanding it was the tip of an iceberg?" Fab 5 Freddy said of "Rapture" in the *Hip-Hop Evolution* docuseries. As a rule, the rest of the iceberg is submerged, out of sight, until gravity causes it to capsize.

Hip-hop as a widespread commercial product, as well as debates over white artists appro-priating the music and style, in many ways date back to Debbie Harry's singular rap verse.

White Rap Family Tree

Tairrie B

Eazy-E signed her to his Ruthless Records imprint, Comptown Records. Her album *The Power of a Woman* features the track "Ruthless Bitch," where she raps, "Male chauvinists who refuse to believe that a girl like me can achieve / status."

Lil Debbie

Swiping her stage name from a sugary snack cake was her first offense. Being one-third of the blaccents-sporting White Girl Mob with Kreayshawn and V-Nasty was the other. Debbie also collaborated on a few tracks with another tatted white rapper, RiFF RaFF.

Teena Marie

The Ivory Queen of Soul did a little bit of rapping in 1981 on the iconic disco song "Square Biz" and once called herself "the first woman rapper ever," which was sweet but incorrect.

Kreayshawn & V-Nasty

Kreayshawn's insufferably catchy hit "Gucci Gucci" made a wave in 2011 and popularized the concept of the "basic bitch." V-Nasty made do as Kreayshawn's sidekick.

Iggy Azalea

Straight out of Mullumbimby, Australia, Iggy earned herself a spot on T.I.'s label Grand Hustle Records with her gift for blaccented trash talking, particularly on promising early mixtapes. Her single "Fancy" made her the second female rapper to top the *Billboard* Hot 100 chart, but a series of beefs and accusations of cultural appropriation led to her career's essential grand closing.

Chanel West Coast

She signed to Lil Wayne's Young Money roster in 2013 but was more popularly known as a host of MTV's viral-videos show *Ridiculousness*.

Invincible

The Detroit rapper, who became known as a "female Eminem," released her debut album *ShapeShifters* in 2008 and was well-received for her thoughtful boom bap style of rap.

Bhad Bhabie

You could love to hate her or hate to admire her, but Danielle Bregoli, the teenage viral-video sensation known as the "Cash me outside girl" (thanks to a reckless appearance on *Dr. Phil* in 2016) was able to craft thoroughly hard, likable songs that made it impossible to completely dismiss her.

Kitty Pryde

Vice described the rapper from Florida who borrowed her name from the X-Men comics as a "much sharper, self-aware, suburban high school version of Kreayshawn." Her 2012 song "Okay Cupid" plays like a stream-of-consciousness diary entry about drunk-dialing and going steady.

Lisa Lee

NEVER FORGET:
She was a member of Afrika Bambaataa's
Universal Zulu Nation.

WHO SHE IS:
Lisa Lee (Lisa Counts) grew up with her
father and two brothers in the Bronx,
where she attended Stevenson and
James Monroe high schools. At home, she
rapped around the house, writing rhymes
to theme songs of television shows like
Gilligan's Island. For the producers of *Wild
Style* in 1983 and *Beat Street* in 1984, she
was an obvious casting choice, based
on her reputation as an MC. In the latter
movie, she performed as part of the trio
Us Girls.

LISTEN:
Lisa Lee never released a physical record,
but you can hear her in *Beat Street*,
rapping about sharing her heart with the
right guy.

About seven minutes into the movie *Beat Street*, there's a party scene in which the lead character, Kenny Kirkland (played by Guy Davis), is deejaying behind a turntable. In a helpful bit of exposition, his friend alerts him, "Yo, Kenny, man, there goes Sha-Rock, Lisa Lee, and Debbie D." And there they were—Sha-Rock, Lisa Lee, and Debbie D—performing a song that sounds like a hip-hop version of a Spice Girls anthem— "Us girls can boogie, too," they sing over a track they chose themselves.

For the average American viewer in the early 1980s, it was rare to see anyone doing hip-hop, let alone on the big screen. Hip-hop parties had been immortalized in photos, in flyers, and on cassette tapes but never on film. And there was no widespread access to the luxury of video recording until 1983, the year Sony offered the very first pro and consumer camcorders to people like my dad. Movies about hip-hop were a major breakthrough, and Lisa Lee was part of two: *Wild Style* in 1983 and, one year later, *Beat Street*.

Lisa Lee had made the intuitive leap into hip-hop at thirteen, when she and her younger brother attended a showcase at Junior High School 123, featuring DJ Afrika Bambaataa, and she rapped for Bambaataa on the spot. Bambaataa lived in the Bronx River Houses, on the east side of the Bronx, in 1971 and was known for blasting soul music from his apartment window. He went from running with the Black Spades gang to founding the Universal Zulu Nation—an organization for black kids in the neighborhood to substitute leadership fundamentals for gang activity—while also deejaying at legendary downtown clubs like the Roxy.

"To be part of the Zulu Nation at the time was a big deal," says Lisa Lee. "I didn't know what I was becoming part of—I just knew Bambaataa was somebody important."

Fab 5 Freddy, hip-hop's famous networker, planted the seeds for *Wild Style* in 1981, when he thought of making a film about graffiti's connection to pop art. The project's potential grew after he pitched it to Charlie Ahearn at the Times Square Show exhibit. Ahearn, an artist and filmmaker from New York, was there screening his kung fu film *The Deadly Survival*. Having attended and photographed hip-hop performances in the Bronx, Ahearn knew he could execute the vision.

"You have to understand, there were no [hip-hop] magazines and no internet. There was no radio play, basically Mr. Magic did exist later, but not in 1980. There was no [widespread] public recognition [of hip-hop]," Ahearn says. "It was all underground, but for that reason, the underground was very important to people."

Ahearn wanted authenticity. He wanted to visualize hip-hop—the graffiti, the break dancing, deejaying, and emceeing—in a way that wasn't fictionalized, which meant recruiting real MCs to perform their own rhymes on-screen. *Wild Style* would be the first-ever movie about hip-hop, anchored by two popular graffiti artists: Lee Quinones, as the character Zoro, and Lady Pink as Rose. Grandmaster Flash, Kool Moe Dee, Busy Bee, Lil' Rodney C from Funky Four Plus One, and Lisa Lee were among the MCs Ahearn cast in the film.

"MCs at that time, if they were real, had to be able to come out and perform for hours. . . . That meant a strong presence on a stage, and Lisa Lee had

that," says Ahearn. "There's no doubt that she was a legend among people that knew hip-hop."

Lisa Lee remembers the process: "Fab 5 Freddy knew somebody that knew somebody that knew me and told me to come audition in the Bronx," she says. "Everybody else in the Bronx was trying to get in on it, so why wouldn't I wanna be picked? This Caucasian man saying he's gonna give us some money? Why wouldn't you as a child?"

Indeed, agreeing to star in a movie about the incredibly fun activity you were taking part in anyway was a logical decision, just as hip-hop was a natural source of expression for her peer group.

Production on *Wild Style* was slapdash; Ahearn drafted impromptu scripts on a typewriter and shot with a 16mm Bolex camera. Filming began in 1981, hampered by sound issues and reshoots. Lisa Lee appears in a scene with her real-life friends, cruising in the back of a limo with MCs Busy Bee and Lil' Rodney C, who perform a rap

> **"**
>
> ## MCS AT THAT TIME, IF THEY WERE REAL, HAD TO BE ABLE TO COME OUT AND PERFORM FOR HOURS.... THAT MEANT A STRONG PRESENCE ON A STAGE, AND LISA LEE HAD THAT.
>
> **"**

battle in the car. Ahearn cut the part that features Lisa Lee rapping with them, but she appears in another sequence set in a hotel room and then on a basketball court. The film screened at the Embassy Theatre in New York City in 1983, with action and dialogue so loose that viewers categorized it as a docudrama. What started as a low-budget film turned into an unintentional classic.

While *Wild Style* was still in production, casting agents held auditions for *Beat Street*, another hip-hop film set in the South Bronx, centered around a crew of DJs, break-dancers, MCs, and graffiti artists. The project was green-lit after actor/singer Harry Belafonte read a plot outline from reporter Steve Hager, who'd been writing about hip-hop for the *Village Voice*.

The audition process, Lee remembers, was much more "Hollywood" than *Wild Style*'s had been. She had recently partnered with two other MCs, Debbie D and MC Sha-Rock, as a trio known as Empress. There are various recollections of how they got cast, but according to MC Sha-Rock, the three of them showed up to a giant room at the Roxy in Manhattan and waited in line for five hours to audition for *Beat Street*, during which time Sha-Rock, she wrote in her book, flagged a crew member holding a clipboard and asked to speak directly to Belafonte. In a movie that highlighted a hip-hop culture that was still bubbling in the commercial sense, they made sure they were part of its cinematic portrayal.

"If you are filming a story on the history or anything that has to do with the Bronx, then Lisa, Debbie, and myself should be in the movie," Sha-Rock told the crew member. About a week later, she says they had a meeting with Belafonte and casting agents, who hired them to play a girl group. The film's casting director, Pat Golden, who says Whitney Houston and Madonna (who tried out for the role of the white girl, Aisha) auditioned for *Beat Street*, went out to clubs and drove around the Bronx in a station wagon, sniffing out talent.

"I'd seen a lot of female rappers in these clubs that I'd go to. We would go to some of these clubs in Harlem and the Bronx, where people were rapping, and meet people backstage and ask them to come in for auditions," Golden recalls. "As a casting director, and as a black woman, I wanted [the movie] to be reflective of the culture, and that was at the time of what Doug E. Fresh called 'happy rap.' I wanted people to not be afraid of these kids, 'cause there was no reason to be."

In March 1983, New York's *Daily News* described *Wild Style* as "a visual education in hip-hop, the slang word for the clothing and musical styles of young blacks." That these panoramic views of the culture came from outsiders was bittersweet. (The *Boston Globe*, in its review, referred to rappers as "rap talkers.") The documentary *Style Wars*, also released in 1983, introduced the arts of graffiti and break dancing to the public, as did the movie *Breakin'* a year later.

Ahearn recognized himself as a spectator, and the makers of *Beat Street* weren't active hip-hop participants. They were voyeurs creating their closest possible approximation of hip-hop.

"I was aware of hip-hop, but no more aware than I would be of certain religions," Belafonte told the Associated Press in 1984. Hip-hop aficionados skeptically embraced *Beat Street* as a commercialized version of the culture they knew to be more complex. But the presentation of hip-hop in both *Wild Style* and *Beat Street* was crucial to its visibility, essential to moving hip-hop beyond the Bronx.

After *Beat Street*, Us Girls performed together for a short stint before splitting up. Rapping was not a lucrative profession at that point, and so Lisa Lee drifted away. "I didn't have interest, because the money wasn't there at the time. We were just too young and started way too early," she says. "I don't remember any of us really taking it seriously. I wish we did, but we didn't. But I love that I was part of the beginning."

THe sequence

NEVER FORGET:
That's them singing on Dr. Dre's 1995 song "Keep Their Heads Ringin'."

WHO THEY ARE:
The three members of the Sequence—Angela "Angie B" Stone, Gwendolyn "Blondy" Chisholm, and Cheryl "The Pearl" Cook—grew up in Columbia, South Carolina, where they sang in church together and were part of a high school cheer team. While signed to Sugar Hill Records, they became the first female rap act to release a physical record, along with three albums: *Sugar Hill Presents the Sequence* (1980), *The Sequence* (1982), and *The Sequence Party* (1983).

LISTEN:
"Funk You Up," the Sequence's biggest record, is a bona fide party jam with a snap-and-bounce rhythm that works best at a disco or skate rink.

One of my favorite scenes in *Love and Basketball* has nothing to do with love and a little bit to do with basketball. In the movie's first act, Quincy McCall, the romantic lead, played by Omar Epps, is in the middle of dominating a game at Crenshaw High School, when the home team cheerleaders shout a chant: "U-G-L-Y . . . You ain't got no alibi. You ugly. You, you, you ugly." The opposing cheer squad returns an equally rude chant, familiar to anyone who was raised on a playground: "M-A-M-A. Ask me how you got that way. Yo mama. What, what. Yo mama." What does this have to do with the Sequence?

The three members of the Sequence were cheerleaders at C. A. Johnson High School, and their biggest hit, "Funk You Up," is based on a cheer they performed at that school. "We're gonna blow / you / right on out / We're gonna blow you right on out," the chorus goes. When you think about rapping, cheerleading probably doesn't come to mind. But the Sequence saw it as the foundation of the singsong rap style they engineered.

Released in 1979 under Sylvia Robinson's Sugar Hill Records, "Funk You Up" was the first recorded song by a female rap act and came right on the heels of King Tim III's "Personality Jock" (the first-ever physical rap record) and Sugarhill Gang's "Rapper's Delight," clocking in at fifteen minutes—songs that introduced the nation at large to the concept of rapping. The *Boston Globe* mentioned "the house party R&B style known either as 'rap records' or 'rapping to the beat'" in May 1980 and noted, "There are now 50 'rap records' in circulation, making house party dancers go hip-hop to the sound of voices talking and walking in rhythm and rhyme."

Rap became more profession than hobby in the eighties, and, in concert, capitalist signals went off. A former soul singer (the voice of "Pillow Talk") and mastermind of hip-hop in its maiden recorded era, Robinson assembled the Sugarhill Gang, whose member Henry "Big Bank Hank" Jackson famously ripped off lines from another MC, Grandmaster Caz, in "Rapper's Delight." Robinson pieced the Sugarhill Gang together like a boy band, but more than a reflection of raw talent, the group represented hip-hop's potential. Black kids who'd started rapping for fun in the Bronx learned that their style could be sold and duplicated, and national recognition was much more attainable.

"After Hank and them came out with Sugarhill Gang, people started to be, like, *Wow, this could go in another direction*," says Mercedes Ladies' RD Smiley.

The Sequence arrived as part of the initial wave of groups who launched a new era of recorded rap, during which the curators of hip-hop started to distinguish between the culture (the four elements of emceeing, deejaying, tagging, and break dancing) and the business of rap, which was the product being sold.

The legend of "Funk You Up" continued. In 1995, N.W.A member and producer Dr. Dre sampled part of the Sequence's vocals—the "ring-da-ding, ding-ding-dong" part—for the hook to his single "Keep Their Heads Ringin'," a hypnotic song featured on the soundtrack to fellow former N.W.A member Ice Cube's breakthrough movie, *Friday*, in 1995.

Vinyl records, in addition to homemade cassette tapes and word of mouth, made it easier for rap to migrate outside the Bronx, its birthplace, into places like South Carolina, where the members of the Sequence heard it and ran with it. "When we heard 'King Tim III,' we lost it," Chisholm told *Rolling Stone*. "And then when we heard the Gang, we was, like . . . 'We can do that!' Because, with cheering, you're basically rapping right there."

The Sequence succeeded in landing a record deal in early 1979, when the Sugarhill Gang made a tour stop in South Carolina at the Township Auditorium, where the girls took it upon themselves to crash-audition. A Sugarhill crew member helped them get backstage, where the trio rapped for Sylvia Robinson and earned a spot on her label, Sugar Hill Records. "Rap isn't simply a male monopoly as Blondie, Angie B and Cheryl rap to the shuffle boogie beat of the Sugarhill Gang band," the *Boston Globe* wrote in 1980. The Sequence likes to take credit for bringing singing and melody to rap, through records built on blustery funk rhythms.

Largely because of horror stories like those from TLC, Toni Braxton, and Prince, the last of whom once compared music-industry contracts to slavery and stayed protective of his music and copyrights until his death, a generation of artists learned to do their best to avoid the inevitability of bad contracts. The problem, in the Sequence's case, was a lack of compensation from Sugar Hill Records and Sylvia Robinson. The more they learned the business, the more they realized that making records was sort of a shady business! As with other genres, women rappers faced being

AS WITH OTHER GENRES, WOMEN RAPPERS FACED BEING EXPLOITED TWICE OVER, BOTH FINANCIALLY AND THROUGH OTHERS' CONTROLLING THEIR ARTISTIC IMAGE.

exploited twice over, both financially and through others' controlling their artistic image. And in those early days, there was often no recouping the damage. After years of recording and touring with rap acts like the Sugarhill Gang and Funky Four Plus One, the Sequence received what amounted to breadcrumbs.

Chisholm told *Rolling Stone* of "Funk You Up": "They cut our percentage down to six percent each on the song . . . So, you know, it hurts to know that, here you is, busting your ass, can barely feed yourself, can barely pay your bills, and everybody's just going on, and people making millions of dollars off something you created."

Nevertheless, the Sequence got to put out three albums and can count themselves as among the first rappers who were officially thought of as artists of the genre, which is nice, although not necessarily nicer than money. The group disbanded, and Angie Stone branched off into a solo career. R&B fans had no idea that the voice behind neo-soul songs like "No More Rain" was the same Angie who had been part of one of the earliest successful rap acts.

FACTOIDS

◆◆◆

The voice on the hook of LL Cool J's 1995 classic "Doin' It" is **LASHAUN**, a rapper who later became a professional photographer.

◆◆◆

SHARAYA J, once signed to Missy Elliott's label, the Goldmind, Inc., released a song titled "Green Light," where she raps about pussy kryptonite.

◆◆◆

In 2007, Ego Trip premiered the talent show *Miss Rap Supreme*. **REECE STEELE** won the competition, and Khia debuted a classic bar demanding that people "R.E.S.P.E. Respect me."

◆◆◆

Like their predecessor Trina, **CITY GIRLS** (Yung Miami and JT) pursues and favors physical and material pleasures while swatting at men who get in their way. Or in their words: "Don't nothin' but this cash make this pussy talk.

◆◆◆

SHAUNTA, a rapper from Compton, is best known for her verse on Timbaland's single "Luv 2 Luv You" and a cameo on Brandy's "You Don't Know Me (Remix)" featuring Da Brat.

◆◆◆

AWKWAFINA began her career as a rapper before transitioning to Hollywood in box-office hits like *Crazy Rich Asians* and *The Farewell*. "New York City bitch, that's where I come from, not where I moved to / On Mom and Dad's trust fund," she raps on "NYC Bitche$."

◆◆◆

CHEEKY BLAKK was a pioneer and legend in the New Orleans bounce scene in the early nineties and among the few women doing it.

◆◆◆

After earning internet buzz with a record about two-timing, "For Everybody," **KASH DOLL** dropped her debut album *Stacked* through Republic Records.

SWEET TEE

SWEET TEE REMEMBERS THE BEST SONG SHE EVER WROTE THAT SHE NEVER MADE.

She Speaks

I was in London, and at that time [in 1986], you would snatch up anybody's music that you could find to see what everyone else was doing. I happened to swipe a tape of this group called Soul II Soul ["Back to Life (However Do You Want Me)"] before the record dropped. So, I'm in the limousine, and I play the tape, and I hear this record: "However do you want me / However do you need me." And I was, like, wow what record is this?! I made the most expensive phone call from the limousine in London to New York, and I was, like, "Hurby, can you please set me up some studio time?"

Back then, it was about finding records. You would go to a DJ's house or you go in your mother's records or your dad's records and play them and you found a loop or something you thought was hot and you wanted to rhyme to. My dad

◆ ◆

NEVER FORGET:
She recorded a festive holiday song, "Let the Jingle Bells Rock," for Profile Records' 1987 compilation album *Christmas Rap*.

WHO SHE IS:
Sweet Tee (Toi Jackson) started her career collaborating with DJ Davy DMX in the 1980s, when she rapped on his song "One for the Treble." She was briefly part of the group Glamour Girls and signed to Profile Records, working with producer Hurby "Luv Bug" Azor. She released a few singles, including "Why Did It Have to Be Me" and "On the Smooth Tip" (in the music video, she wears customized jeans spray-painted with her name on the back), before briefly signing to Def Jam.

LISTEN:
Sweet Tee brags Slick Rick–style about "having people stomping to my beat" over a funky bass and kick on her 1986 debut single, "It's My Beat," featuring DJ Jazzy Joyce.

◆ ◆

used to play records 24/7. Music played all day, all night. Even when we left our apartment, the stereo kept playing.

In my case, with Hurby, he would be searching through records and bring beats to me and say, "I want you to rhyme on this." Or I would take it to Hurby and say, "I wanna do this." There was no plan. If you look at Cold Crush Brothers and those groups, it wasn't about recording [at first], 'cause that wasn't a thing. We didn't know it was

gonna be a business or genre. Rap records just started happening.

At that time, Charisse from Changing Faces, before they were out, and two other singers, they all met me at the studio. We slowed ["Back to Life"] down so we could hear what they were saying at the beginning. Charisse, Cassandra, and Khadija re-sung that whole thing, and then I put some rhymes on it: "Yes, it's time to get soul to soul / Forget cee-lo, Sweet

Tee is on a roll." And I made a whole record. I was pumped. I took this record up to Cory Robbins [founder of Profile Records], and you know what he told me? He said, "You cannot take peoples' songs that they're singing on and rhyme on it. You can't do that."

DJ Red Alert played it a few times [on the radio]. [The label] would never press it for me. Cory didn't see the vision, so of course [other rappers] did it first. When I got that tape and brought it back to New York, I had a Wrangler truck with an incredible sound system. I'm riding around playing that record, and people are stopping me in the street, going, "What record is that?" And I'm, like, "It's something I just copped from London."

I still have a quarter-inch reel of it in my belongings. I don't know if Red Alert still has it. But I performed it at the Sisters in the Name of Rap concert [in 1992]. I got to do it one time onstage, but every time I hear that record, I'm happy and it stabs me in my heart at the same time.

Roxanne Shanté

NEVER FORGET:
She was the first solo female rapper to
have a hit record.

WHO SHE IS:
Roxanne Shanté (Lolita Shanté Gooden)
started rapping at age eight by emulating comedian Nipsey Russell's rhymes
on the game show *Hollywood Squares*.
Shanté earned her title as a godmother of
hip-hop at age fourteen, after her battle
rap song "Roxanne's Revenge" inspired
a legendary wave of response records.
Shanté released two albums, *Bad Sister*
(1989) and *The Bitch Is Back* (1992).

LISTEN:
Shanté caps her album *Bad Sister* with
a fresh one-verse freestyle, "Gotta Get
Paid," on which she admits to rapping
offbeat and gloats, "I am letting you
know / I'm doing this off head."

◆ ◆ ◆

Between the years 1984 and 1985, the rap
world waged an ongoing battle, the Roxanne
Wars—or what the *Washington Post* described
as a "neofeminist watershed." The only attacks
happened on records, beginning with UTFO's
"Roxanne, Roxanne," produced by the R&B
group Full Force, who performed as backup
dancers for the rap group Whodini (known for
"Freaks Come Out at Night"). UTFO's song was
a big hit, but it only grew into legend because
of Roxanne Shanté.

The subject of "Roxanne, Roxanne" is a fictional young
woman (named Roxanne) who shoots down UTFO's advances:
"Baby, don't you know, I can sing, rap, dance in just one show,"
Kangol Kid raps. On a record about catcalling, each of the
three UTFO members tries in vain to woo Roxanne.

Roxanne Shanté, then going by her given name, Lolita
Gooden, responded to their song with a five-minute diss
track addressing UTFO's flaws—which came to be known as
"Roxanne's Revenge": "You thought you was cute, yeah, you
thought you was a prince," she raps. It was like the subject of a
painting jumping out of the frame and coming to life. Shanté,
known for battle rapping around her neighborhood, didn't
yet have a stage name. "In battles, I was rhyming for thirty

to forty minutes, so four minutes was nothing for me," she told *Billboard* in 2018. "I stuck with the story line, and the next morning I was 'Roxanne.'"

It would've been ambitious enough for Shanté to make history with a diss track calling out a group of male rappers, but what's most impressive is that she did it at fourteen years old. A girl from the Queensbridge Houses in New York became a pre-viral sensation before rap was on TV and before the world at large recognized female rappers.

It wasn't just one back-and-forth. "Roxanne's Revenge" inspired a generation of MCs and amateur rappers to dump a rich, random tapestry of diss records aimed squarely at Shanté, from Sparky D's "Sparky's Turn (Roxanne, You're Through)" to Crush Groove's "Yo My Little Sister (Roxanne's Brothers)." Even an alleged child named Tanganyika targeted Roxanne in a song titled "I'm Little Roxanne."

Aisha Baum was fifteen years old when she recorded "Ice Roxanne" in 1985 on a 45 vinyl record, under the nickname Little Ice. She'd been writing poetry at home in Brooklyn, but she wasn't much into rapping, until her older cousin from the Bronx asked her to record a diss song about a girl named Roxanne Shanté.

"It was exciting for me to do it," Baum remembers. "I was, like, 'Oh, she's a bit of a bragger, this girl!' We called it 'Ice Roxanne' because it was, like, *we're icing you*, and *get outta here* . . . Now that I listen to it, it sounds so infantile. It's hilarious." (Baum went on to become a member of the female rap group Poizon Posse.) "When I think about living through that era and hearing her name, and all of the people—not just young women, but the males that wanted to battle her," says Baum, "she had to be a strong little somebody to deal with that."

"Roxanne's Revenge," originally titled "Roxanne Speaks Out" and re-recorded over another beat due to licensing, premiered on Mr. Magic's *Rap Attack* radio show in 1984; Shanté released the song through Pop Art Records. UTFO answered back with a song featuring a rapper they called "The Real Roxanne," which only confused the matter. They'd gone as far as to hold a casting call to fill the fictional role of Roxanne and hired two young women—the Original Roxanne (a woman named Elease Jack) and then the Real Roxanne (Joanne Martinez). Martinez didn't rap on UTFO's response to Roxanne Shanté, but she did continue recording songs under the moniker the Real Roxanne, including "Bang Zoom, Let's Go Go."

Although no one publicly documented all the "Roxanne" disses in real time, there is a Roxanne Wars Wikipedia page, and there's a WordPress blog from 2013 that catalogued about thirty known responses, some available only on cassette tape and vinyl.

Similar answer records—diss songs that piggybacked on popular singles—kicked off in the 1980s and were largely used for marketing boosts: Glamour Girls' "Oh! Veronica" was a response to Bad Boys' 1985 single "Veronica," and Salt-N-Pepa's debut single "The Show Stoppa" (back when they were called Super Nature) was an answer to Doug E. Fresh's "The Show" in 1985.

The songs weren't based on personal beefs, but, whether real or orchestrated, the concept of a beef in hip-hop came to be nothing without a good diss track. "Roxanne's Revenge" transferred the art of battling to physical records. It's impossible to imagine a rap world without "Roxanne's Revenge," or Boogie Down Productions' "The Bridge Is Over" (part of the infamous Bridge Wars, a series of territorial diss records between New York rappers) or Nas's "Ether"—songs that, at their best, function as professional antagonism in hip-hop, a way for personal vendettas to be settled as harmless entertainment.

Even for a seasoned MC, battle rapping is one of the hardest sports to master. In theory, anyone can rap, but not everyone can freestyle.

Even for a seasoned MC, battle rapping is one of the hardest sports to master. In theory, anyone can rap, but not everyone can freestyle. (Try to improvise a rap right now and see how hard it is.) The best freestyle battles aim to offend opponents with a combination of brevity, comedy, and skill. For the audience and participants, it's a specific adrenaline rush that generates *oohs* and *ahhs* when punch lines and insults hit their mark. (Eminem's *8 Mile* was popular for a reason.)

Roxanne did this repeatedly as a teen in street battles, and she neither wrote down nor memorized her rhymes. She told Pitchfork in 2018, "It's been thirty years, and I've never done the same show twice."

Before "Roxanne's Revenge," Shanté was making a living battling MCs of all stripes in Queensbridge for money, starting at a pot of fifty dollars; the same storied Queensbridge projects she lived in produced other rap legends like Nas, Mobb Deep, and Marley Marl, a renowned DJ and producer known for playing music from a boom box out of his apartment window. Marley Marl spotted Shanté by his building and, knowing her reputation, asked her to record a response to UTFO. He would give her a pair of Sergio Valente jeans in exchange, since he worked at the company's factory.

Marley Marl, in collusion with manager Tyrone "Fly Ty" Williams, according to legend, wanted to use Shanté as an intermediary to retaliate against UTFO for missing a show date. Shanté used the opportunity to her advantage, too. By recording a response, she made the young woman in UTFO's record real, thereby claiming a song that wasn't about her, as well as all the responses that came after.

Shanté entered a series of competitions, including the infamous MC Battle for World Supremacy in 1985, which she lost to Busy Bee. She joined and toured with Marley Marl's Juice Crew All-Stars but took four years to release her debut album, *Bad Sister*, in 1989, which proved to be too long of a gap. The album buried Shanté's battle rap roots in favor of upbeat dance tracks, as her label, Warner Bros., tried to mold her into the image of a star rather than playing to her strengths. (This set the stage for her more aggressive next album, *The Bitch Is Back*.) Despite having a successful record on the radio, she earned little money from rapping, knew nothing about publishing rights, and says she got no royalties until well after her peak. She was savvy, but she was still a teenager learning the business and paying the price for entering the industry so young.

In 1990, Ernie Paniccioli, noted hip-hop photographer, shot a video interview with Shanté for *Word Up!* magazine as part of a series, *Best of Word Up! Video Magazine*, which profiled rappers like Ice-T, KRS-One, Queen Latifah, Public Enemy, and MC Lyte. Paniccioli remembers going to Shanté's home in Newark, New Jersey and seeing the posters and heart-shaped phone in her room.

The interview (available on YouTube) opens with a shot of Shanté sitting on her bed, with a pair of teddy bears, her hair slicked back, gold teeth reflecting in a bright, pink space. In a matter of four years, her life had become the stuff of movies. "She is and was, even at that age, a very deep person. She read everything, she listened to everything, and she liked listening to older people, not just hanging out with teenagers," says Paniccioli. "What I was not prepared for in doing the video was the depth of her history and the incredible stuff she survived."

It was, in fact, made for movies. Marley Marl had taped the making of "Roxanne's Revenge" on VHS, and you can find the footage of the performance on YouTube: video of Shanté rapping into

THE WINNERS OF WARS WRITE HISTORY, AND SHANTÉ SAW HERSELF AS AN UNLIKELY CHAMPION IN RAP WHO BIRTHED A GENERATION OF BATTLE MCS. THAT SHE WAS ABLE TO SEE HERSELF AT ALL WAS AN ACCOMPLISHMENT.

a mic for five minutes straight, wearing a festive sweater and a ponytail. Views of one version of the footage on YouTube rose by thousands soon after the release of her Netflix biopic, *Roxanne Roxanne*, in 2017. "Who knew her before Netflix?" a commenter wrote. Hers was the first widely released biopic about a woman MC, forty-five years after the birth of hip-hop.

Other biopics, which are naturally part propaganda, focus on the making of legends already recognized as legends. *Roxanne Roxanne* depicted Shanté as a prodigy who became a rapper at fourteen, a mother at sixteen, and a young woman who survived an abusive relationship with the older man (played by Oscar-winner Mahershala Ali) who was the father of her first child. Nia Long played Shanté's mom in a film that got rave reviews and educated a new generation of music fans. "I heard of her, but the Netflix series . . . made me understand her more and made me like her more," says

New York rapper Young M.A. "I used to do little cyphers in my neighborhood, too, with dudes, and I really could spit, and they couldn't fuck with me. So when [I saw her story], it was like, wow, that's crazy 'cause I was just like that."

As executive producer, Shanté got to see herself become a star on-screen, though a star in name only. She told NPR, "I never took it as being a star or anything, I think, because it was not financially compensating . . . [The movie was] very therapeutic, because it gave me a visual of the things that I survived."

In a twist of fate, UTFO's Kangol Kid said he was proud of Shanté for making the film, but he wasn't super happy with the movie's marginalization of key figures like his group. "When you think of the single and you think of the phenomenon that took place, you think of all of the battles. You think of hip-hop's first beef of wax," he said in a podcast interview with rappers Lord Jamar and Rah Digga in 2018. "As a hip-hop historian, as someone who was there, you would expect to see that."

But the benefit of an autobiography is that the subject and filmmakers get to write or correct a narrative, insert facts where they should be, and drop the ones that stray from the story. The winners of wars write history, and Shanté saw herself as an unlikely champion in rap who birthed a generation of battle MCs. That she was able to see herself at all was an accomplishment.

LADY B

LADY B, AMONG THE FIRST HIP-HOP DJS TO BREAK RAP RECORDS ON THE RADIO, REMEMBERS RECORDING "TO THE BEAT Y'ALL" AND BECOMING A VOICE OF PHILADELPHIA RADIO.

She Speaks

The hip-hop bug bit me in a club in Philadelphia called Kim Graves. The DJ there, Lawrence Levan, would break down the breakbeats in the middle of his mix. Sugarhill had just come out with "Rapper's Delight," and that's what hip-hop was. Before rapping was called rapping, it was called "toasting." I started doing it just as fun. I wasn't looking for a career. Then [Dr. Perry Johnson from TEC Records] approached me to take what I was doing in the club and put it on a record.

Me, my mother, sister, and Mimi Brown, another radio personality in Philly, sat up all night coming up with rhymes on three-by-five cards, twisting them up, moving them around, tacking 'em on a board. We didn't have computers then! I went to the studio, and I cut it—it was Nick Martinelli's studio downtown, this producer who was big in Philly. Hip-hop was [simply] happy. Not even

"Rappers' Delight" was a song that was composed about anything, if you asked Grandmaster Caz when he wrote it. They were just braggadocio songs, just having fun. That's before we realized the words could mean something, and we could do something.

I got [the line about Jack and Jill: "I said Jack and Jill went up the hill / To have a little fun / But stupid Jill forgot the pill / And now they have a son"] from a friend of mine, World B. Free, a basketball player for the Sixers. That's who introduced me to hip-hop. I went up to New York, went to the projects, and saw the speakers [in the park jams]. I was seventeen years old, wasn't even thinking about what being a woman was—I was still a little girl. [Hip-hop] was not that deep for me. It was taking a bunch of rhymes I had, that World had, and putting them on three-by-five cards. I don't love "To the Beat Y'all" to this day, 'cause it was something that was thrown together. It was kind of a gimmick. It was a one-cut song. I'm proud of it—don't get me wrong. But I'm even more proud of what I did for hip-hop as a genre on the radio.

I went to the radio station one day to get a job, for extra money, and they had a music director [position] open. The music director's job is to receive the music from the [record label's] promotions [department]. As the

hip-hop songs began to come in, I started to beg management to let me play them on the air and do a special hip-hop show. That took a minute, but they finally caved. There was my beginning in radio, on WHAT 1340 AM. All you had was me and Mr. Magic for an entire decade. [I broke] everything on Profile, Enjoy, Sugar Hill, Tommy Boy Records. I'm the youngest of four children who came up in a house where the stereo was blasting 24/7, so I always loved music. I got a little bit of everything: R&B, funk, all your classics, Dionne Warwick, Nancy Wilson.

[In radio], there were a whole lot of obstacles and a whole lot of standing your ground. I had to fight to play Public Enemy's first song, "Bring the Noise"—even threatened to quit my job if they didn't let me play it. I was pissed. It was okay for me to play the Beastie Boys, so I didn't understand [the resistance to Public Enemy]. There was no profanity in the song, nothing that broke an FCC law. I even called the Black Media Coalition into it at the time. I was very serious about putting my foot down.

SPARKY D

NEVER FORGET:
Her claim to fame is a diss record released in response to Roxanne Shanté's "Roxanne's Revenge."

WHO SHE IS:
Sparky D (Doreen C. Broadnax) was born and raised in Brownsville, Brooklyn, and was influenced by early MCs like MC Sha-Rock, Pebblee Poo, and Dimples D. She had dreams of starring in the Broadway musical *West Side Story* when she was younger and told her mother, "If I'm not a star by twenty, I promise I'll go to school and be a doctor." She released her album *This Is Sparky D's World* in 1988, and her battle against Roxanne Shanté in the mid-eighties has gone down in history as the earliest major rap beef between female MCs.

LISTEN:
Sparky D drops antagonistic rhymes to a disco beat on her 1988 single "Throwdown."

Just before midnight on December 31, 1984, famous hip-hop radio jock Mr. Magic announced one of his world-famous premieres on WBLS: Roxanne Shanté's "Roxanne's Revenge," one of the last songs to close out the year. Over in the Van Dyke projects in Brownsville, Brooklyn, Sparky D and her then-boyfriend, rapper-producer Spyder D, were spending New Year's Eve drinking ten-dollar champagne in her mother's three-bedroom apartment. It was the last day of what Spyder D recalled was "a lean year." They wanted 1985 to be different.

"Roxanne's Revenge" made Roxanne Shanté a star and made Spyder D's Spidey sense go off. "It kind of sobered me up," he remembers. "I looked at [Sparky], like, 'We gotta answer this.' The next day, the studio was closed, but I was chomping at the bit." Shanté had commercial success, and Sparky D wanted the crown.

"We heard, 'Well, my name is Roxanne, a-don't you know / I just a-cold rock a party, and I do this show,'" Sparky D recalls, citing Shanté's lyrics. "I looked to Spyder, and he looked to me, and we was, like, 'What the hell?'"

The timing was perfect. Sparky D, who started as a B-girl, was fresh off her run in the rap group the Playgirls, which she'd formed with two friends, City Slim and Mo Ski. She'd met them in a hallway in Van Dyke, where she heard them flipping the *Diff'rent Strokes* theme song into a rap. The three joined forces and took to the city, battling. "Everywhere we would go, the Playgirls would win," Sparky says.

Her partner, Spyder D, had made money touring off his single "Smerphies Dance." He and rapper Kurtis Blow were both managed by a young Russell Simmons, before Simmons cofounded Def Jam Recordings. Spyder D met the Playgirls in 1983 through Blow and produced the group's single, "Our Picture of a Man," released through Sutra

Roxanne Shanté versus Sparky D was the first major rivalry between two women in rap. They fed off each other, reveled in battling, and understood its place in hip-hop. Despite not being the best of friends—"We weren't friends at all," Sparky says—they both promoted the feud for entertainment, while onlookers treated it like a heavyweight fight, setting a precedent of beef as a form of marketing. "It got to the point where boroughs was going against each other. Like Brooklyn and Queens, because she was from Queens and I was from Brooklyn, and it was real," says Sparky D. "My DJ was Cool Red Alert

THE ATTENTION PUT THE SPOTLIGHT ON TWO YOUNG WOMEN IN RAP WHO PROVED THEY COULD STIR INTRIGUE THROUGH SKILL AND STRATEGIC COMPETITION.

Records. Over the backdrop of eighties synths and a stalking bass, each member describes her ideal man. The song flopped, which set up the aforementioned "lean year."

Spyder D wrote most of the lyrics for Sparky D's response to Shanté, titled "Sparky's Turn (Roxanne, You're Through)." While recording the song on January 2 at Power Play Studios in Queensbridge, Spyder D took Russell Simmons's advice about not overproducing and kept the beat spare. One diss is about Shanté's "cracky-wacky voice."

"I felt Sparky was a better rapper in the sense of voice quality. Sparky had a crisp, clear voice," says Spyder. "Her diction was perfect yet street, and that's a tough combination."

on 98.7 Kiss and her DJ was Marley Marl, and he was on WBLS and the stations started to get friction." Sparky remembers Mr. Magic telling her, "You and Roxanne [should be] like Larry Bird and Magic Johnson. They get on that basketball court and play ball, and when they finish playing ball, they have a drink."

That dynamic never materialized. Instead, the feud erupted in May 1985, during a battle contest in Raleigh, North Carolina. While the Roxanne Wars mania was dying down, Shanté and Sparky recorded an EP titled *Round 1*. Released in September 1985, the disc featured their diss records and an album cover that shows the two of them side by side, wearing boxing gloves and staring into the camera, not at each other. It was like,

'Look, y'all gon' take this picture. Y'all don't even have to talk to each other. Just take these pictures," Sparky D says. "We did what we had to do, to do business. It was competition, it was a battle, it was a fight without fighting."

Spyder D recorded the weekend of battles on Betamax tapes, including the pair's visits to record stores with lines of fans wrapped around the block. "The optics of it were incredible. We're talking about two teenage female MCs. They were the headliners. There were no big names on the bill, and the excitement around that event was mind-boggling," says Spyder D. Instigators in both of their inner circles—managers, friends, recording executives—happily fueled the tension, egging them on. The attention put the spotlight on two young women in rap who proved they could stir intrigue through skill and strategic competition. "Everything was all lined up as this great rivalry: Sparky and Shanté, which opened the door for female rappers," says Spyder D. "I don't know why it took that dynamic. People were spreading rumors to keep the rivalry up."

Their battle was the beginning of a new normal. Beef is one of rap's biggest selling points, as Shanté proved, and it's especially enticing with women involved, since the field is so sparse to begin with: Lil' Kim vs. Foxy Brown, Khia vs. Trina, Nicki Minaj vs. Lil' Kim/Remy Ma/Cardi B/Azealia Banks. Healthy competition is great for the sport of rap, but for women, it's also damaging in a music industry that tends to generalize their feuds. Women rappers beef because all rappers do, and humans sometimes don't get along. But the scarcity of women rappers makes all their beefs seem monumental rather than the stuff of a typical business day. When Nicki Minaj and Cardi B were at odds in 2018, Migos rapper Quavo tweeted about collaborating with both women at the same time and

noted the magnitude of the moment: "'MotorSport' is the modern-day ROXANNE V SPARKY D."

Sparky D battled a drug addiction for more than a decade before finding her footing. She remembers her battle with Shanté as a torrid but glorious chapter in her life. Says Sparky, "Roxanne Shanté and Sparky D had an impact on hip-hop because we stood out and said, 'We can do that.'"

Salt-N-Pepa

NEVER FORGET:
They were the first female rappers to go platinum and the first to win a Grammy.

WHO THEY ARE:
Cheryl James (Salt) and Sandra Denton (Pepa) met as students at Queensborough Community College. Cheryl was quiet. Sandra was not. It was the perfect recipe for a lifelong friendship. Outside of school, they worked as phone operators at a Sears in Queens with producer Hurby Azor, who formed the duo Salt-N-Pepa. After the original Spinderella, DJ Latoya Hanson, left, the second Spinderella joined, making them a trio. Salt-N-Pepa released five albums from 1986 (*Hot, Cool & Vicious*) to 1997 (*Brand New*).

LISTEN:
On "I'll Take Your Man," Salt-N-Pepa sell their promise (to take your man) effectively through a series of believable threats.

When "Shoop" came out in 1993, every girl in my elementary school began rapping it. Around fifth grade, I committed the lyrics to memory and would recite them aloud, alone or in a group, as part of school-bus karaoke sessions in Queens. Imagine a caravan of schoolgirls rhyming a cappella: "You're packed and you're stacked! / Especially in the back! / Brother, wanna thank your mother for a butt like that!" By the age of ten, I'd seen women experiencing enough uncomfortable stares from men on the street to know the song was audacious. Whatever "Shoop" meant, everyone wanted to do it.

Salt-N-Pepa's long history of subversion began with their 1987 single "Tramp," where they accuse men of being promiscuous. "It just so happens that," they say, "most men are tramps." Three years later, in the music video for "Let's Talk About Sex," the group's three members, Salt, Pepa, and DJ Spinderella, wore construction worker outfits while taunting men on the street, assuming the role of catcallers, before revising those personas in 1993 for their biggest single, "Shoop." This was two decades before women were launching public and viral campaigns against what was labeled "street harassment."

More than simply anthems for women and middle-school girls, these songs reflected a shift, not just in hip-hop, but to the age of third-wave feminism, which at its core championed women's sexual freedom and rights like equal pay for equal work. Public awareness around feminism was growing in predominantly white spaces: the riot grrrl punk movement, sparked in 1991, was buoyed by songs about women owning their sexuality and confronting issues of violence; 1992 was declared the Year of the Woman after a historic rise in women candidates running for office and winning; *Bust* magazine launched in 1993. Young black women were, at the same time, experiencing their own awakening on the heels of work by black feminist activists who cited fighting racism and classism as key to any true feminist movement.

Women who decided to rap about inequality faced a unique challenge: their genre was led by the voices of young black men like N.W.A, who were speaking against racism and oppression while in the process downgrading their black female colleagues and doing it through irresistible, misogynist songs that enchanted young women, too. Salt-N-Pepa used the framework of feminism so often in their music that they were branded feminists, even though feminism wasn't so much a mission for Salt-N-Pepa as it was a logical path.

They didn't particularly like the label, but, as a group, they lived up to some of its principles.

Salt-N-Pepa weren't afraid to be sexual—their single "Push It" asks a dude to pump hard, like the beat—they rapped about safe sex and HIV awareness, promoted showmanship, and made videos for the *Yo! MTV Raps* generation, producing much of their early work under the direction of a male mentor. While their main producer, Hurby Azor, had his own financial agenda—making music for mass appeal through the voices of women—Salt-N-Pepa's material performed a larger purpose that spoke loudly to women and became a calling card of the group.

"The guys love us, they think we're sexy, but the girls take us seriously," Pepa told the *Washington Post* in 1994. "I've always said that when I was a teenager growing up, I wish I had girls like Salt-N-Pepa to look up to. If I'd had someone I could relate to, a lot of things would probably be different."

Azor's original plan, when the gang all worked at Sears together, had been to form a two-man group with Martin Lawrence (the actor-comedian). "He couldn't rap, so that died out. Then it became me and Cheryl," Azor told *Rolling Stone* in 1997. He coined the name Salt-N-Pepa to play off his and Cheryl's skin complexions. The final permutation of the group was Cheryl and Sandra, and neither had experience as rappers. They were fans of hip-hop, but they had no plans to pursue rap as a profession.

Pepa, born in Jamaica and raised in Queens, regularly attended hip-hop park jams. "I just used to be so in awe and fascinated and, like, 'Wow, this

MORE THAN SIMPLY ANTHEMS FOR WOMEN AND MIDDLE-SCHOOL GIRLS, THESE SONGS REFLECTED A SHIFT, NOT JUST IN HIP-HOP, BUT TO THE AGE OF THIRD-WAVE FEMINISM.

is amazing!' But I would *never*, *ever* touch the mic," Pepa told *Rolling Stone*. "I just had my little raps that I used to write, but I was nervous, I was scared . . . And Hurby was, like, the first person that was, like, 'Let me see if you could rap.'" Salt was the type of child who routinely broke out into song and dance in front of family members in Brooklyn.

The original third Salt-N-Pepa member, DJ Latoya Hanson, aka DJ Spinderella, dropped out after the group's first album, 1986's *Hot, Cool & Vicious*. (According to Pepa's memoir, Latoya had missed rehearsals and appearances.) Deidra Roper, a dancer also from Brooklyn, auditioned and replaced her as the new Spinderella.

Before they became a trio, Salt and Pepa went by the name Super Nature for their first single, "The Show Stoppa," a response to Doug E. Fresh and Slick Rick's "The Show," which Salt later described to *Rolling Stone* as "a bold move for these two little girls from Queens that no one had ever heard of before." The song was Azor's attempt to capitalize on the popularity of response records in the era of "Roxanne's Revenge." It was indeed fearless, garnering radio play that led to performance bookings and the beginning of a career for Salt-N-Pepa.

The year they released their debut album, there were no songs like "Ladies First" or "U.N.I.T.Y" that urged men to do the bare minimum and stop calling women bitches. MC Lyte wasn't yet craving roughnecks, and Queen Latifah was still a princess. Salt-N-Pepa cornered the market first when it came to excoriating men and talking shit, and they looked cool doing it.

Between Public Enemy's two masterpieces—1988's *It Takes a Nation of Millions to Hold Us Back* and 1990's *Fear of a Black Planet*—in 1990, Salt-N-Pepa released their third album *Blacks' Magic*, a funk project full of abrasive and black-affirming songs like "Negro Wit' An Ego," where they rap about being "not a militant but equivalent to an activist." There's also, notably, the upbeat edutainment anthem "Let's Talk About Sex" on there. While many of the album's stop-and-start beats and rhyme schemes didn't age incredibly well, this feminist-promoting rap was Salt-N-Pepa's version of "conscious hip-hop," which essentially meant political rap. But consider if Salt-N-Pepa would be seen as political alongside a group like Public Enemy.

Public Enemy had established the subgenre with relentless anthems that charged an entire generation of black Americans embroiled in protest against the country ("Fuck the Police," "911 Is a Joke"). Conscious hip-hop was the banner under which rappers like them could capture social and political conflict. But it was largely a medium for black men who rapped about blackness without necessarily having to address gender. Some of the rappers who earned that label openly disdained it—as Mos Def told me for a *XXL* feature in 2009, "Conscious rap as opposed to what? Asleep rap?"—nevertheless, conscious hip-hop would find mainstream success through artists like KRS-One, Common, Mos Def, and Talib Kweli.

In an era without hip-hop stylists, Salt-N-Pepa bought and wore their own accessible clothes, the same styles worn by cool black and Latinx kids in the eighties: big eight-ball jackets, spandex, rectangular gold door-knocker earrings, and acid-washed denim. "A lot of women were into oversized clothes, looking a little more like the guys, and here we came with our spandex and our eight-ball jackets and our Kente hats and our diva boots," Salt said to *Broward New Times* in 2012. The group's now-classic, asymmetrical hairdos were a result of a failed perm experiment by Pepa's beautician sister.

"Push It," a pop hit synonymous with the 1980s, a B side to "Tramp," influenced a legion of spandex-clad rapping girl groups. But even four albums deep—and after they became the first female rap act to win a Grammy—Salt-N-Pepa didn't have a commercial hit until "Shoop," one of the few songs they wrote on their own.

Azor wrote the majority of their first four albums—*Hot, Cool & Vicious* (1986), *A Salt with a Deadly Pepa* (1988), *Blacks' Magic* (1990), and *Very Necessary* (1993). But after 1989, Salt-N-Pepa chose to rely less and less on Azor's songwriting. Their resentment over his level of control grew. (Azor and Salt had dated on and off before breaking up.)

The first song Salt wrote and produced for the group was "Expression," from their 1990 album, *Blacks' Magic*. Salt described the process as a "liberation from being Hurby's girlfriend."

"I wanted to start taking over the voice of Salt-N-Pepa more in the studio—[be] more in control of what we wanted to say," she told *Rolling Stone* in 2017. When she and Pepa wrote their hallmark single "Shoop" for their next and best album, *Very Necessary*, it was the ultimate step toward independence.

Azor's earlier work had set up Salt-N-Pepa as the voices of a movement. "Shoop" was a smash. Salt's songwriting talent had been sorely underused. "It was a fight with the record company, with Hurby, to make it the first single off the album. I mean, a *real* fight that we finally won," Salt told *Rolling Stone*.

The fight was symbolic. They were wrestling for freedom, while at the same time relying on Azor's guidance to continue making hits. In inferior hands, a song like their 1995 single "Ain't Nuthin' But a She Thing," could read as disingenuous. Just look at the title, and its chorus, "I can be anything that I wanna be!" and imagine Meghan Trainor singing it. The now-famous photographer Ellen von Unwerth directed the music video, for which Salt suggested she, Pepa, and Spinderella all wear

matching uniforms of jobs considered traditionally male: an astronaut, a firefighter, a police officer, and a mechanic. In one shot, to contrast, they wear patent leather boots, while standing onstage in front of a brigade of women, with a large poster behind them that reads: *S-H-E*.

"The primary message was showing how strong women can be and to not restrict their ambitions. Also [to] have fun at the same time," von Unwerth says of the video. "It's astonishing how we talked about these issues [so many] years ago. They were super sexy because of who they were as human beings and how well they represented the message they carried and sang about. They did not need to add anything on top to be memorable."

Azor's heavy thumbprint on even Salt-N-Pepa's most feminist songs (and on albums, outside of their last one, *Brand New*) represented a tried-and-true formula that also worked across other genres: a male producer shaping women's content and sound. Even when Salt-N-Pepa were at their most blunt, their sexiest, and most brash, with enough selling power to make them appear powerful in the public eye, they were disempowered behind the scenes. I don't think this invalidated their message over the years as much as it showed how men in hip-hop could manipulate aspects of a woman's image and voice.

Before the age of public feminism in popular music, being feminist wasn't a badge, and it wasn't a marketable movement across pop. Like Roxanne Shanté, Queen Latifah, and Lil' Kim, Salt-N-Pepa's music supported acts of feminism through their raps that would later be absorbed into mainstream pop and automatically embraced by the Nicki Minajs and Cardi Bs of the world and stars like Taylor Swift and Beyoncé, who at the 2014 MTV VMAs performed in front of a screen with giant block letters that read, simply: "FEMINIST."

SALT-N-PEPA SLOGANS

◆ ◆ ◆

"I treat a man like he treats me / The difference between a hooker and a ho ain't nothing but a fee"

"NONE OF YOUR BUSINESS"

◆ ◆ ◆

"C'mon girls, let's go show the guys that we know / How to become Number One in a hot party show"

"PUSH IT"

◆ ◆ ◆

"So read me all the rules so I can have my money right / 'Cause I'm a new lady boss keepin' game tight"

"BIG SHOT"

◆ ◆ ◆

"Let's tell it how it is, and how it could be / How it was, and of course, how it should be"

"LET'S TALK ABOUT SEX"

◆ ◆ ◆

"Go to work and get paid less than a man / When I'm doin' the same damn thing that he can"

"AIN'T NUTHIN' BUT A SHE THING"

◆ ◆ ◆

"We've got to let the fellas know what they can do for us"

"I LIKE TO PARTY"

MC LYTE

NEVER FORGET:
She was the first female solo rapper nominated for a Grammy Award.

WHO SHE IS:
MC Lyte (Lana Michelle Moorer), raised in Brooklyn, landed a deal with First Priority Music through the duo Milk D and Gizmo, aka Audio Two, off the success of her song "I Cram to Understand U (Sam)" in 1987. Lyte's career stretched over twenty-seven years and eight solo albums, beginning with her debut, *Lyte As a Rock*.

LISTEN:
"10% Dis," an attack aimed at Lyte's rival Antoinette, contains one of rap's most famous threatening opening lines: "Hot damn, ho, here we go again . . ."

When MC Lyte first started rapping at fourteen years old, she sounded like a fourteen-year-old girl. To deepen her tone, she worked with a vocal coach, Lucien George Sr., whose three sons, the George Brothers, were members of the R&B group Full Force (producers of Roxanne Shanté's hit record "Roxanne's Revenge"). Every Saturday, George Sr. would go to Lyte's house in Brooklyn and teach her how to manipulate the deeper part of her voice, using Salt-N-Pepa songs as reference points.

"He would tell me to learn a song that I really loved," MC Lyte told *Vibe* in 2011. "I would literally say it over and over again, and George would coach me on how to make my voice sound strong and how to pronounce the words to where someone else would feel it." George taught her how to come from the diaphragm, she says, to sound more imposing.

The human diaphragm is the muscle and connective tissue separating the chest and abdomen that, when contracted, activates the thorax, so your lungs can take in more air. Anyone who speaks, shouts, or performs theater for a living has the process of doing so to project their voice mastered. According to *Psychology Today*, "A person who uses the diaphragm voice commands attention, 'sounds' more attractive socially, and is more likely to be perceived as a promotable leader."

Every song MC Lyte has ever touched is more powerful as a result. When she interrupts the beginning of her 1988 single "Lyte As a Rock" to preface it with a lesson in language and diction, she enunciates: "Do you understand the metaphoric phrase 'light as a rock'?" she asks. Then she answers her own question: "It's explaining how heavy the young lady is." On her 1993 single "Ruffneck," an aggressive tribute to street-corner dudes and the first song by a female rapper to go gold, she raps every word with full body, so you can hear her spitting into the mic.

SHE DIDN'T SEEM LIKE SHE WAS SELLING AN IMAGE. IT SEEMED SHE WASN'T TRYING TOO HARD TO SELL AT ALL.

Chuck D, who has quite a voice himself, called MC Lyte's voice "one of the greatest voices of all time." The voice earned her consistent commercial work (AT&T Nationwide) and gigs as an actual emcee for events like the BET Awards and NAACP Image Awards. It's worth going on and on about, as I am now.

"Some other female rappers, you can copy their style, but it's hard to copy MC Lyte," says her DJ, K Rock, who appears on "Lyte As a Rock." "You'll never hear another Lauryn Hill voice or an MC Lyte or a Lil' Kim voice. They stand alone."

If there were such a thing as an ideal female MC, Lyte was it. Preserving the purity of hip-hop became ever more crucial, the more the culture spread out, and this purity was always based on respect for the craft, delivery, and wordplay. Lyte checked off all three, and hip-hop treated her like an all-star athlete because of it. Her era in the mid to late 1980s is still regarded as a golden age, a much simpler time when women seemed to prioritize rapping over sexuality, though it's naive to think one approach is better than the other, when selling sex and being "nice for a girl" both appeal to men.

Lyte wrote the lyrics to her first song, "I Cram to Understand U (Sam)," when she was twelve. Four years later, with the help of her friends (whom she calls her brothers) Kirk "Milk Dee" Robinson and Nat "Gizmo" Robinson—the duo behind Audio Two—and their father Nat Robinson, she recorded the track, released it as a single, and landed a deal with Atlantic Records.

"I Cram" worked as a meditation on drugs in the form of a love song about a dealer boyfriend whose side chick is crack. It came with a beginning, an end, and a twist. And Lyte was a young black woman coolly rapping about the destruction she saw happening among young black men. "I don't try to copy men. But I do have this tough attitude. I won't take anything from anybody," she told the *Los Angeles Times* in 1990.

She didn't seem like she was selling an image. It seemed she wasn't trying too hard to sell at all. When people saw her in interviews and in music videos, it looked as if she wore clothes for actual comfort. Jeans and a striped T-shirt with a leather cap. No makeup. Lots of jerseys. The OG tomboy look, popularized by Lyte, inspired generations of artists to embrace the cozy life, from TLC and Aaliyah in the nineties down to teen pop star Billie Eilish.

"I wanted the male rappers to listen to my rhymes as opposed to looking at my body," Lyte told *Vibe* in 2001. "I wanted to be taken seriously, like, 'Don't even look at that, just listen to what I'm saying.'"

The elementary school Lyte attended in Crown Heights, Brooklyn, Weusi Shule (later renamed the Johnson Preparatory School), was founded by a woman named Ayanna Johnson. The school dedicated itself to teaching black American and African history, encouraging everything from studying Langston Hughes to celebrating Kwanzaa, all of which had an enlightening effect on Lyte. Her mom attuned her to the vocal arts early on, taking her to Broadway musicals like *Dreamgirls* and *Cats*, and in junior high a kid named Eric taught Lyte another vocal art: rapping. The trick to structure, she learned, was to control her breath and make use of semicolons and em dashes—the James Baldwin school of writing.

Lyte explained to *Vibe*, "You just write one line, and there's a hyphen that separates the next line. Whereas some people just write line, line, line, line. Mine kind of runs on, you know . . ." She spent many of her teenage years perfecting this technique and applied it to her debut album, *Lyte As a Rock*, released the same year as Salt-N-Pepa's second album, *A Salt with a Deadly Pepa*, and a year before Queen Latifah's debut album, *All Hail the Queen*.

Lyte wrote most of her first album as a preteen and wound up making a classic. "Paper Thin" showed her ability to pick off opponents with a cavalier cockiness. Another record, "10% Dis," where Lyte came at rapper Antoinette for jacking Audio Two's beat (Lyte was merciless about it), begat a yearslong battle between the two that turned into great marketing, similar to Roxanne Shanté versus Sparky D. Antoinette thinks the beef was less about actual animosity and more a result of men in both of their camps exaggerating a beef that wasn't there. But the drama, for what it was worth, launched Lyte into legendary status as a lyricist and storyteller. As *Vibe* wrote in 1996, her music "spoke for the black girls who craved hearing themselves represented correctly in the B-boy-dominated genre they lived for."

"I didn't try to be different—I just was," Lyte said in a 2013 interview with the site Halftime Online. "I did recognize that my voice was different. Well, maybe not even my voice, but the way in which I delivered rhymes was very monotone, and I was told that and not in a positive way. It was, like, 'She's too monotone!' or 'Is that it? Where's the excitement?'"

Heather B, a rapper inspired by MC Lyte, says, "When I heard the tone of MC Lyte's voice, I was like, wow, I could do that."

But in becoming a voice in hip-hop, MC Lyte was also a prime example of men in the culture idealizing what women should look and rap like to be seen as credible. When Lil' Kim and Foxy Brown became the new prototype and people longed for the purer days of MC Lyte, it was a way of negating the power of women expressing their sexuality in rap.

In 1996, Lyte underwent a slight sonic reinvention with "Keep On, Keepin' On," a single produced by Jermaine Dupri and featuring his artists Xscape. This was a smooth R&B collaboration from one of the toughest voices in rap, and it sounded flawless. Still, Lyte appears in the music video wearing a black suit and rapping about being "choosy about who I let knock my boots," proving she was still very much herself. The voice paid off and carried her career past the expected benchmark for women.

ANTOINETTE

ANTOINETTE EXPLAINS THE BACKSTORY BEHIND HER BREAK-THROUGH SINGLE "I GOT AN ATTITUDE" AND HOW SHE UNWITTINGLY PARTICIPATED IN AN ORCHESTRATED BEEF WITH MC LYTE.

She Speaks

From the time I was a little girl, I used to write a lot. Sometimes I would write poetry. "Rapper's Delight" was the first real rap song I heard, and it was like a marriage made in heaven for me. I was, like, I can actually [set] my poetry to music. Way before people heard of Antoinette, I penned myself as Annie C. I decided on that name after I heard Blondie B and Angie B. In junior high school and high school, I was in a group called the Feminine Force with another girl named Antoinette and a girl named Sharon. Sharon used to do the beatbox. In about the eleventh grade, the group fell apart. Sharon moved out to Staten Island, and Antoinette and I had gotten into a little argument. When I was in school, [classmates would] be, like, "She's good for a girl." I just wanted to be a good MC.

I started working with a guy I met in high school named Fat Doug. It's all history from there. We recorded the demo "I Got an Attitude" about the altercation between myself and the other Antoinette. I was saying, "I can't deal with her, 'cause she got an attitude." We were shopping for a deal, and he took me to Jay Ellis, who took the demo to Next Plateau to let Eddie O'Loughlin hear it. Hurby [Azor] happened to be in the next room. Hurby came and was, like, 'Yo, who is that? I want her on my album.' He was doing the compilation album at the time, *The House That Rap Built*. I think Hurby heard "I Got an Attitude" in September, and it was the first single from his compilation in November, so [the success] happened to me just that fast.

After that, MC Lyte came out with a song, "10% Dis," dissing me. I had no idea why. I [had] never met her. I didn't know her. The younger version of myself was pissed off. Why would she target me? On YouTube, there's an interview with MC Lyte where she's talking about how it all started. Supposedly, Audio Two and Hurby had a meeting. Audio Two wanted Hurby to make a diss record against their record. Back then, that's how people got put on [the air]—somebody would make a record, and somebody would make a record about their record. "I Got An Attitude" had the same beat as Audio Two's "Top Billin'"—it's a sample from "Impeach the President"—so they took it as the response to their meeting with Hurby. They told Lyte, "He got a girl on us. You gotta get her." They're the ones that put Lyte up to the whole thing. "I Got an Attitude" had nothing to do with them.

[After "10% Dis"], I didn't respond right away. My second record, "Hit 'Em With This," had no information about her. Then the next song I did, "Unfinished Business," there was a reference made, but it wasn't a diss song.

There was one diss song on my album *Who's the Boss?* called "Lights Out, Party Over," and [I recorded it] because the streets were talking. MC Lyte was swinging hard, and she was still making records, and it was, like, *You have to say something*.

She and I met [for the first time] years later at the Queens of Hip-Hop show, and we talked, and we're cool. We just talked in general. It wasn't necessary to rehash [what happened] when we were younger. At the end of the day, we're sisters in the game. She became one of the female hip-hop icons. I decided to pursue an education.

Queen Latifah

NEVER FORGET:
Queen Latifah earned an Oscar nomination for Best Supporting Actress in 2003 for her role in *Chicago.*

WHO SHE IS:
Queen Latifah (Dana Elaine Owens) changed her name to Latifah at the wise age of eight; as a student at New Jersey's Essex Catholic Girls and Irvington high schools, she sang, acted in plays, and learned how to beatbox. She's confident she was the first person in Newark to show people how to do the wop. Over the course of twenty years, Latifah pulled double duty making music (eight albums) while also becoming a film star, though everyone still calls her by her rap name.

LISTEN:
"It's Alright," featuring Faith Evans, finds Queen Latifah singing in a flirty tone about a requited crush: "When I'm sexin' you, when I'm next to you, I know it's alright."

Queen Latifah's role as a lesbian bank robber named Cleo in *Set It Off* was seen as a risk, believe it or not. The year was 1996, and Latifah was better known as a rapper who'd had a few bit parts in films (*House Party 2, Juice, My Life*) and as the star of a sitcom in its third season (*Living Single,* about a group of girlfriends). In *Set It Off,* her breakout lead role as Cleopatra Sims—Cleo, for short—Latifah seized her moment in the final act.

Surrounded by police aiming their guns at her 1962 Impala, Cleo opts for driving into a stream of bullets—and a tragic death—instead of surrendering. The scene became instant black cinema canon.

But in a sit-down interview that year, talk-show host Rolonda Watts questioned Latifah's decision to star as a gangsta lesbian (more the lesbian part than the gangsta thing). "A lotta people are going to say, 'Queen Latifah is ruining her career playing a lesbian on the movie screen,'" Watts said. "Are we ready for that?"

We were ready. *Set It Off* made a more than respectable $8.5 million in its opening weekend, nearly eclipsing its $9 million budget. Director F. Gary Gray had previously gone from high-concept music videos (TLC's "Waterfalls," Ice Cube's "It Was a Good Day") to a feature film debut at age twenty-three: the stoner comedy *Friday,* starring first-time actor Ice Cube.

Set It Off was Gray's ambitious follow-up about four women in Los Angeles desperately in need of cash. A classic antihero heist film, it was a story about money and friendship, anchored by two rising actors—Jada Pinkett Smith and Vivica A. Fox—and two promising ones, Kimberly Elise and Queen Latifah.

Instead of looking like royalty, or the editor of a hip urban magazine, as on *Living Single*, Queen Latifah wore cornrows and baggy jeans as Cleo, a self-proclaimed "dyke" who smoked blunts and had a chip on her shoulder. "The hood is where I belong. I mean, what am I gonna do in Hollywood? Or Thousand Oaks or some shit?" Cleo tells Stony (Jada Pinkett Smith) in a heart-to-heart leading up to their big bank heist.

Two girls at Irvington–Frank H. Morrell High School inspired the Cleo character, which Latifah knew she could pull off. After auditioning for the role, casting director Robi Reed recalls, Latifah told her over the phone, "I am this bitch."

"The role of Cleo said to anyone paying attention that Dana really had skill and that anything up to this point wasn't luck or a fluke," says Reed. "She was seen as a serious actress." Latifah's box-office draw spiked from there, and she became part of the first generation of rappers—alongside 2Pac, Will Smith, Ice Cube, LL Cool J, and Ice-T—to build a bankable Hollywood résumé.

Latifah the rapper was a savior to hip-hop in the nineties. In a 1992 interview for her late-night talk show *The Whoopi Goldberg Show*, Whoopi praised her for simply managing to avoid the words "ho" and "bitch" in her rhymes—which explains where rap as a genre was at the time.

Queen Latifah wrote in her memoir, "Gangsta rap was ruling at the time, and with it came all this misogynistic bull— 'bitch' this, 'ho' that. And, crazy as it sounds, I saw female rappers buying into it."

Latifah's music was sold as a fresh alternative that unfortunately helped set up a binary: Women were either righteous MCs like her or chose to sell sex. For those seeking broader success, there was little room in between.

Around 1986, producer Mark Howard James, aka Mark the 45 King, saw Queen Latifah at a Newark talent show, when she performed with singer Eddie Stockley as a duo named Quiet Storm. "She was a singer, learning how to rap better," says James. "She's a fast learner. You give her a hammer, and she'll build a house." They made a demo tape, "Wrath of My Madness," which James accidentally or intentionally left at Fab 5 Freddy's house, and Freddy routed the tape to his friend Dante Ross, an A&R guy at Tommy Boy Records. The song set off alarms.

"I was, like, 'Whoa, what the fuck is that?'" Ross remembers. "It was one of those records that, within twelve hours, was on the air." He and Tommy Boy president Monica Lynch signed Latifah to a deal.

She then became a member of the Native Tongues, a collective of acts like Jungle Brothers, De La Soul, and A Tribe Called Quest who brought low-end jazz to rap while dressed in African-inspired prints and medallions. Queen Latifah had a similar look and feel—she bought the outfit for her first album cover in Newark at "an African fabric store on Halsey Street." "Everyone else was wearing their sex, but I was wearing my heart. I wanted to be about more than a designer label. I wanted to deliver a message," she wrote in her book *Ladies First: Revelations of a Strong Woman* (although women wearing their sex was itself a message). Compared with her peers, she was eccentric.

"Latifah and MC Lyte weren't selling sex. And Salt-N-Pepa sold it a little more than Latifah and Lyte did," says Ross. Latifah's debut album, *All Hail the Queen*, produced by Mark the 45 King, incorporated

NO ANTHEMS
WERE MORE
REBELLIOUS AND
RELEVANT TO
THE TIMES THAN
"U.N.I.T.Y."

high-speed dance rhythms, house music, and Jamaican patois. Says Ross, "It was reflective of what was going on in hip-hop. Everything was positive and about self-empowerment. Public Enemy started the trend of black empowerment, black consciousness, and the Jungle Brothers and De La [Soul] did it in a less 'threatening' kind of way, a more psychedelic way, and Latifah and Monie Love were part of that."

No songs were more rebellious and relevant to the times than "U.N.I.T.Y"—on which Queen Latifah shoots a pithy five-word comeback at rappers' favorite epithet for women: "Who you callin' a *bitch*?"—and "Ladies First," her motivational duet with London-born rapper Monie Love.

But Queen Latifah's acting work overtook her career so much that people forgot her past life as a rapper. Her career in Hollywood kicked off after director Spike Lee and Robi Reed saw Latifah perform a summer concert at the Pier in New York City. They had her audition and cast her as a fed-up waitress at Harlem's legendary soul food spot, Sylvia's, in *Jungle Fever*, Lee's 1991 film about interracial dating.

Latifah's brief monologue about Wesley Snipes's character bringing a "stringy-hair ass" white woman on a date to a black establishment earned her a SAG card—the Screen Actors Guild's credential for working actors. "Spike and I rolled the dice," says Reed. "With the waitress [role] in *Jungle Fever*, all she had to do was be who she was onstage."

But Latifah's lasting gift to the world is *Living Single*, a girlfriends-centered sitcom set in a beautiful Brooklyn brownstone. Playing one of television's most iconic characters, Khadijah James, editor of a hip black magazine, titled *Flavor*, Latifah brought the best quips ("Khadijah don't need ya!"), daggers, and shade, alongside a cast of still-underappreciated comedic geniuses, over five seasons.

In a business as volatile as music, acting was a logical backup for rappers. Being on-screen took them out of their environments and into faraway, lucrative places. Old rock stars could technically tour into infinity (think the Rolling Stones), and pop stars reinvent themselves over decades—Celine Dion had a sixteen-year Las Vegas residency; Madonna is 201 years old—but the idea of rapping as a lifetime sport is still relatively new.

"It's really hard to have a long career in hip-hop as an MC as a woman without diversifying greatly," says writer Karen Good. "You've got to be Eve doing daytime TV or movies. You gotta be Latifah doing other things. Everybody begins to shift."

It's why, after one album with N.W.A, Ice Cube said in 1989, "You can't rap forever. If it ends tomorrow, I still gotta do something to survive." Jay-Z, Nas, Ludacris, and Eve have shared a similar paranoia in interviews. Eminem said he couldn't see himself "jumping around the stage like a fucking kid" in old age (although he did).

Queen Latifah said the same in 1996. "I'm not going to be a rapper forever," she told *Vibe*. "I'm always going to write rhymes. But that doesn't mean I'm always going to be able to compete in this business." While rappers like Jay-Z, T.I., and Snoop Dogg have shown what hip-hop longevity looks like, making music beyond age forty, there was really no blueprint for the women who eventually hit a ceiling. And without structural support, the ceiling collapses.

Latifah stopped releasing rap records and discovered acting, then went on to star in romantic comedies and family fare and earned an Oscar nomination for the musical *Chicago*—one of only two rappers to ever be nominated for an Academy Award as an actor. The other is a rapper from West Philadelphia who spent his childhood on playgrounds, Will Smith.

QUEEN LATIFAH AT THE BOX OFFICE

Bringing Down the House (2003)
$132,716,677

Hairspray (2007)
$118,871,849

Girls Trip (2017)
$115,171,585

Last Holiday (2006)
$38,399,961

The Secret Life of Bees (2008)
$37,770,162

Taxi (2004)
$36,879,320

Set It Off (1996)
$36,461,139

The Perfect Holiday (2007)
$5,812,781

Beauty Shop (2005)
$36,351,350

Joyful Noise (2012)
$30,932,113

Brown Sugar (2002)
$27,363,891

Just Wright (2010)
$21,540,363

Chicago (2002)
$170,687,518

J.J. Fad

♦ ♦ ♦

NEVER FORGET:
J.J. Fad was among the acts nominated in the first-ever Grammys rap category for Best Rap Performance.

WHO THEY ARE:
At nineteen years old, Juana Sperling held auditions at her mother's house in Rialto, California, to form a girl group. The original J.J. Fad consisted of five members whose initials spelled J.J. Fad, including Juana and her best friend's cousin, Baby D. Their song "Supersonic" got them a record deal with N.W.A member Eazy-E under his label, Ruthless Records, under which they released two albums and became crossover sensations who appealed to a broad, pop audience.

LISTEN:
"Supersonic" kicks off with an acoustic rap over beatboxing, then turns into a jazzercise rhythm with verses about J.J. Fad's devastation on the mic. It ends with a tongue-twisting rap, which Eminem later paid homage to in his 2013 single "Rap God."

♦ ♦ ♦

After years of zero recognition, the Grammys introduced its inaugural rap category in 1989: the award for Best Rap Performance, which was supposed to be a milestone for hip-hop. By the time of the broadcast, everyone in the country knew Juana Sperling (MC JB), Dania Birks (Baby D), and Michelle Ferrens (Sassy C) as J.J. Fad, the group whose single "Supersonic" stuck to your eardrums and biker shorts.

The song earned them radio spins, national recognition, and that first rap Grammy nomination, alongside LL Cool J ("Going Back to Cali"), DJ Jazzy Jeff & the Fresh Prince ("Parents Just Don't Understand"), Salt-N-Pepa ("Push It"), and Kool Moe Dee ("Wild Wild West"). But the acknowledgment was bittersweet. The Academy claimed there wasn't enough airtime to accommodate all the categories during the broadcast, which hip-hop practitioners viewed as a slight. (The rap winners would be announced during the preshow.) Feeling excluded from the main-stage narrative, most of the rap nominees agreed to snub the Grammys right back and boycott. Not J.J. Fad.

Leading up to the 1989 Grammys, Def Jam Recordings, the home of LL Cool J and DJ Jazzy Jeff & the Fresh Prince, spread news of an impending boycott through a press release, in which the label's spokesman, Bill Adler, accused the

Recording Academy of "ghettoizing" rap. Chuck D said at a press conference, "We don't give a fuck about a goddamn Grammy." During an after-party at the Cat & Fiddle nightclub in Los Angeles, on the night of the Grammys, Salt from Salt-N-Pepa explained their decision not to attend in an interview with Fab 5 Freddy on *Yo! MTV Raps*: "We paid our dues and got our nominations just like everybody else, and it's just not fair that we're not going to be able to be shown," she said.

Only Kool Moe Dee and J.J. Fad, both citing the importance of the event, showed up to the ceremony in February 1989. The three members of J.J. Fad came dressed in custom tuxedo jackets with rhinestone-studded bow ties and cummerbunds.

Whitney Houston opened the show with "One Moment in Time." Tracy Chapman won Best New Artist for "Fast Car." The Grammys added a hard rock/metal category that year and televised the winner (albeit contentiously; metalheads argued that said winner, Jethro Tull, wasn't metal). And before all that, during the preshow, DJ Jazzy Jeff & the Fresh Prince won the first-ever rap Grammy in absentia. The following year, when the rap category aired, Will Smith showed up and dedicated his set "to all the rappers last year that stood with us and helped us to earn the right to be on this stage tonight."

Every musical genre has criticized the Grammy Awards at one time or another. (Rock artists have also hated them.) But over the years, rappers have treated the institution like, well, an institution, deserving of boycotts and skepticism. It took six years for a woman to win in any of the key rap categories: Not until 1995 did Salt-N-Pepa become the first female rap group to earn a Grammy—Best Rap Performance for "None of Your Business." The Academy introduced an award for Best Female Rap Solo Performance in 2003, but it extinguished the

category after two years (Missy Elliott won both times), lumping male and female acts back together. J.J. Fad's presence at the Grammys was major at a time when rap was fighting to be recognized as culturally prestigious; then, when it became so, the 2010s saw big rappers like Drake and Jay-Z actively boycotting the show for the same reasons. There's still value in winning a Grammy, especially for lesser-known artists, but the coronation has become much less hallowed over the years.

It just so happened that the late eighties was the era of M.C. Hammer, the Oakland Athletics batboy-turned-rapper who was ridiculed for his dance moves, his commercial music, and his crotch-sagging harem pants, though he later became the prototype for mainstream success in hip-hop. *Entertainment Weekly* wrote in 1990 that "the 27-year-old Hammer came to symbolize rap's first big push into heartland America." It was this expansion of hip-hop into white America that prompted the Grammys to finally recognize the genre.

J.J. Fad's Grammy appearance stood out in an era when rap fans considered crossover rappers to be sellouts. Over the years, the group defended their choice to attend. "We decided to go because it was an honor for us," says Ferrens. "We said we might never get another opportunity. It wasn't to be disrespectful to someone else's cause. The message was heard. They started televising [the rap category], and we were glad we went." Says Sperling, "We said, 'We're not boycotting because we may never get back here.' And we never did get back there."

It's fitting that Whitney Houston, accused of being a pop sellout herself, opened the first Grammys that celebrated rap and that J.J. Fad attended. "It was not a good thing to cross over. You didn't get the respect other hip-hop artists got," says Sperling. "It was, like, *Oh, you crossed*

over, you're not real rappers. You're pop. It was kind of offensive. We were three black girls in the black community. That's the song we picked, and it happened to cross over."

J.J. Fad was part of the first pop-rap wave of the 1980s, while signed to one of the most hardcore rap labels around, Ruthless Records. The "sellout" argument meant that a black act was essentially too popular or that their music wasn't true to the roots of hip-hop, but this point was really about the frailty of genres, in the scheme of things, especially once rap became the lodestar of popular music. The fear was a desire to keep the soul of hip-hop without losing the culture to outside forces, which proved inevitable.

Two original J.J. Fad members were friends of N.W.A's Dr. Dre and Mik Lezan, aka DJ Arabian Prince, who produced a pair of records for the group early on, using his 808 drum machine and Yamaha keyboard: "Another Ho Bites the Dust" and the upbeat dance record "Supersonic." After they shopped the demo around LA, with "Supersonic" as the B side, "Another Ho" hit big on radio, while DJs loved "Supersonic."

"A lot of people could sing along. Cheerleaders, everybody. It went viral before anybody used the word 'viral,'" says Lezan. "Sometimes when you're doing dance music, people say, 'That ain't really hip-hop.' But I often said that's where hip-hop came from. A lot of early hip-hop was up-tempo.

IT WAS THIS EXPANSION OF HIP-HOP INTO WHITE AMERICA THAT PROMPTED THE GRAMMYS TO FINALLY RECOGNIZE THE GENRE.

"I don't believe in the concept of 'sellout' at all," says Danyel Smith, a former editor in chief of *Vibe* and an Oakland native. "I believe in the power of pop, and I believe they are a girl group that was at the forefront of female pop, rap, and should be celebrated as such. I don't like the old rock-critic notion of: You have to be somehow pure, or that you have to sell small amounts of music to be real. All we had were guys to jam to, and many of them were great, but you also had these women MCs in videos dancing and having that strong attitude and having their own opinion and rapping that fast and so well. It was a miracle. Even if it's only 'Supersonic,' they're hip-hop Hall-of-Famers."

It was Grandmaster Flash and 'Planet Rock.' That was all hip-hop."

The sheer force of "Supersonic" helped J.J. Fad land a deal with LA's Dream Team Records—shortly afterward, three of the original members dropped out. To once again fill out the group, Dream Team brought in Michelle Ferrens, a well-known cheerleader at St. Mary's High School. "She was one of the most popular girls at my high school. The best body, the most mouth—she was dynamic," Danyel Smith remembers. "We all looked up to her. A few years later, when we saw her as a part of this group, it didn't feel like much of a surprise."

A spot on the Ruthless Records roster was sometimes a winner's curse. N.W.A rapper Eazy-E ran the label at a time when N.W.A was infamous, but Ruthless was also a financial dead end for certain artists. (Ice Cube left N.W.A due to money complaints.) Nonetheless, Eazy was looking to sign a female act that could help legitimize the label. He bought out J.J. Fad's contract after seeing them perform at the club Casa Camino Real in LA.

With the ear of Dr. Dre, who added his signature drums to the beat, J.J. Fad re-recorded their vocals for "Supersonic." J.J. Fad split its 1988 debut album, *Supersonic*, into two halves, with "Time Tah Get Stupid" on the hip-hop side (which features Dr. Dre scratching) and songs like the title track on the pop side.

Mainstream outlets obsessed over J.J. Fad's clean-cut image. Per a description from *People* magazine in 1988 that now reads like a message on a scroll: "J.J. Fad, like the duo DJ Jazzy Jeff & the Fresh Prince, is part of a startling new breed of rappers: As clean-cut as can be, the three are into bowling, pinball, and miniature golf, don't smoke or do drugs, and boast that their favorite drinks are virgin daiquiris." "Supersonic," a Top 40 hit, was so universally appealing that decades later, Black Eyed Peas member Fergie made a gentrified version, her 2006 solo single, "Fergalicious" (a pop song that has some rapping), and that record also became a hit.

J.J. Fad's crossover success was instant, which meant white fans attended their shows, and Ferrens noticed a difference in reception at these concerts. "When we first started touring, we would go places and be huge, people rushing to the airports to see us. And then we'd come back to our hometown, and it's, like, crickets," she says. "Now it's more accepted. It's expected. If you don't cross over, then you're not successful."

J.J. Fad were the only women and the only pop act on Run-D.M.C.'s 1988 *Run's House* tour, surrounded by Public Enemy, Stetsasonic, and DJ Jazzy Jeff & the Fresh Prince. The tour was like a proving ground for them. "That's how we started getting a little bit more respect, because people were, like, okay, they have some hip-hop," says Sperling.

It was hard not to love their music, their look, and their dance moves. When people think of eighties style, a clear reference point is J.J. Fad and their sporty outfits, an idiom that was revived some thirty-plus years later when fashion regurgitated that decade's looks with trends like athleisure. In the video for "Supersonic," the group wore black leggings and matching collegiate jackets.

The national acclaim of "Supersonic" catapulted others by association. The song helped Eazy-E land a distribution deal for Ruthless through Atlantic Records' subsidiary, Atco. Dr. Dre confirmed that J.J. Fad's success brought in the money that powered Ruthless and, in turn, N.W.A. Dre said in the HBO documentary *The Defiant Ones*: "The money that we made on the J.J. Fad album helped fund a lot of the albums that came next."

A month before the 1989 Grammys, "Supersonic" was certified gold—the first-ever gold record for Ruthless. Lezan says, "It was a catalyst for a lot of things that went on at Ruthless and probably opened the doors to N.W.A's early tours." Despite keeping the lights on at Ruthless, J.J. Fad got no mention in *Straight Outta Compton*, the $161 million–grossing N.W.A biopic released to theaters in 2015. When it came time to record their sophomore album, Dr. Dre, tied up with multiple other projects, wanted to postpone it, but J.J. Fad got anxious and rushed to release the album in 1990. They titled it *Not Just a Fad*. "We never broke up, but after the second album didn't do that well," says Sperling, "it was perfect to take our time to raise our kids. Live a normal life."

L'TRIMM

◆ ◆ ◆

NEVER FORGET:
Their black Malibu Barbie–style eighties outfits consisted of biker shorts and neon hairbows.

WHO THEY ARE:
Born in Spanish Harlem and raised in Hollis, Queens, Lady Tigra (Rachel de Rougemont) rapped, break-danced with her little brother, and did graffiti writing as a kid. She chose "Tigra" as her tag because it was a childhood nickname meaning "little fatso" in Creole. Bunny D (Elana Dickerson) was born in Chicago and also a graffiti tagger and B-girl who danced ballet and tap. The pair met at a Miami dance club and began performing as L'Trimm, named after a denim company called Trim. Atlantic Records released their first of three albums, *Grab It!*, in 1988, followed by *Drop That Bottom* and *Groovy*.

LISTEN:
On the sweet, made-for-prom jam "Cutie Pie," they rap about a good guy who's "the apple of my eye."

The best thing L'Trimm ever did for Miami bass was make a record about Miami bass. On their biggest single, "Cars That Go Boom" (or "Cars with the Boom"), released in 1988, they rhapsodize about the joy of playing a bass record out of a car blessed with subwoofers. The chorus is a simple, confectionary, two-line tribute to the power of a good sound system: "We like the cars / The cars that go boom."

Lady Tigra and Bunny D were high schoolers at the time, rapping as if they'd snuck into hip-hop with fake IDs. "Cars That Go Boom" appealed to the car-and-bass lovers inside and outside of Miami and served as an ode to the legendary sound systems that exemplified Miami bass, the type of frenetic music made for figuratively (and literally) dry humping in the club.

"On the East Coast and on the West Coast, people had that in common: They were all tricking out their systems in their cars," says Lady Tigra. "They were all cruising. So here comes this bottom-heavy, bass-heavy song that you could play in your car, singing about the activity that you're doing right now and glorifying it."

When Tigra moved to Miami, bass ran the city. She and her friend Nicole Gordon-Hay (who went by the nickname Tricky Nikki) would frequent clubs on teen night so much that their appearances at Skylight Express eventually led to featured-dancer spots on the weekly teen dance show *Miami Teen Express*. It was there that Lady Tigra met Bunny D, and they became L'Trimm.

With the help of Larry Davis, who was producing R&B records in Philadelphia before moving to Miami to join Hot Productions (a label run by Paul Klein and Henry Stone, who'd worked with KC and the Sunshine Band), L'Trimm recorded a playful comeback to Salt-N-Pepa's record "Push It." The resulting song, "Grab It!," included a subliminal reference to Salt-N-Pepa: "You say you wanna push it / Let's push it and I'll show you what to do." The song was an attempt to lightly punch up, but Bunny D says, "I don't think people really caught on to it."

"Grab It!" hit radio and very quickly earned Tigra and Bunny a record deal with Hot Productions, under Atlantic Records. They built their music around the high-strung 808 drums that were characteristic of Miami bass, along with hyper synths, bubbly electro-rap, and pretty-girl rhymes about being young, fly, and gifted while dealing with teenage dilemmas. The material was kept lightweight and young but also notably tongue-in-cheek—*Grab It!*, for one, was titled *Grab It!*.

"Grab your opportunities, your dreams, your goals," Bunny D explains with a giggle. "It was one of

" IT WAS ONE OF THOSE INNUENDOS THAT WAS KINDA RISQUÉ.

"

those innuendos that was kinda risqué." Their schoolgirl tones, lisps, and nasal, Rosie Perez–esque vocal effects made some of their more suggestive content slightly more scandalous and uncomfortably mature, in retrospect, including two songs about a boy named Chris who was both a "ho" and a "mutt" and was based on Bunny D's real-life cheating boyfriend.

Davis says, "I think they found their niche 'cause they didn't take themselves so serious. It was still all fun." In 2020, "Cars With the Boom" got revived on the addictive homemade video app TikTok, where young people drawn to the song's bubbly vibe posted their own dances to it, giving new life to a duo responsible for bringing a ray of sunshine to Miami bass.

ARTISTS FORMERLY KNOWN AS . . .

Salt-N-Pepa ↔ Super Nature

Jean Grae ↔ What What?

Queen Latifah ↔ Princess of the Posse

Vita ↔ Hot Totti

Azealia Banks ↔ Miss Banks

Eve ↔ Eve of Destruction

MC Lyte ↔ Sparkle

Foxy Brown ↔ Shorty/Queen Nefertiti

The Women of Miami Bass

Missy Mist

The rapper, born Michelle Broome, worked primarily with Miami bass producer DJ Eric Griffin on songs like "Make It Mellow" (which got her a deal with Atlantic Records) and "Let's Get This Party Started," where she attests that "the rock and roll guitar will have you jammin' so hard."

Anquette

After 2 Live Crew dropped their obscene party single "Throw the D," Anquette responded with the up-tempo "Throw the P." Over the same 808s and record scratches, the trio questioned, "How could you throw a dick that was miniature size?" Indeed, how could you.

MC Luscious

In 1990, Luscious released a self-explanatory answer record to the Boys from the Bottom's "Boom! I Got Your Girlfriend," flipped into "Boom! I Got Your Boyfriend," about stealing another girl's fine man.

Get Fresh Girls

The song most Miami locals will remember is the chipper cautionary tale "I Seen Your Boyfriend," about catching a shady boy "tricking."

Dimples Tee

They released a response to 1987's "Jealous Girls," titled "Jealous Fellas," where they rap that "ladies in the eighties are tryna get ahead / while jealous fellas like you want us to stay in bed."

Fresh Celeste

While her rap song "Get It Boy" finds her taunting a boy to hit the dance floor, she also sang R&B crush songs (see: "Dangerous Loverboy").

Tricky Nikki

The lost third member of L'Trimm was supposed to be in the group, but was phased out before Lady Tigra and Bunny D signed their deal. She recovered with her single "Bust the Rhythm of my ABC's." She later quit rapping and joined the Nation of Islam.

OAKTOWN'S 357

♦ ♦ ♦

NEVER FORGET:
Biggie dropped Oaktown's 357's name (which comes from the .357 Magnum) as part of a rhyme about his extensive gun collection on his song "Come On."

WHO THEY ARE:
The members of Oaktown's 357 worked as backup dancers for M.C. Hammer before they became a formal group, helmed by Hammer. Their style was an extension of his hyper dance aesthetic, and they released two albums under his label Bust It Records, *Wild & Loose* (1989) and *Fully Loaded* (1991).

LISTEN:
"Juicy Gotcha Krazy" is a high-speed, tongue-in-cheek dance record about an irresistible woman.

♦ ♦ ♦

A year before the world heard "U Can't Touch This," M.C. Hammer was on the precipice of becoming a king of crossover rap. Hammer's independent album, *Feel My Power* (later re-released and retitled *Let's Get It Started*), had sold 60,000 copies and made him a regional star in his hometown of Oakland, California (where he worked as a batboy for the A's), complete with his own boutique imprint, Bust It, under Capitol Records. He was ready to be a father of an empire. All he needed was a few solid acts, including a girl group who would make him look good and rival the biggest female rap group of the time, Salt-N-Pepa.

The idea behind Oaktown's 357 was to build off Hammer's sound and style and sculpt a group in his image, harem pants and all. High-energy dance music and sweat choreography were crucial to presenting this group as a total package. Hammer's performances had all the energy of a Barnum & Bailey show, with a convoy of dancers determined to match his stamina. The man loved to dance.

So Hammer began to build a roster. He first tried to groom one of his dancers, Phyllis Charles, aka Lil P, as a solo rapper,

WE WOULD GO OUT TO ALL THE BIGGEST CLUBS AS THEY GOT BIGGER, AND EVERYBODY WOULD GO NUTS. IN SOME WAYS, 357 DID AS MUCH FOR HAMMER AS HAMMER DID FOR 357.

after he heard her rapping to Salt-N-Pepa's "Tramp." But Lil P, whom he discovered at the Oakland Army Base, didn't want to go solo. Hammer decided to pair her with two of his other dancers: Suhayla Sabir (aka Sweet LD), whom he'd met at Club Silk in Emeryville, and Tabatha Brooks (Terrible T), who met him at the San Francisco club the Palladium during the promo for his single "Ring 'Em."

The source of the group's name, Oaktown's 357, was far more threatening than the group itself. "The numbers 357 are in reference to the .357 Magnum," says Sweet LD. "The power of the weapon, we associated with our power as performers, dancers, women, and artists. The numbers also fit our personalities, so to speak . . . Not necessarily sexy, but definitely fun, confident, sassy."

To prep for shows, Hammer would put his dancers through mandatory boot camps, which involved running and weight training. While recording his debut album in Vallejo, California, he would often develop routines in real time and adjust the pace of his songs as needed. "We would play the music in the studio real loud, and Hammer would constantly get up and dance with his dancers and check to make sure the tempo was right," says James Earley, one of Hammer's producers tasked to work with Oaktown's 357. "He needed to know that everything about the dancing was right." To reiterate: *Hammer loved to dance.*

Making Oaktown's 357 into legitimate showstoppers took effort. The vision in Hammer's mind was a girl group in the vein of Rick James and the Mary Jane Girls or Prince's Vanity 6. Since neither Sweet LD nor Terrible T had rapped before, Hammer helped co-write the first album, *Wild & Loose*, with production from Earley and another of Hammer's right-hand men, Felton Pilate. But the music was almost tangential to the show. Terrible T, whose older brother got her into boogaloo and pop-locking, incorporated street moves into their routines. While helping Hammer plan his shows, she and Sweet LD also served as their own choreographers, donning colorful, practical biker shorts and stretch fabrics for comfort while in motion.

"We wore the biker shorts, the workout clothes, because of the way we danced. Back then, you didn't care if you sweated. You was gon' get on the dance floor to burn rubber."

Says Earley, "They were literally teaching an entire generation how to move. They would go on *Soul Train* and make everybody crazy. We would go out to all the biggest clubs as they got bigger, and everybody would go nuts. In some ways, 357 did as much for Hammer as Hammer did for 357."

By that point, Hammer was on a roll, meaning that white people loved him. "U Can't Touch This" was making a torturously good run through pop to kick off the 1990s.

"When I met Hammer, his goal was to do almost Christian-flavored, very nonthreatening hip-hop," says Pilate. "We used to joke about the fact that we had old white people buying his music, because it was just a phenomenon that happened to happen at the right time. 357 wound up being an offshoot of that. They weren't pretending to be straight from the hood. This was dance music and have-fun music and *let's just enjoy this*."

Oaktown's 357 had a moderate hit in 1988 with their debut single, "Juicy Gotcha Krazy." Lil P left the group before the release of the music video, which opens on a talk-show parody featuring Madonna, Diana Ross, and Tina Turner impersonators. "We started writing that on the airplane, and it was almost like it was a joke: Ooh, Juicy got you crazy," says Terrible T.

While Hammer was getting flak for seemingly straying from hip-hop's roots—which were, in fact, built around dancing and partying—Oaktown's 357 was an occasional casualty, even the subject of a passing reference on a Notorious B.I.G. song, "Come On," where he rapped, "You can't touch my riches / Even if you had M.C. Hammer and them 357 bitches." Still, the group legitimized Hammer as an artist, performer, and producer with a vision based around showmanship. Hammer's reign came just before the East Coast/West Coast rap rivalry that defined the nineties and led to the deaths of the Notorious B.I.G. and 2Pac. At a time when New York was the epicenter of so-called "pure" hip-hop, Hammer and Oaktown's 357 were the opposition who came in glistening with positivity.

"M.C. Hammer was changing the dynamic and the look and the sound of hip-hop, so other performers felt threatened by his show. 'He's from the West Coast. He's not an "MC." He's this, he's that . . .' were comments made to discredit him as a rap artist and performer," says Sweet LD. "However, if you look back on what he did, you might not have liked it, but he opened a lot of doors for endorsements and so forth. I know he opened the doors to where it became more acceptable for rappers to perform in certain venues."

"As a rapper, to be blunt, he was not amazing," says Pilate. "But as an entertainer, we created something that, although [some] people hated it, you had to respect the fact that we accomplished it."

Oaktown's 357 released a second album, *Fully Loaded*, in 1991 before Bust It Records dropped them. Despite a low mainstream profile, their style is still unmistakable. "I think for some people from the East Coast, Oaktown's 357 might've been a guilty pleasure, because they didn't want to like M.C. Hammer," says Sweet LD. "In some ways, 357 was kind of a pleasant buffer for Hammer to be accepted."

MIA X

MIA X REMEMBERS PUSHING BACK AGAINST THE MUSIC INDUSTRY'S BODY TYPE EXPECTATIONS FOR WOMEN.

She Speaks

I was already a proven battle rapper, a proven writer. But in the industry, I was a plus-size rapper who refused any type of plastic surgery, who was told, "I think you're very pretty, but if you lose weight, they will probably shoot more videos of you, because guys like visuals, and sex sells."

I felt we already had little petite girls and thick, fine, naturally Southern, cornbread-fed girls like Gangsta Boo and Trina, so I didn't feel the need for me to do that. Everyone was buying into a body type and a look, and my look was more around-the-way-girl. This is my hair, I have a roller set, these forty double-D titties, they mine, this stomach is mine, this big ole ass is mine, and guys like that just as much as they like a lady with a six-pack.

When it came to endorsements and things like that, as popular as I was—I had moved 500,000 records in six weeks, and I had one video—I did notice that I didn't get four and five and six videos like a lot of the ladies that were putting out records at the same time as me. It was label executives as well as big directors at the time [who] would look [at me] and say, "You know, I think she really got something, but she is kinda fat, and she's not that tall."

It was challenging, because they would always try to find somebody to say, "Well, you have a pretty cool shape, maybe if you came down about forty or fifty pounds, we were thinking that you would really, really be market-able." Or when we would go out to dinner, they would have certain ladies and executives in the indus-try that I had formed a bond with say, "I mean, your skin is flawless, but there are these steam rooms that melt the fat, and there are these places . . ."

I was, like, I understand, but until my health is at risk, I'm comfortable. I understand that when you all look at me, you don't see the beauty that you see in the other girls, because I'm not the one in the see-through bodysuit or whatever. But I was already a mom, and I really didn't want no see-through stuff for my cat and my ass. I was trying to get people to understand that sex is gonna have to sell from the way I spit it out in the rhymes, 'cause I'm not showing y'all my titties, because I don't have no relationship with y'all like that. If I was a size two, I would not let you see my boobs. You not 'bout to see all my privates. My grandma gon' have a fit! So I was passed up for a lot of things, and I wasn't considered sexy when it came to the magazines saying who was the sexiest, but I was always considered one of the dopest, so I'll take that. I understood the power of imagery, but at the same time I stood my ground, because there are women that look just like me, too, and I became, like, a people's champ.

◆◆◆◆◆◆◆◆◆◆◆◆◆◆◆◆◆◆◆◆◆◆◆◆◆◆◆◆◆◆◆◆◆

NEVER FORGET:
She was one of the originators of bounce music.

WHO SHE IS:
The rapper from New Orleans's Seventh Ward was part of Master P's unstoppable, camouflage-obsessed No Limit regime. Mia X (Mia Young) knew she wanted to be a rapper when she heard the Sequence's "Funk You Up." Then, at fourteen, when she was part of the rap group New York Incorporated (with producer Mannie Fresh), they would rent ballrooms to throw five-dollar disco parties and open shows for acts like DJ Jazzy Jeff & the Fresh Prince and Run-D.M.C. Mia X met Master P while she was working at the record store Peaches & Tapes, before signing to his label, No Limit Records, where she released three albums, beginning with her 1995 debut, *Good Girl Gone Bad*.

LISTEN:
On her debut single, "Da Payback," in 1992, she raps, "Females are women and girls, not bitches and hoes" and clowned a man about his "weak-ass dick" and other malfunctions.

◆◆◆◆◆◆◆◆◆◆◆◆◆◆◆◆◆◆◆◆◆◆◆◆◆◆◆◆◆◆◆◆◆

Women in Duos & Groups

Doggy's Angels

Snoop Dogg once fathered a rap girl group featuring Coniyac, Big Chan, and Kola Loc, who released a handful of funk-inspired R&B rap songs.

Us Girls

Debbie D, Lisa Lee, and MC Sha-Rock first called themselves Empress. You can see them performing in the 1984 film *Beat Street*.

Paulette Tee & Sweet Tee

The two then-teen daughters of Paul Winley, who owned the Harlem-based label Winley Records, recorded "Rhymin' and Rappin'" in 1979, with the backing of their dad's band. The song dropped the same year Sugarhill Gang released the first hit rap song, "Rapper's Delight."

Get Em Mamis

Baltimore natives Roxzi and Symphony specialized in hyperactive, hard-core club anthems like "Cold Summer" and "When You See Us."

The Playgirls

Prior to going solo, Sparky D started out in this trio from Brownsville, Brooklyn, with her friends City Slim and Mo Ski. They signed to Sutra Records and released the single "Our Picture of a Man."

Missy Dee & the Melody Crew

The quartet featuring MC Lady T drop bouncy disco-backed raps on their 1981 song "Missy Missy Dee."

Dee Barnes and Body & Soul

Dee Barnes and Rose "Almight T" Hutchinson, released their debut single, "Dance to the Drummer's Beat," in 1989. Their performance of the song "We're All in the Same Gang," an all-star posse cut produced by Dr. Dre, earned Body & Soul a Grammy nomination. But Barnes became a part of Dre's toxic history in 1991. While she was host of the music video show *Pump It Up!* the rapper/producer assaulted her over a segment about N.W.A that aired. It took years for Dre to finally apologize.

Sisters Disco

They were the aptly named counterparts to DJ Breakout and DJ Baron's Brothers Disco in the early seventies.

Glamour Girls

In 1986, Sweet Tee and Juice Crew member MC Glamorous, who met at Sweet Tee's birthday party (the same night as MC Glamorous's prom), released "Oh Veronica," a response to the Bad Boys' "Veronica," which tells the tale of a fly girl who's also a "sleaze."

HWA

Like Bytches With Problems, Hoes with Attitudes (HWA) was created as an answer to N.W.A. Signed to Eazy-E's Ruthless Records, the Compton-based trio (Jazz, Diva, and Baby Girl) released an album of explicit raps in 1994 titled *Az Much Ass Azz U Want*. Their song "Eat This" has nothing to do with food.

Poizon Posse

The New York–based group consisted of four rappers (including Aishah Baum, who released a Roxanne Shanté diss record under the name Little Ice). The group worked with fellow rapper Toi "Sweet Tee" Jackson and released one album, *Stompin'*, in 1993.

Figure of Speech

Decades before Ava DuVernay was directing Oscar-nominated films like *Selma* and *13th*, she was known as Eve and was half of an LA duo with a rapper named Jyant. There's video footage of the pair performing a tongue-twister aptly titled "Don't Get It Twisted" at LA's famous MC spot, the Good Life. "The Good Life was a gorgeous haven for young black and brown artists in LA at the time. It changed me forever," says DuVernay. "It was the first time I allowed myself to think and work as an artist, and all the risk and courage and dedication and tenacity that goes with that brave act."

Finesse & Synquis

These two solo rappers came together to collaborate on the album *Soul Sisters*, the title track of which chops part of Labelle's hit song "Lady Marmalade" into an upbeat ladies' anthem.

Deadly Venoms

The Wu-Tang Clan–affiliated foursome (rappers N-Tyce, Finesse, Champ, and J-Boo) combined forces to release three albums (only one through a major label), as well as a handful of street records like "Venom Everywhere" and "Bomb Threat," on which N-Tyce raps, "I got dreams like Jordan got cream."

NIKKI D

NEVER FORGET:
She was the first female rapper signed to Def Jam Recordings.

WHO SHE IS:
Nikki D (Nichelle Strong) moved to New York in the fall of 1986 with the sole mission of signing to Def Jam, the biggest label in hip-hop. When Def Jam head Russell Simmons got a hold of her demo tape from the production duo L.A. Posse, he called and left them a message. "The bitch is dope!" he screamed. "I wanna sign her!" Nikki D became a special project and released one album under the label, titled *Daddy's Little Girl*.

LISTEN:
"Daddy's Little Girl," a song about loss of innocence that samples the bass line and vocals from DNA's "Tom's Diner," made it to No. 1 on the *Billboard* Hot Rap Singles chart.

Before Def Jam Recordings drafted Nikki D, the label's founder, Rick Rubin, had signed all the label's reputable rap acts. His business partner, Russell Simmons, an entrepreneur from Hollis with a lisp, teamed with Rubin (who'd started the label in his NYU dorm room) to transform Def Jam into a rap institution, responsible for launching the careers of early legends: Run-D.M.C., LL Cool J, Public Enemy, Beastie Boys. But the most important label in hip-hop went years without a female rapper on its roster. Simmons, having recruited only R&B acts to the label, needed a win.

"It was important for Russell," says Faith Newman, who was Def Jam's business manager and director of A&R. "At the time, it was Rick who had signed LL Cool J and the Beastie Boys and Slick Rick and Public Enemy, and Russell was signing more R&B [acts], like Oran 'Juice' Jones and Alyson Williams. Nikki was his signing. He was very close to that project, and it meant a lot to him that she was the first female rapper there for Def Jam."

It also meant a lot that a machine was putting weight behind a female rapper, at least in theory. Compared to her labelmates like the Beastie Boys and Public Enemy, Nikki's commercial appeal wasn't as clear and immediately apparent. Public Enemy's Flavor Flav cameoed as a hype man in the video for her single "Lettin' Off Steam," where Nikki dons a leather fitted cap and her trademark gold tooth. But the bigger hit for her was "Daddy's Little Girl," where Nikki rapped, "Before I made love, I should've been protected / 'Cause now I'm in a jam with this careless punk," at a time when there weren't many artists rapping about hiding a pregnancy. The song hit No. 1 on the *Billboard* rap chart.

Nikki had star production for her debut album, *Daddy's Little Girl*, working with the Bomb Squad, producers of classic Public Enemy records, including "Fight the Power" and "911 Is a Joke." Based on her title tracks alone—"Wasted Pussy," "Your Man Is My Man," "Gotta Up the Ante for the Panties"—it was clear she was sending a message. "What I do is the girls' side of things," she told the *Boston Globe* in 1990. "Men have always dogged us, and now I'm ready to do the doggin'." But having a message wouldn't be enough to match Def Jam's other heavyweights.

"That was genuinely her. That wasn't, like, anybody trying to get her to fit into some kind of pro-woman mold," Newman says. The real task was making those records take off.

Whatever momentum Nikki had collapsed when Simmons started branching out from Def Jam to focus on other ventures, like Phat Farm, the clothing line he started in 1992. Newman left for Columbia Records, and Simmons's business partner, Lyor Cohen, stepped up. Def Jam's restructuring sent Nikki D's project into the cracks. "That was a game changer for them. Lyor came in and kind of took over everything and started all these little labels," says Newman. "I think maybe she got caught up in that time, which was a messy time for

Def Jam. She didn't have somebody to champion her, and there was too much craziness going on with the Def Jam label, that the album probably got lost in that."

The lack of attention bothered Nikki, who asked for a release from Def Jam. Her reasoning is one that's become a standard among female rappers. "[B]ack then they didn't understand women. They were trying to market me like the guys, and I wasn't a guy," she told *XXL* in 2009. "I never got to make my own decisions and since I felt like I wasn't in control of my own career I wanted to step out." While the label couldn't quite cater to her needs, Nikki D remains a pivotal member of the empire that Def Jam built.

BYTCHES WITH PROBLEMS

In 1991, *The Phil Donahue Show* welcomed an eclectic guest panel for an episode about female rappers: MC Lyte, Yo-Yo, and two conflicting acts—the righteous, Afrocentric rapper Harmony (an affiliate of Boogie Down Productions) and the duo Bytches With Problems. Two things were big then: gangsta rap and daytime talk shows. This episode flawlessly merged the two.

Phil Donahue walked onstage wearing a fitted cap and a dollar-sign chain around his neck, then opened the show with an embarrassing song and dance: "Producers say I need to chill / I never do seem to sit still," etc. He started the conversation with a question about the use of the word "bitch," which BWP member Lyndah McCaskill defined as "a strong, positive, aggressive woman who goes after what she wants." Harmony vehemently disagreed, and one caller described BWP as "a poor representation of black women."

The tension made for good TV. "I knew we were gonna have opposition on that show, because we were on shows together in the past," McCaskill remembers. By the end, they were hugging it out.

As you can imagine, Bytches With Problems was . . . problematic. Controversy, and their billing as the female N.W.A, earned them regular publicity and bookings on the talk-show circuit. Larry King called them "rap's nastiest duo."

They were selling a hard-core image—and, to some, the degradation of black women—to a white audience, which became a source of outrage. Jamie Foster Brown, editor in chief of *Sister 2 Sister*, printed BWP lyrics in the magazine as part of a campaign to draw attention to rap she deemed harmful: "If they keep hearing women refer to themselves as bitches, what's to keep them from finally believing it?" Brown told the *Boston Globe* in 1990.

In addition to the attention-grabbing appearances, BWP had the music to back up their positions as provocateurs. *The Bytches*, their 1991 debut album, was radically unfiltered and often progressive. The duo promoted sexual freedom, wrote a song about their periods, and had flagrant song titles like "Fuck a Man" and "Is the Pussy Still Good?" They had a song about date rape ("No Means No"). And at one point, they bought footage of the Rodney King beating (the incident ignited the LA protests described as riots) to use in their music video "Wanted," a song about police brutality.

Hip-hop director Hype Williams's first official credit was for BWP's "We Want Money," a song about women needing a man with capital. The video shows the duo meeting with crowds of women and confronting dudes on the streets. The nuance of their attempt to repossess the word "bitch" got lost in the messaging. Their reclamation was both fuel for the fire of misogyny in rap and a shameless attempt to get attention and publicize a bigger message.

"We were just too ahead of our time, 'cause the word 'bitch' was out there already, but we were trying to portray it as an assertive, aggressive type of woman who goes after what she wants and tells it like it is," says McCaskill. "We got a greater response from people who weren't in the media. I think regular people were feeling the name [Bytches With Problems]."

BWP was among the many early female rap groups created as a response to popular male rappers. Ed Lover was the co-host of *Yo! MTV Raps* and part of the rap group No Face with Mark Skeete when the two of them decided to assemble a female version of the West Coast trio N.W.A. Bytches With Problems was the answer. (Ruthless Records' Hoes With Attitude was another.)

McCaskill had signed to Warner Bros. Records as a solo artist at age nineteen and recorded a song about teenage moms with producer Teddy Riley. After being featured on the No Face song and in the video "Half" as the bride who takes half of the couple's money, she recorded "Two Minute Brother" for Skeete, who later added BWP's other half, Tanisha Michele Morgan, to the record.

Originally from Newark, New Jersey, Morgan was a backup dancer for the house music artist KC Flightt, taught ballet, and worked as a high school substitute teacher on the side. While traveling to a tour date featuring KC Flightt and No Face, Morgan dropped a few good "yo mama" jokes in the limo, which, along with her talent, thrilled Ed Lover enough for him to recruit her.

Once Ed Lover got BWP a record deal with Eazy-E's Ruthless Records, their career took off. Russell Simmons heard their demo tapes, bought out their contracts, and signed them to his label, Rush Associated Labels, or RAL, in a distribution deal. BWP recorded their first album at a hole-in-the-wall studio in Queens where the parking lot doubled as a rat condo, and McCaskill wrote most of their lyrics.

McCaskill and Morgan both leaned into a marketable group persona: gangsta girl shock jocks. They knew they were selling an image, and the more provocative, the better. "I wasn't this street girl. I never referred to myself as a bitch. I just looked at it as acting. It was a great marketing tool," says Morgan. "Had we any other kinda name, like if we were called Destiny Girls or Diamond Princesses or anything, we wouldn't have gotten any kind of attention at all. I had mixed emotions about it, 'cause I wanted the songs to be played on the radio, but they were always too dirty."

and taking that stand. Some people were okay with it. Others were not, but we rolled with it."

When BWP started recording their second album in LA with DJ Quik's production team, their artistic direction didn't quite jibe with Simmons's. According to McCaskill, he said something offen-

THE DUO PROMOTED SEXUAL FREEDOM, WROTE A SONG ABOUT THEIR PERIODS, AND HAD FLAGRANT SONG TITLES LIKE "FUCK A MAN" AND "IS THE PUSSY STILL GOOD?"

Yo! MTV Raps, she says, wanted the group to delete a scene in the "Two Minute Brother" video where McCaskill mimes the size of a two-inch dick with her hands. The explicitness of their content was implicit in their name, and that came to be a great selling point at first, and then hard to sell. By the mid-'90s, there were feminists across the world looking to publicly reclaim the word—the Canadian riot grrrls band Fifth Column released their anthem "All Women Are Bitches," and *Bitch* magazine launched in 1996. BWP knew how much a word like "bitch" could take on a more powerful, communal meaning in the hands of women, even as a weapon in the hands of men in hip-hop who were using it as a pejorative.

"When I was young, that was a common word in the neighborhood. You hang out with ya girls, and you call each other 'bitch,'" says McCaskill. "It was just something that we said, but I don't think we grasped the power that those words had back then. I'll still use that word, but I don't use it as much as I did in the past. I don't know how much good we were actually doing by using that word

sive along the lines of "What did y'all do with my Bytches?" Their second album covered teenage pregnancy, welfare, and gold digging. But the earlier music got little to no airplay, and their chemistry was fading. The duo parted ways, unable to sustain the hype. "The television [promotion] was a double-edged sword," says Morgan. "People were looking at us like activists, because we were on all these talk shows. It got real frustrating."

BWP had a decent run, even appearing in the 1991 rom-com *Strictly Business*, starring Halle Berry, in a brief club bathroom scene (they're credited as Uptown Girl 1 and Uptown Girl 2). McCaskill went on to become a substance-abuse counselor. Morgan performed voice-overs for Eddie Murphy's cartoon *The PJs* and in McDonald's commercials; she also got a job in the mayor's office in Newark, New Jersey.

"We were one of the first girl rap groups that did the kind of gangsta rap that paralleled what N.W.A did," Morgan points out. "Did we go platinum? No. But did we make a mark? I feel like we made a scratch. We paved a way for the ones today to be able to do the kind of music they're doing. I feel happy about that."

N-TYCE

WHEN I SIGNED TO WILD PITCH RECORDS, I WAS STUDYING BROADCAST AND COMMUNICATIONS AT BENNETT COLLEGE, A PRIVATE ALL-GIRLS SCHOOL IN GREENSBORO, NORTH CAROLINA. The summer before my senior year, I stayed at an NYU dorm on West Fourth Street with a couple girls from my school. We all went to New York for the summer, so I got to work on my music. That's when I did "Hush Hush Tip." Some of the guys at my record label would take me out to these industry parties, and, all around New York, all you kept hearing about was Wu-Tang Clan. I'm, like, "What is a Wu-Tang Clan?" I never heard of 'em in North Carolina, but they had really made a mark in the industry.

A guy named Sincere who worked at my record label introduced me to a guy named Prince Rakim, who would hang out with us. Rakim came up to me at a party, like, "What's up, N-Tyce?" He had a Wu-Tang Clan shirt on. He's, like, "I'm Wu-Tang Clan!" I was, like, "What! So, I *do* know Wu-Tang Clan!" I didn't know it was a bunch of 'em. Rakim is RZA.

Rakim hooked me up with Fourth Disciple, a producer. I was in a studio, Wu-Tang was in a studio, and I had recorded "Hush Hush," but I wanted a guy on it. Method Man was like, "I'll do it!" I told him what I wanted, and he went in and did it, and that's how "Hush Hush Tip"

NEVER FORGET:
She talked to Notorious B.I.G. about doing a record together before his death.

WHO SHE IS:
Born and raised in Greensboro, North Carolina, N-Tyce (Amma Allen) originally called herself MC Spice and was a member of a local rap group, the Bizzie Boys, whose manager helped her get a deal with Wild Pitch Records when she was sixteen. She then became a member of Deadly Venoms, a group of all female rappers affiliated with Wu-Tang Clan.

LISTEN:
N-Tyce is best known for her 1993 duet with Method Man, "Hush Hush Tip," a low-key record about creeping.

got created. One of my favorite records was a record by Atlantic Starr called "Secret Lovers," and I kinda did a rap version of it.

Under Wild Pitch, I had "Black to the Point," "Sure You Right," and "Hush Hush Tip" as a B side record. Unfortunately, the album, *Single File*, never came out. I had some cool records that L.E.S produced—he produced a lot of stuff for Nas. I had Killah Priest on the album, who was down with Wu-Tang, and we did a really hot record. [Also], Monie Love. It was a well-rounded album, but unfortunately Wild Pitch went through some issues with EMI Records. My record wasn't a priority.

After that album never came out, a guy I knew named Storm was talking about putting an all-girl group together and asked would I be interested. Even before I started, I always loved female rappers—MC Lyte and Salt-N-Pepa [were] my favorite. I loved Finesse and Synquis when they came out

on Uptown Records, so when he said Finesse was part of it, I was in, and then Champ and this girl out of Queensbridge, J-Boo. That's how we started Deadly Venoms. Storm came up with [the name and concept], all of that. I thought it'd be a good idea to be in a female rap group, 'cause I don't think there were any, period. You had Salt-N-Pepa and Finesse and Synquis, but not a group like Wu-Tang. We were supposed to be the female version of Wu-Tang. Right after I graduated from college, we started working on the project.

I came home to North Carolina to be in a wedding, and I met the love of my life, and I never went back to New York. I ended up dating my now-husband for, like, three years, and we've been together ever since. I figured I had spent so much time on my music career that it was time for me to focus on family. I'm a mommy, I have two kids. I do inspirational hip-hop now.

YO-YO

NEVER FORGET:
Her recurring role as Sheneneh's loquacious friend Keylolo on *Martin*.

WHO SHE IS:
Yo-Yo (Yolanda Whitaker) grew up in South Central Los Angeles with her mother and two siblings. A star in her neighborhood, she was known for battling boys at Washington Prep High School and got her big break after meeting Ice Cube at a swap meet and then collaborating with him on the single "It's a Man's World." She signed to Cube's imprint under East West Records and released five albums over five years. One of her career highlights is a duet with reggae artist Patra, "Romantic Call," the video for which features 2Pac.

LISTEN:
On "You Can't Play with My Yo-Yo," a smooth self-empowerment manifesto, Yo-Yo labels herself a "womanist" and stands her ground while Ice Cube plays the background over soulful nineties horns. The song samples the voice of none other than Queen Latifah.

The battle-of-the-sexes record is a staple in hip-hop, as much a collaboration as it is a sociological experiment. The point is for each side—man and woman—to trash-talk each other on a level, playful meeting ground and highlight gender double standards. Positive K's 1992 single "I Gotta Man" is about the man, Positive K, trying in vain to hit on a woman. "I got a man," she replies. "What ya man got to do with me?" is his response. (A lot?) On 2000's "Chickenhead," La Chat attacks Project Pat's net worth, and he calls her a "bald-head scally-wag."

"It's a Man's World," by Ice Cube and Yo-Yo, released when she was eighteen years old, is another classic in this pantheon. It's a direct spin of the James Brown classic on which the two of them deploy and defend stereotypes back and forth. Cube: "Women, they're good for nothing." Yo-Yo: "I'm not your puppet, so don't even try to pull." In the wake of N.W.A launching a brutal campaign against "bitches," collectively (see: their record "A Bitch Iz a Bitch"), Yo-Yo played both offense and defense against an onslaught of "bitch" from men, using her verse on "It's a Man's World" to address some rappers' primitive depictions of women. The song appears on Ice Cube's 1990 album, *AmeriKKKa's Most Wanted*, alongside a

IF YOU WERE A FEMALE RAPPER IN THE LATE 1980S, YOU WERE LIKELY LABELED A FEMINIST, BECAUSE MAYBE YOU DIDN'T LIKE TO BE CALLED A BITCH.

track where he threatens to kick his pregnant girl-friend in the stomach.

If you were a female rapper in the late 1980s, you were likely labeled a feminist, because maybe you didn't like to be called a bitch. The soundtrack of the time confirmed this. "A woman can bear you, break you, take you / Now it's time to rhyme, can you relate to / A sister dope enough to make you holler and scream," Queen Latifah rapped on "Ladies First" in 1989. Two years later, Yo-Yo said on her single "You Can't Play with My Yo-Yo," which samples Queen Latifah's voice. "Label me as a woman, and sometimes I feel inferior / Falling back on the hands of time makes no man superior."

The East Coast had Salt-N-Pepa, Queen Latifah, and MC Lyte. The West Coast had Yo-Yo. When she released her debut album, *Make Way for the Motherlode*, she was nineteen years old and a role model, with a pro-woman, pro-black stance that appealed to other young women who were desperately in love with hip-hop. It was complicated for women like Yo-Yo to indulge in a sport like rap (or to be a fan of it) that sponsored an environment of hatred and violence against women and sold it as entertainment while also providing a means of money and escape for young black women, too.

Yo-Yo's entire first album is her playing the role of a sapient older sister and supportive homegirl. "Girl, Don't Be No Fool" opens with a PSA and Yo-Yo explaining, "This is for the men who like to dog women / And this is for the women who like to get dogged by men / And this is for Ice Cube and Jinx / Because those brothers know they some dogs." Her music was the perfect counter-programming to the recklessness from Cube and others. Music fans absorbed the message, media had no choice but to pick it up, and the change in conversation—through Salt-N-Pepa, Queen Latifah, MC Lyte, and Yo-Yo—was crucial to giving women a voice in rap.

Says Danyel Smith, former *Vibe* editor in chief, "To have a girl from around the way who very much looked like us? All respect to the around-the-way girls that LL was rapping about, but if you were from California, you looked at those girls, and you admired those girls, but that wasn't who we were. Yo-Yo was who we were. The braids, everything. Her body looked like everybody's body. The amount of swag she had, and the amount of uplift she had in her raps was different from, say, J.J. Fad. She was very much about: *Stop getting pregnant by these brothers who don't care about you. Stop hanging out on the corner. Just 'cause you can't afford to get your nails done doesn't mean that you're wack.* All the stuff that we were feeling."

Yo-Yo started the Intelligent Black Women's Coalition, a nonprofit organization for black girls and women, in direct response to, well, men like Ice Cube. "I started the Intelligent Black Women's Coalition because I was concerned about the messages that some rappers were putting out about women, and the impact that they were having," Yo-Yo told *Commercial Appeal* in 1990.

Yo-Yo recorded her second album, *Black Pearl* (1992), without the aid of Ice Cube or producer Sir Jinx (who'd produced songs on her prior album) as co-writers and producers. The title track was an affirmation for black girls, but the album didn't sell like *Motherlode*. The album's message might've been too uplifting for national consumers. "It didn't really bother me that *Black Pearl* didn't sell," Yo-Yo said in an episode of TV One's *Unsung* that aired in 2015. "I enjoyed my freedom. I wanted people to understand that, hey, listen, I was on my own." (She reteamed with Ice Cube for her third album and on the song "The Bonnie and Clyde Theme.")

"Her sound was so specifically California, and also, she was dealing with the tax that we all pay for being women in this business," says Smith.

" THE FIRST TIME I WAS CALLED A FEMINIST, I WAS, LIKE, HMM, I DON'T KNOW IF I'M A FEMINIST, I DON'T KNOW," SHE TOLD TV ONE. "AND THEN, WHEN I TALKED TO A REAL FEMINIST, I WAS, LIKE, OH, YEAH. YEAH. THAT'S ME.

"

"There was just no way they were going to put singles from *Black Pearl* into heavy rotation on the radio across the country. That just was never going to happen."

While Yo-Yo supported women's rights in songs and interviews, she rejected the "feminist" label and didn't understand the need for it. Like many black women, including rappers who resisted the brand of white feminism that neglected black women's struggles, she saw the label as a hindrance and called herself a womanist instead. "It's interesting because Lil' Kim was probably the only woman rapper at that time that I could find on record saying that she was a feminist," says author and professor Gwendolyn Pough. "A lot of the women rappers said no I'm not a feminist . . . but they want to say, 'But I believe women should have equal rights.' Well actually, you're feminist."

Yo-Yo changed her mind over the years, once she realized how much her music pushed back against the labels men applied to women, and during a crucial time in American politics. *Make Way for the Motherlode* came out just two months before Anita Hill's sexual harassment allegations against Clarence Thomas helped change power dynamics in the workplace, and it was two years after Kimberlé Crenshaw coined the term "intersectionality" to explain how the experience of being black and female gives black women a uniquely broad perspective on racism and sexism. However fraught the overall movement, Yo-Yo's advocacy on records mirrored real life and ran parallel to the work of feminists in other fields. "The first time I was called a feminist, I was, like, hmm, I don't know if I'm a feminist, I don't know," she told TV One. "And then, when I talked to a real feminist, I was, like, oh, yeah. Yeah. That's me."

BOSS

By the time Boss made it from Detroit to Los Angeles in 1991, rap was terrorizing all of America. Neighborhoods like Compton and Watts, California, had become breeding grounds for gangs and had been depleted by drug and crime laws under President Reagan, whose policy targets were poor and black. Out of this came a subgenre of rap that was harsher and bleaker than anything that had come before it, and it was hip-hop at its most politically unapologetic.

Gangsta rap desanitized hip-hop (which was largely happy music—that was uplifting, informative, political) and tilted the axis of the genre toward the West. While Philadelphia rapper Schoolly D is responsible for setting the gangsta rap ethos in motion, it was West Coast rappers Ice-T and the trio of Ice Cube, Dr. Dre, and Eazy-E, known collectively as N.W.A, who gave the subgenre life in the mainstream. "It was dubbed 'gangsta rap,' but for me it was an intimate look at what was actually happening in our community in Los Angeles, in Compton in particular," Kendrick Lamar said onstage in 2016, as N.W.A was inducted into the Rock & Roll Hall of Fame.

Over in the East, Def Jam Recordings, under Russell Simmons and Lyor Cohen, had built its own roster of rebels: LL Cool J, EPMD, and Public Enemy proclaiming "911 Is a

Joke." They were all products of the same system, but Def Jam didn't have a gangsta rapper. They didn't have anyone like Boss.

Boss talked and looked the part. Wearing a beanie and dark shades to obscure her eyes, she rapped about Glocks and drive-by shootings, and her body swam in oversized jeans. Gangsta rap was hip-hop's hypermasculine rage against oppressive systems, a subgenre in which women were expendable, so to have a woman at the forefront was seen as subversive. To Def Jam, Boss was the perfect storm. "Her personality was that of 'I'm a G': *Yo, don't treat me like a female, I'm drinking forties, smoking blunts like you guys,*" says Kevin Liles, Def Jam's former president.

"My approach was, fuck it," Boss recalls. "I'm just gonna write what I'm going through—doing what we had to do to survive. It was hard, I guess, for people to believe that it was a female saying all that shit."

To a kid raised on the West Side of Detroit, the hip-hop of the late 1970s and '80s was the equivalent of a spaceship landing in their backyard. From Afrika Bambaataa to Roxanne Shanté, Salt-N-Pepa, MC Lyte, and Queen Latifah, Boss would write down and recite the lyrics to all their songs. She started writing her own material at age fourteen. "I was so fascinated by music, period. But when rap came out? Oh, my goodness, that was just everything," she says.

During her freshman year at Rochester, Michigan's Oakland University, Boss's roommate introduced her to a beatboxer named Irene Moore, aka Dee. Boss and Dee formed a duo and joined a large clique of rappers in Detroit—about twenty to thirty people, including groups, who all worked under producer Jewel Silas and his company 24K Productions as part of a boot-camp-style clique called Thee Posse. This commune of rappers would meet at Silas's studio for sessions to chill and record and occasionally do shows. "We would all sit around and get in line and wait for him to do our beats so we could get on the mic," Boss remembers.

Detroit had a rap scene—members of Thee Posse took turns performing at local clubs like Brotherhood, hoping to land record deals. But the promise of hip-hop—and Boss's preferred style of rap—lived in LA. She and Dee relocated there and stayed wherever they could afford, sometimes selling dope to make money, from Inglewood to Lynwood, Compton, and Paramount, sleeping in hotels and slumming it with people they met around the neighborhood. They even worked a random job putting price tags on GUESS overalls at a factory warehouse.

On a mutual friend's recommendation (a promoter who dressed like Prince), Boss called producer Jef "Def Jef" Forston to persuade him to meet up at the Diamond Inn, where they were staying, and collaborate with her and Dee in Compton. "I remember going to meet her at a hotel to hear her rap," Forston says. "Her voice was one of the most amazing voices I'd heard, and her rhymes were dope. She was talking some street shit about pulling down ski masks. She had this thing where she turned her back and started rapping. She put the shades on. She kept saying, 'Don't look at me when I rap.' She sounded so powerful."

Forston offered Boss and Dee room and board in his two-bedroom apartment in North Hollywood while they worked together. The first tracks he produced, though, weren't hard enough. "The music I was playing was more like dance music, up-tempo hip-hop. She was, like, 'I need that gangsta shit.'" Boss was stubborn. "I wanted to make something that could hang with the guys," she says. "A good record, a good song. Something that would stand up throughout history."

In Compton, Boss and Dee found a hookup at Total Trak Productions—a record pool owned by Tracy Kendrick and Courtney Branch, two producers who'd worked on DJ Quik's 1991 album *Quik Is the Name*. They signed Boss and Dee to a management deal and helped them get a four-song demo to Russell Simmons at a record convention in New York.

Boss and Dee signed to Def Jam West as a duo, confusingly under the name Boss. They also reunited with Forston. "I had a little more experience making harder tracks. I made a track for my boy, and it was the hardest track," he says. "I remember calling [that friend] and telling him I'm gonna give her that track [instead]." The song became Boss's debut single, "Deeper."

Forston produced the majority of the duo's 1993 debut album, *Born Gangstaz*, which also features production by MC Serch and Run-D.M.C.'s Jam Master Jay. The first song Dee recorded for the album was "Explanation of a Mad Bitch," under the direction of Simmons, who gave her a new nickname she didn't like, Dee the Mad Bitch. (She did a song with 2Pac, "Judgement Day," under that name.)

"Russell was, like, 'Dee, can you rap?'" Dee remembers. "I ended up on the song. I thought it was trash, and he ended up putting it on the *Zebrahead* soundtrack, and that's when everybody thought it was Boss, but that song was all me. People were confused, because we kinda sound alike from being around each other for so many years. It kinda hit me when I see the soundtrack and the soundtrack had her name and her face on there, but it was me." (The classic Nas song "Halftime" appears on that soundtrack.)

On the album cover, Dee, a willing silent partner, is seen in the background holding a gun. Much of the press implied Boss was a solo artist rather than a two-person entity. "I kinda felt cool with being in the back like that, 'cause I wanted her to shine. I wasn't able to show my mom what I can do, but she can," says Dee, whose mother had passed by then. "I was trying to put all my energy into pleasing her parents."

In a 1993 article, the *Los Angeles Times* pegged Boss as "the first woman to seriously challenge male rappers in the raunchy, anything-goes world of gangsta rap," though the artists who made gangsta rap didn't completely embrace the term. There was the usual criticism. A *Wall Street Journal* article published in 1994 labeled Boss a poseur because of her middle-class background, which seemed to clash with her hard-core image. Boss stands by her image and says she was up-front about her upbringing— she cites the intro of *Born Gangstaz* ("Intro: A Call From Mom"), where a voice mimicking her mom's leaves a message stating, "I did not spend all that money on you for that gangsta stuff."

"Before I even went to LA or New York, I was selling dope in Michigan. I needed some cash. Middle class had nothing to do with it," says Boss. "It wasn't nothing to hide. I didn't say I was [making] Gotti money. I said I was selling weed. In my path to get to where I was going, I was ready to do what I needed to do, and I didn't want nobody to get in my way. I'm surprised I'm not somewhere in jail. I don't know what I was thinking, but I was ready to fuck somebody up."

Boss (and before them, Bytches With Problems) used the aggressive aesthetic of male rap that they and their labels figured would sell. After their debut album, Boss and Dee split up to work on solo projects, they both had kids, and Boss disappeared from rap, leaving a trail of contradictions behind that are less scandalous in retrospect.

SHOUTOUTS!

RASHEEDA

NEVER FORGET:
She opened her own boutique with locations in Atlanta and Houston.

WHO SHE IS:
In the premiere of VH1's reality series *Love & Hip Hop Atlanta* in 2012, Rasheeda introduced herself in her confessional: "I've been signed to major record labels like Motown and Jive, but they never understood me as an artist, so we decided to go independent." It's true. She rapped as one-third of the group Da Kaperz before releasing her debut solo album, *Dirty South*, in 2001. She became a beloved staple in Atlanta's independent rap scene and is one of the few *Love & Hip Hop* cast members to have had a legitimate music career before joining the show.

LISTEN:
Rasheeda reps the fight life on her unruly single "Do It," featuring Pastor Troy and Re Re.

GANGSTA BOO

NEVER FORGET:
She referred to herself as "the Devil's Daughter" prior to finding religion.

WHO SHE IS:
While signed to Three 6 Mafia's label, Hypnotize Minds, Gangsta Boo released two albums, 1998's *Enquiring Minds* and 2001's *Both Worlds *69*. After a brief flirtation with horrorcore as part of Three 6 Mafia, Gangsta Boo left the label over financial issues and rechristened herself Lady Boo. She once told *Vice*, "Men are more chauvinistic than they even know, really. I've had to go through certain things where I've had to push a titty up or two to get things done, whereas a man doesn't."

LISTEN:
"Can I Get Paid (Get Your Broke Ass Out)" is designed for the strip club and finds Gangsta Boo supporting the demands of strippers: money.

PRINCESS & DIAMOND

NEVER FORGET:
Solange sampled one of their interviews on her 2018 album *When I Get Home*.

WHO THEY ARE:
Princess and Diamond met in their Ellenwood, Georgia, neighborhood, and became members of the rap crew Crime Mob. In a clique with four men, Princess and Diamond—still in high school at the time—popularized crunk rap (fight songs and club tracks) and came packaged as a duo with relentless energy on Crime Mob songs like "Rock Yo Hips" and "Knuck If You Buck." Years after Crime Mob split up over business conflicts, Princess and Diamond reunited with an EP titled *Vagina Power*, in 2019.

LISTEN:
The tenderest Crime Mob song, "Circles," puts a crunk twist on a Luther Vandross sample ("Going in Circles") and sees Princess and Diamond rapping about a relationship that's seductive but going nowhere.

JACKI-O

NEVER FORGET:
Jacki-O dubbed herself the Queen of the South and, in 2006, engaged in a beef with fellow rapper Khia about who the real Queen of the South was.

WHO SHE IS:
The rapper from Liberty City, Florida, who shares her alias with a US First Lady released her debut album *Poe Little Rich Girl* in 2004 and thrived as an independent artist, pegged as the latest filthy mouth from the South, following Trina. After two albums and a slew of mixtapes celebrating lust, Jacki-O retired the provocative image in favor of Christian rap.

LISTEN:
Her debut single "Nookie," as the title suggests (it was originally titled "Pussy"), very bluntly celebrates Jacki-O's sex skills.

RAH DIGGA

NEVER FORGET:
She rapped with Lauryn Hill on the Fugees song "Cowboys."

WHO SHE IS:
Standing out around a rapper like Busta Rhymes is tough (not only because he sounds loud, but because he looks loud). However, Rah Digga (Rashia Tashan Fisher) had an unmistakable gruff tone when she rapped, which came from grooming herself on rappers like MC Lyte; she even dubbed herself a "direct descendant of MC Lyte." Rah Digga first performed at the popular open mic circuit, Lyricist Lounge. Her contributions to the Fugees' sophomore album, *The Score*, then landed her a deal with Elektra Records and a spot as the lone female member of Busta Rhymes's rap crew and imprint, Flip Mode Squad. She released two albums: *Dirty Harriet* (2000) and *Classic* (2010).

LISTEN:
Her single "Party & Bullshit 2003," which features the line "I'll beat that bitch with a bat," was tailor-made for clubs with metal detectors.

JEAN GRAE

NEVER FORGET:
She wrote and directed a web-based sitcom titled *Life with Jeannie*.

WHO SHE IS:
Born in Cape Town, South Africa, Jean Grae moved to New York with her mom when she was just three months old. At fourteen, she danced at the famous Alvin Ailey Theater, and her first incarnation as an MC was with the rap trio Natural Resource, when her alias was What? What? In an industry that actively marketed sex, she prioritized wit, and followed up her 2002 debut album, *Attack of the Attacking Things*, with five more albums, including 2008's *Jeanius*, a flawlessly soulful collaboration with producer 9th Wonder.

LISTEN:
On "My Story (Please Forgive Me)," she reflects on a decision to have an abortion at age sixteen, rapping, "My primitive mind was struggling / Just to understand the meaning of life, forgive me."

FACTOIDS

◆◆◆

MC SMOOTH's brief career as a rapper and singer included a song called "Female Mac" about creeping and man-stealing where she kinda sounds like MC Lyte.

◆◆◆

One of London's biggest rap exports, **MS. DYNAMITE** opened a swath of hip-hop fans up to the UK garage scene with her debut album, *A Little Deeper*, in 2002.

◆◆◆

NEFERTITI released a solo album in 1993 titled *L.I.F.E.*, which stood for *Living in Fear of Extinction*, which could also be an acronym for the age of Trump.

◆◆◆

SASHA GO HARD and **KATIE GOT BANDZ** have perfect rap names and were the pride of Chicago as patrons of Drill music, an extension of gangsta rap.

◆◆◆

CHYNA WHITE appeared on Lil Jon's boisterous club record "Bia, Bia" in 2000, rapping in the rain and wielding an axe in the music video.

◆◆◆

PASSION dropped her album *Baller's Lady* in 1996, which finds her rapping with exaggerated vocals on "Baller's Lady," featuring E-40.

◆◆◆

Angel, better known as a model and rap video vixen, moonlit as a rapper named **LOLA MONROE**.

◆◆◆

Timbaland tried grooming two female rappers under his imprints, both of whom left after years in limbo. **MS. JADE** signed to Beat Camp and released her debut album, *Girl Interrupted*, in 2002, along with a catchy single, "Ching Ching." **TINK**, who signed to Mosley Music Group, had the rapping and vocal chops to succeed Nicki Minaj.

HeaTHeR B.

NEVER FORGET:
She's respectfully regarded as the first black woman on reality TV.

WHO SHE IS:
Heather B. (Gardner) will live on in the reality-TV history books as a founding cast member of *The Real World*. Raised in Jersey City, she discovered hip-hop by way of radio, specifically Run-D.M.C. and KRS-One. In high school, she joined a roughly fifteen-member rap clique of all women called FMC (Female Midtown Crew). She left Saint Peter's College in Jersey in her junior year to tour with KRS-One's crew, Boogie Down Productions, and landed a deal with Pendulum under Elektra Records. After releasing two albums, *Takin' Mine* in 1996 and *Eternal Affairs* in 2002, she went on to become a co-host of the Sirius XM radio show *Sway in the Morning*.

LISTEN:
On the title track of her debut album, *Takin' Mine*, Heather B. daydreams of escaping the stress of broke living and government housing and becoming "head negress on the island."

The purest form of reality TV existed in the 1990s, when MTV debuted its seven-strangers-in-a-house show *The Real World*, a lab-rat-style vehicle for its cast members to learn about racism and sexuality while making friends in the vicinity of a hot tub. As part of the inaugural 1992 season, set in New York City, twenty-one-year-old Heather B. from Jersey City came to coexist with a roommate from Birmingham, Alabama, named Julie, who assumed Heather B. was a drug dealer.

She wasn't. Heather B. was a rapper affiliated with Boogie Down Productions, a crew with a revolving-door of members, including KRS-One, D-Nice, and DJ Scott La Rock. At St. Peter's College, she switched majors twice, from accounting to corporate finance and marketing to elementary education. While throwing regular one-dollar chicken-and-beer parties to earn money, she met KRS-One's brother, Kenny Parker, in 1988; Parker brought her to KRS-One, who initially offered to hire Heather B. to do promotions for his label, Edutainment, but when he found out she could rap, he recruited her to Boogie Down Productions. (She appeared on the song "7 Dee Jays," on their 1990 album, *Edutainment*.)

Vocally, Heather B. sounded like a rough, seasoned New Yorker—people figured she was from Brooklyn or the Bronx, not Jersey—and she made songs that were rooted in realism. On her anti-guns single, "All Glocks Down," she calls herself a "bulletproof lyricist." "When I fell in love with hip-hop, I remember Antoinette, MC Lyte, Queen Latifah, all of them. But there was also Salt-N-Pepa, who was sexy in their own way. It wasn't vulgar. It wasn't in your face. I had time to figure out which way [I wanted to go as an artist] and do my own style."

By 1992, Heather B. was the face of a different movement. What started as a call from her manager to audition for a documentary—an MTV show about "a group of young people who agreed to allow their private lives to become public entertainment," as one news broadcaster described it—turned into life on *The Real World*. She remembers telling Parker, "I have to audition for some sort of documentary. Does that even make sense?" He encouraged her to follow through. "He was like, 'You should do it. I remember when I met you, you used to tell me they called you Heather B. because you spent your whole time in high school saying you was gonna be famous,'" she says. "That's how I got my MC name—saying I'ma 'be' this and I'ma 'be' that."

She, of course, had no idea the show would become so big, or that it would beget the beast of reality television, or that she would become the first black woman of reality TV. "It wasn't popular at that time to be on MTV. In fact, KRS was like, 'I think you buggin' doing this. Why would you even do this?'" she says. "But it wasn't explained to me as a TV show. [The producers] said they wanted to do a documentary on artists, and 'We're gonna put seven artists in a house.' And shit, what did I have to lose? They was gon' pay me . . . I was like, this is dope for me to give people an opportunity to see what a female rapper, what that life is like for real."

Soon after meeting one another, in Episode 2 of *The Real World*, a few cast members got a taste of that rap life, when they corraled themselves into a studio to watch Heather B. record a song about date rape titled "The System Sucks." Heather later tells the camera, in her confessional, "I didn't create an image. A lot of people spend a lot of time with images. I didn't create someone separate from myself to sell records."

Most of *The Real World* scenes of yore come across as ancient in modern light, but this one holds up. Heather B. was ahead of the curve, rapping about consent on a national cable show, as part of a genre that would one day overtake the television industry, including MTV. The song, which was never released, lives on in *The Real World* annals. The exposure helped, but even as her face was all over MTV, she says the network still rejected one of her music videos. She had to convince MTV's president Doug Herzog at the time to put her in rotation.

I WAS LIKE, THIS IS DOPE FOR ME TO GIVE PEOPLE AN OPPORTUNITY TO SEE WHAT A FEMALE RAPPER, WHAT THAT LIFE IS LIKE FOR REAL.

Lady of Rage

Lady of Rage was positioned as the latest rap prodigy on Suge Knight's West Coast institution, Death Row Records, home to 2Pac, Dr. Dre, and Snoop Dogg. But a few things got in her way. Namely, Death Row Records.

Stories about the East Coast versus West Coast beef center on how it electrified rap in the nineties and yet culminated in the deaths of 2Pac and Notorious B.I.G., which left a veil over hip-hop while giving the culture a sense of clarity. Survivors became footnotes in the aftermath. After 2Pac's murder in 1996, Death Row deteriorated, leaving Rage in a gray area, a by-product of producer Dr. Dre's notoriously charming inability to finish projects. The summer after Biggie's passing, she finally released her long-in-the-works album, *Necessary Roughness*, but without the momentum of Death Row.

Growing up in Farmville, Virginia, Rage didn't hear much rap on the radio. "The radio station that was popular was called WFLO, and they basically played country music," she remembers. "The major city that was close to us was Richmond, and unless you had a good stereo system, you really couldn't pick up stations from Richmond or Lynchburg . . . I would have to go to the record store."

Rage was part of a high school trio with two friends who called themselves Legion of Doom. After she graduated and moved to Houston, Rakim changed the way she thought about rap. "I always say Grandmaster Flash, Sequence, and

Run-D.M.C. inspired me to become a rapper. Rakim transformed me into an MC," she says. "Once I heard Rakim, it was over. I didn't wanna do anything minimal. Everything I said had to be something to make you scratch your head and say, 'Dang, how did she come up with that?'"

Rage had an ambitious plan: to go to New York and meet Run-D.M.C., who she figured would get her a deal at their label, Def Jam. In the meantime, she worked at Gary Job Corps in San Marcus, Texas, studying a trade—meat cutting—and spent most of her leisure time writing raps.

Twice she tried to convince friends to join her on her excursion to New York, even once suggesting she and a friend hitchhike (she would carry her grandfather's revolver to protect them). She'd read about Madonna living in a shelter in the city, and, she says, "I was, like, shit, if being homeless and not knowing anybody will make you large like that, shit, I can do that." Instead, Rage pawned the gun and stayed with a friend in Arkansas, working shifts at McDonald's, before heading to New York alone.

Rage picked up a menial job in Manhattan at Chung King Studios: She swept floors, cleaned up after sessions, answered calls, got coffee, and booked studio time. She used the coffeepot to heat water, pour it into the bathroom sink, and wash up. Any leftover food, she ate. She even slept in the studio overnight. Eventually, a friend and mentor, producer Chubb Rock, let her crash at his condo and brought her into his fold, hiring her to sing background vocals for his artists. (Under the name Rockin' Robin, she sings on the rap duo Downtown Science's single "Summertime," which sounds like a clone of the DJ Jazzy Jeff & Fresh Prince version.)

Another producer Rage met in the studio, DJ Premier, was an East Coast rap purist. When she told Premier that she was moving to LA and that she wanted to sign with Dr. Dre, Premier wished her luck. "He was, like, 'You know how many people I get telling me they can rap?'" she remembers. "He didn't take me seriously, so I asked him to show me how to DJ." Around 1988, she met a pair of producers, Darryl and Muff, together known as the L.A. Posse, who worked with, among other artists, Pharoahe Monch and R&B singer Monifah. Dre heard Rage rap on L.A. Posse's 1991 album, *They Come in All Colors*, and quickly drafted her to Death Row in 1994. (DJ Premier recalls running into Rage while she was working security in LA. She told him he would hear her on a Dr. Dre record soon, and that turned out to be *The Chronic*.)

When Notorious B.I.G. heard Rage on a DJ Premier track and said she was dope, it was like an anointing. "When I met Jay-Z and he told me he was a fan, I was, like, *Huh, okay*. To be recognized by your female comrades is great, but we're in a male-dominated field, so when they do give you recognition, it's like an extra stamp."

But recording an album was different. For what seemed like centuries, Dr. Dre teased his own long-awaited, never-released solo album, *Detox*, till it eventually became folklore. Rage, clearly a lyrical force, needed and desperately wanted direction, but Dre was juggling multiple projects. While it wasn't uncommon for Dre to neglect the artists on his roster, creatively and logistically, producers like him were a necessary lifeline for women like Rage whose main gateways were men. This was an example of squandered potential. Rage says the release schedule was supposed to go: Dre's *The Chronic*, then Snoop Dogg's album, and then hers. But in the most tragic sequence of events, Dr. Dre left Death Row, 2Pac was murdered, Suge Knight got locked up, and Snoop Dogg left the label.

"So in the midst of the empire crumbling, now, 'Rage, it's your turn. Now you can get in the studio,'" Rage remembers. "Now that my album is

"ONCE I HEARD RAKIM, IT WAS OVER. I DIDN'T WANNA DO ANYTHING MINIMAL. EVERYTHING I SAID HAD TO BE SOME-THING TO MAKE YOU SCRATCH YOUR HEAD."

being worked on, the conductor, Dre, the visionary, is not there anymore, the person who was gonna structure all of this. I'm just in there second-guessing, wondering. I'm lost."

Timelines collided, and while Rage says she happily contributed to her labelmates' classic projects—Dr. Dre's *The Chronic* and Snoop Dogg's *Doggystyle*—she never recorded music for what was supposed to be her debut album, which Dre wanted to title *Eargasm*.

When Rage recorded "Afro Puffs," she thought it would kill her career. She recorded the song for a soundtrack to the 2Pac movie *Above the Rim* but told Dre and Suge not to include it. Interscope's CEO, Jimmy Iovine, instead spent an entire phone call convincing Rage that the song was a hit, though it took a while to get it physically pressed. (As for the concept, she cribbed her signature hairstyle—two thick mini-Afros, parted down the middle—from a cousin who wore her hair in puffs.)

"Afro Puffs" dropped in July 1994 and did its job of boosting Rage's popularity. After the song took off, though, Rage says Death Row blocked her from collaborating with artists outside of the label. She recorded a song with jazz singer Branford Marsalis, "Black Widow," and, she says, "Death Row made Branford Marsalis take the song off the album, because they said it would hurt my image."

Later on, when producer Irv Gotti wanted her on the song "Usual Suspects," with the Lox, Mic Geronimo, and DMX, she says Death Row blocked that, too. "Irv Gotti was at my hotel with the check in hand, like, 'Just come.' And I had already called [Death Row], like, 'Can I do this?' They wouldn't let me do it. Irv Gotti was, like, 'Jay-Z is at the studio,'" she says. "People, a lot of times, wanted to work with me, but because I was still attached to Death Row, they didn't want to deal with what they called the headache."

PEOPLE, A LOT OF TIMES, WANTED TO WORK WITH ME, BUT BECAUSE I WAS STILL ATTACHED TO DEATH ROW, THEY DIDN'T WANT TO DEAL WITH WHAT THEY CALLED THE HEADACHE.

Stuck on a label with rappers who were larger priorities, even as a protégé of Dre's, Rage receded into the background, albeit with a reputation as a promising, respected MC. Years later, Shaquille O'Neal wanted to sign Rage to his newly formed imprint TWIsM. It was 2001, and Rage was out of the Death Row grips. "Shaq was, like," she recalls, "'Rage, record labels don't know what to do with you, because you're like the female who's good enough to play in the NBA, but you will never play in the NBA. So, what do we do with somebody like that?'"

Women rappers would sit on label shelves for ages, and of course stagnation is normal in the music industry, but without the overall numbers, it only contributed to the lack. "What do we do with them?" was a recurring issue for women who didn't fit the industry's standard mold of a rap star. Many of them started answering the question themselves.

FACTOIDS

◆ ◆ ◆

Signed to fellow rapper M.I.A.'s imprint N.E.E.T Recordings, **RYE RYE** dropped a peppy duet with her titled "Sunshine" in 2010.

◆ ◆ ◆

YO MAJESTY was an openly gay trio with two rappers, Shunda K and Shon B, whose music has the telltale stamp of Baltimore club rap.

◆ ◆ ◆

Before her death in 1991, **MC TROUBLE** released an album and had a moderate hit, "I (Wanna) Make You Mine," featuring the dulcet R&B sounds of the Good Girls.

◆ ◆ ◆

KATEY RED, a trans rapper from New Orleans, is celebrated as a queer pioneer of New Orleans bounce. With a voice perfectly suited for the tradition of call-and-response rap, she inspired artists like Big Freedia (a former backup dancer of Katey's) to take up the city's unofficial native tongue and help make it mainstream. Katey Red dropped her debut album, *Melpomene Block Party*, in 1999.

SNOW THA PRODUCT, a Mexican American rapper, spits in Spanish on "Immigrants (We Get the Job Done)," a song on Lin-Manuel Miranda's *The Hamilton Mixtape*, released in 2016 for the maniacally successful Broadway musical.

◆ ◆ ◆

The Oxygen docuseries *Sisterhood of Hip Hop* welcomed a rotating cast of aspiring rappers, including **BRIANNA PERRY**, **SIYA**, **LEE MAZIN**, and **AUDRA THE RAPPER**.

Oakland rapper **KAMAIYAH**, known for her single "How Does It Feel," takes a refreshing sip of Sprite in a 2018 commercial with basketball icon LeBron James.

◆ ◆ ◆

Though recognized primarily as a singer-songwriter, **JESSIE REYEZ** has the gift of gab when she's rapping, like her dark turn on the song "Scar," from Beyoncé's soundtrack for the *Lion King* remake, titled *The Gift*.

THE CONSCIOUS DAUGHTERS

NEVER FORGET:
They recorded a song about the HIV/AIDS crisis titled "All Caught Up."

WHO THEY ARE:
Carla Green and Karryl Smith met when they were twelve years old at Portola Junior High in San Francisco's Bay Area and became immediate best friends. Carla's dad was a singer and bass player for Mary Wells. Her dad's friend was Frankie Beverly, as in *the* Frankie Beverly, whose band Maze would often crash at her parents' house in the Bay Area (where Carla was born and raised) and babysit her, which is why she "grew up a total band baby," she says. Karryl was born in Seattle, where her mom worked at a radio station for twenty years and often brought her daughter along to events featuring stars. Together, Karryl and Carla teamed as the Conscious Daughters and released three albums, *Ear to the Street* (1993), *Gamers* (1996), and *The Nutcracker Suite* (2009).

LISTEN:
"Something to Ride To (Fonky Expedition)," the Conscious Daughters' ode to cruising in the streets with the top down, was fashioned after Dr. Dre's "Ain't Nuthin But a G Thang," and you can tell.

◆ ◆ ◆

As home of the Black Panther Party in the 1960s, Oakland, California, stood as the center of black consciousness. While the earliest rap from the Bay Area skewed light and upbeat, à la M.C. Hammer, Digital Underground, and Too $hort, the gangsta rap from Los Angeles, decades later, appealed to young people's darker sensibilities. The Conscious Daughters married the light and the dark, combining their lyricism with social awareness (hence the word "Conscious" in their name) and rhymes about what they considered "street shit."

The Conscious Daughters wrote from experience about being young and reckless, while also rapping about serious issues like teenage pregnancy (two of their high school friends had babies) and mental illness (Karryl's dad was in and out of a hospital). The West Coast influence was clear in their music: smooth, top-down-cruising melodies and nimble wordplay. But they were also obsessed with New York radio shows like *Mr. Magic's Rap Attack Show*, and Karryl used scratching and cutting techniques inspired by Run-D.M.C.'s DJ Jam Master Jay.

"We wanted to be lyrical acrobats. We talked shit like the West Coast, but our delivery was very in-your-face like in New York," says Green. "Between Too $hort, N.W.A, KRS-One, and New York inspiration, that's what gave us our flow."

Karryl was an all-star athlete, the only girl on her baseball team in elementary and middle school and a basketball player in high school. In ninth grade, when she was put in charge of the school's radio station as program director, Carla would cut class to record their raps on cassette tapes (Karryl went by the name Special K, while Carla was Kool Moe C). When they turned eighteen, they started selling their tapes at clubs. A friend handed one of their demos, "Wife of a Gangster," to Oscar "Paris" Jackson, a Bay Area rapper known for his provocative, socially militant style. He signed them to his Priority Records imprint.

"Lyrically, 'Wife of a Gangster' was ice-cold, and it talked about the tribulations of the other side of the dope game, and the people that violence affects, outside of the key players," Paris recalls. "Their honesty struck me, and their street sensibilities struck me. I didn't really hear that from female artists at the time, except for maybe Boss, and Boss was really more on a straight gangsta edge."

After high school, Carla quit her job working as an assistant producer of the video-games department for director George Lucas's production company Lucasfilm to work on their debut album. (Yes, the same George Lucas who created the *Star Wars* franchise. Carla was drawn as a character named Carla the Swordmaster in the Lucasfilm game *The Secret of Monkey Island*. She was also on the original development team for the game *Tetris* when she was nineteen.)

By the time their second album, *Gamers*, was released in 1996, "It was all about lyrical assassination," says Carla. "Like: *Mic-checka- one, two, with the chrome deuce holder with the gangsta /*

Dumdum slugs in the chamber." Their music merged references to drinking forties with messages about domestic violence and records like "All Caught Up," a song about the HIV/AIDS epidemic, co-written by Paris. "Every album had at least two songs that were educational," says Carla. "It was really his genius that took our conscious, social, fun side and paired it with his knowledge of black power. So we were able to make albums that were gangsta, political, and fun at the same time."

"The Daughters were really well-rounded," says Paris. "They talked about being married to the game, incarceration, single motherhood, struggling, lack of economic opportunity. They weren't coming like [the rapper] Isis. They were coming like, okay, these are some women from East Oakland banding together to overcome adversity."

Carla believes the emergence of Napster—the dawn of the digital-song era—slowed Conscious Daughters' momentum. Priority Records folded. "Everything froze. Nobody was selling nothing," she says. She and Karryl planned separate solo albums—Carla released *The Jane of All Trades* in 2011. But that year, Karryl died tragically after complications from a blood clot. Carla stopped recording in her partner's absence.

Da Brat

When Da Brat switched up her look for her third album, *Unrestricted*, it seemed like she'd been hiding something. From her introduction in 1994, up until that year, 2000, she wore her hair mainly in twists, had a nose ring, and opted for Timberlands with Girbaud jeans and duvet-sized jerseys, sometimes with a folded bandanna on her forehead. All she had to do was wear a bikini top, let her hair down, and gyrate in a music video with Tyrese ("Watch'u Like") to set off alarms.

"Can anyone tell me what's really going on with Da Brat?" a *Vibe* reader wrote in a letter (actual snail mail) after the magazine profiled Da Brat in its August 2000 issue. "Why is she all of a sudden dressing like she wants to be Lil' Kim?" (It wasn't that drastic. Lil' Kim was wearing titty pasties and neon wigs.) But even after Lil' Kim and Foxy Brown's height in the nineties, the pressure to exude sex appeal loomed heavy.

Da Brat debuted in 1994 with her album *Funkdafied*, when mainstream rap was largely Bad Boy Records' rich-people problems or gangsta rap from Death Row Records, home of 2Pac, Dr. Dre, and Snoop Dogg. Da Brat and Jermaine Dupri—who'd engineered the rap duo Kris Kross's backwards-clothing revolution and created his Atlanta-based label, So So Def—rode the wave of West Coast rap. *Funkdafied*, a brief nine tracks, is anchored by

G-funk, the subgenre of seventies funk reinterpreted as dangerously smooth rap that was centralized in LA. Dupri and Brat traded flows on the album's title track, where she raps, "Lay up, and listen / As I catch up on my pimping" (the song reached No. 6 on the *Billboard* Hot 100), and on "Give It 2 You," Brat announced herself as "the baddest little pimp in this hip-hop biz."

Dupri was originally reluctant to sign a female rapper, because to him they weren't lucrative. But Da Brat proved to be a secret weapon. Her voice was nasally. Her style was androgynous. And she could really flow. "There was a lot of female rappers—Salt-N-Pepa, Antoinette, MC Lyte—but this was the first time we had seen one with braids and the energy that she came to the screen with," Dupri said in a 2019 documentary, *The Remarkable Rise of So So Def*. Da Brat brought success and money to his So So Def enterprise, so he's lucky that she came around. *Funkdafied* became the first album by a female rapper to sell a million records. (While Eminem, Outkast, and Biggie are among the rappers who've sold ten million records, no female rapper has ever been certified diamond.)

The video for "What'chu Like," released a year after Sisqo's indestructible hit "Thong Song," created one of those head-turning moments in hip-hop. It was the first single from Da Brat's third album, *Unrestricted*, a heavily R&B-focused album that concerned itself mostly with debauchery. "That's What I'm Looking For" was conceptually different than the songs on *Funkdafied* that glorified the good life, and Da Brat wrote her own lyrics, mostly without Dupri's assistance. And here she was in the video, dancing with Tyrese, the model and singer from the Pepsi commercial.

"Up until now, I've never revealed a titty. For people to see this thuggish, hard-core, foul-mouthed platinum princess in tight clothes—they bugged out, you know?" Brat told *Vibe* in 2000, assuring her fans that "you'll still see the braids and the tomboy image." The tomboy image wasn't solely about comfort; it said to fans, voluntarily or not, that women wanted to be taken seriously as a rapper rather than be ogled.

But sex made for good business. Da Brat's decision to play against type was almost too obvious bait to fans; women still had limited options when it came to how they looked, even when they were following the blueprint. Male taste so heavily defined the concept of image in that era that for women, simply deciding what to wear as an artist became do-or-die. "I was always told you want to be fuckable to men and women to sell records," Da Brat told *Variety* in 2020 after coming out as gay. "Men still run the labels and they probably will forever, and if they have to create you, they will. So it's still tough for female MCs, producers and writers if you don't have the support of a major male artist backing you—or if you're not super-duper sexy and have some big titties and a nice ass and can twerk. You can't go in there looking [tough] like I did [back in the day] and be like: 'I'm a rapper.' They're going to say, 'Let's get you out of those tomboy clothes and dress you up in a teddy.' But that changes who you are—and then your rhymes start changing because you look different. Then you're not so relatable because you're not being yourself anymore. Now you're somebody else. Who are you?"

Da Brat's catalog is basically an unofficial early marker of before and after Lil' Kim. (Brat's first two albums came just before Kim's arrival.) But it's ironic that Brat had a makeover to fit industry standards, after already proving that she was financially viable as an artist, with her debut album.

Of course, Brat never abandoned the baggy duds; after *Unrestricted*, she commenced with wearing clothing she could practically dive into.

LEFT EYE'S RHYMES

"AIN'T 2 PROUD 2 BEG" (1991)

"So I choose to explain, it's evident / Left Eye don't mean the rest of my body is irrelevant"

On a song in celebration of desire and horniness, Left Eye pops in for a clean eighteen seconds, rapping about how, believe it or not, women have libidos, too, and sometimes they want to be kissed on "both sets of lips."

"HAT 2 DA BACK" (1992)

"Every day, last week, and not a place to go / This nut still had me dressin' like a fashion show / But not this week, I'm chillin', 'cause it's nothin' to hide

TLC dressed like lost members of Kris Kross (the duo, protégés of Jermaine Dupri, appears in this song's music video) and were proud of their tomboy aesthetic, or so goes their ode to sagging pants and sporty clothing. Left Eye raps about choosing to dress for comfort on what's basically an athleisure anthem.

"WATERFALLS" (1994)

"I seen a rainbow yesterday / But too many storms have come and gone, leaving a trace of not one God-given ray / Is it because my life is ten shades of gray"

Left Eye had the rare gift of rapping like a spoken-word prophet in an endearing way, notably on TLC's biggest hit, "Waterfalls," where they turned an extended metaphor about safe sex and the HIV/AIDS crisis into a No. 1 pop record.

"KICK YOUR GAME" (1994)

"Miss Left Eye (Yo) / All I wanna do is kiss your hand / Let you know I'm not just another fan, I am the man"

Although she's absent from two big TLC standards, "Creep" (an exegesis about women cheating) and "Red Light Special" (about sex), Left Eye left her mark on album cuts like this, where she role-plays as both a suitor with beautifully weak game and the subject who rejects him.

"NO SCRUBS" (1999)

"If you can't spatially expand my horizons / Then that leaves you in the class with scrubs, never rising / I don't find it surprising and if you don't have the G's"

On the lead single from their third album, *Fanmail*, TLC coined a new word for slacker men and ignited the greatest cultural discourse between the sexes since *Men Are from Mars, Women Are from Venus*. It's here that Left Eye turns the "scrub" convo into a brief thesis about finding a man who can blow her mind, intellectually and otherwise.

◆ ◆

NEVER FORGET:
The time she was arrested for arson for burning down her NFL boyfriend's home, then appeared on the cover of *Vibe* with TLC wearing firefighter outfits.

WHO SHE IS:
As the sole rapping member of TLC, Lisa "Left Eye" Lopes animated every TLC song. Before they became an acronym, Tionne "T-Boz" Watkins and Lisa "Left Eye" Lopes were part of a group named 2nd Nature with a third member, Crystal Jones, signed with Pebbles Riley. When the group changed its name to TLC and replaced Crystal with Rozonda "Chilli" Thomas, the legendary trio was born as a pivotal act on Babyface and Antonio "L.A." Reid's LaFace Records. Over the course of four albums (including their 1994 classic *CrazySexyCool*), they became one of the highest-selling girl groups of all time. Before Lopes's death in 2002 in a car accident in Honduras, she was working on a solo project titled *N.I.N.A.* under Suge Knight's label Tha Row.

◆ ◆

A BRIEF HISTORY OF POSSE CUTS

1995
"Da Ladies in Da House"

Big Kap
Bahamadia
Precise
Treep
Uneek
Lauryn Hill

1996
"3 THE HARD WAY"

Bahamadia
Mecca Star
K-Swift

1997
"NOT TONIGHT
(LADIES NIGHT REMIX)"

Angie Martinez
Missy Elliott
Lil' Kim
Left Eye
Da Brat

1999
"THOROUGH BITCHES"

Charli Baltimore
Lady of Rage
Gangsta Boo
Queen Pen
Da Brat
Scarlet

2001
"GANGSTA BITCHES"

Eve
Trina
Da Brat

SYLK-E. FYNE

NEVER FORGET:
She recorded two songs with 2Pac.

WHO SHE IS:
Sylk-E. Fyne (La'Mar Lorraine Johnson) started rapping at fourteen. At Dorsey High School, she won Best Rapper title in ninth grade—the first person in the yearbook to ever get that title, per her recollection. She later met and collaborated with the likes of 2Pac, Eazy-E, and Snoop Dogg before releasing one major-label album, her debut *Raw Sylk*, in 1998. For her second album, *Tha Cum Up*, released digitally, she laments having "the most horrible deal ever" with Rufftown Entertainment.

LISTEN:
Sylk's biggest single, "Romeo and Juliet," is a romantic bedroom ballad where Sylk brags about her "bomb-ass punani" and loyalty over a smooth R&B beat.

Way before Tupac Shakur signed to Death Row Records, he was rapping with his friend Dana Smith, aka Mouse Man, a beatboxer he met at Roland Park Middle School in Baltimore. Shakur was just a scrawny, bummy New York transplant who stapled the hem of his pants to fit his body, and one of his earliest recordings is a back-and-forth freestyle he recorded in Smith's grandmother's basement as a teen, titled "Babies Havin' Babies." Once Pac relocated to the West Coast and got a record deal, the pair reconnected, and it was there, at a reggae club in downtown Los Angeles one night, that they met Sylk-E. Fyne.

Born and raised on the Westside of Los Angeles, Sylk started rapping at fourteen, influenced by artists like Queen Latifah and Nikki D, the first female rapper signed to Def Jam. When Sylk started hanging with 2Pac and Smith, treating them to both hospitality and weed, she would roll to their hotel, Le Montrose, with homemade meals and wow them with fried chicken and macaroni.

"I had invited her through, and she met Pac. We started freestyling," says Smith. "She was one of the first chicks that

I met who could just freestyle like a mutha, could hang with the dudes. She could go bar for bar, line for line, all fuckin' night with rhyming, which was crazy, because I never met a female that didn't need help."

It wasn't until years later that the hangout sessions turned into legitimate studio work. Sylk recorded a song with 2Pac when he was well on his way to becoming an icon, after Suge Knight bailed him out of prison and signed him to Death Row Records.

Sylk recalls laying a verse for 2Pac's single "Breathin'" (a song that appears on his posthumous 2002 album, *Until the End of Time*)—she remembers rapping something like "Back in the days before I had my son / Spitting the game and clowning niggas, how I had my fun."

It's one thing to record a song with 2Pac before his prime. It's another to do *two* songs with 2Pac. Sylk recorded "Thug Luv" with 2Pac and Bizzy Bone from Bone Thugs-N-Harmony (Sylk's Ruthless Records labelmates) in a studio session where Sylk recalls seeing 2Pac dressed in all white on his way to a Versace runway show.

At seventeen, Sylk started working with the Real Richie Rich, an in-house producer for Eazy-E, and, after finding Eazy's number in Rich's phone, she called Eazy-E every day for about three months to leave freestyles on his answering machine. The fact that he never returned her calls (at first) didn't faze her. She left a particularly disrespectful freestyle on the morning of her grandmother's funeral: "You little ho, I don't wanna be with you, you a little fake gangster," it went—or something like that. This finally caught Eazy-E's attention, and Sylk got a callback, which led to an audition opportunity.

When Eazy-E and his producer Rhythm D held auditions for a girl group they were assembling called GBM, aka Gangsta Bitch Mentality, Eazy-E

and Rhythm D called on Sylk and brought her to Audio Achievements in Torrance, California, the same studio where N.W.A recorded *Straight Outta Compton*.

"
SHE COULD GO BAR FOR BAR, LINE FOR LINE, ALL FUCKIN' NIGHT WITH RHYMING . . .
"

Sylk made the final cut for the group and signed to Ruthless, along with the other GBM members: Diamond, T-Ski, and Big Chan, aka Chan Loc, who went on to become a member of Snoop Dogg's rap trio the Doggy's Angels. "The shit that we were into and even the female [rappers] of the time that we liked the most liked to spit. Like could really flow flow," says Smith.

The moment was peak gangsta rap—the reign of N.W.A, Ice Cube, Ice-T—when West Coast rappers made their name with songs about the politics of the streets and systemic oppression. Or sometimes just bullshit. The song "House Party," by Eazy-E and GBM, works as a simple, freewheeling boast with a low-key, menacing beat that could serve as the soundtrack to an intruder prowling at night.

Contract and money issues have been part of Eazy-E's legacy—Ice Cube split from N.W.A over money. But Sylk says she never had the same issues with Eazy-E. She says she occasionally helped him write in the studio. "I would be in the session with E, and I would come up with these great ideas, and he'd give me $1,500, like, 'Good looking out, thanks for the ideas.'" She's credited for a track under her real name, La'Mar Lorraine Johnson—"Ole School Shit," on Eazy-E's second and final album, *Str8 off tha Streetz of Muthaphukkin Compton*, released in 1996.

Sylk was a fast writer. Rhythm D says, "She was one of the dopest writers. That's what kinda put Sylk a little ahead of the game, to where she was able to land her own deal. . . . The songs would get done quicker because Sylk would damn near be finished with her verse before everybody. She didn't need no assistance. And if anybody was going too slow, she'd come through and help them. She'd get down, and soon as I put a beat on, she's going in."

After Eazy-E died of complications from AIDS in 1995, Sylk signed with another production company, Grand Jury, working with Michael Concepcion (one of the founders of the Crips gang).

Her debut album, *Raw Sylk*—released in 1999—has some of her gangsta DNA. On the opening track, the song "Keep It Real" featuring Too $hort, she raps: "Dealers and smugglers, land of the hustlers / Females with fame, watch out before we buck ya / For all ya loot, yo Versace suit." By that time, she was older and wiser and wrote songs about love and emotional growth. Her single "Romeo and Juliet," a thug-romance ballad that peaked at No. 6 on the *Billboard* Hot 100 chart and at No. 1 on the Hot Rap singles chart, features the Shakespeare-inspired hook: "It's like Romeo and Juliet / Hot sex on the platter just to get you wet."

"When she did the Romeo and Juliet, it fucked me up. I was, like, what?!" Smith recalls.

"I never saw that side of her. I'm, like, hold up, you tryin' to be sexy and shit?"

When she met Puff Daddy in New York, she says he shook her hand and said, "Nice to meet the female who took my spot." (The song she knocked down on the chart was "Victory.")

"Back in the late nineties, there wasn't music talking about staying loyal, marriage, relationships, faithfulness," says Sylk. "Lil' Kim and Foxy Brown was, like, 'Take ya nigga money!' I wanted to do something different. I had my first and only child, a single mom raising a son. I just wanted to be sassy, grown, sexy. I wanted to be like an R&B rapper. I was ready to transition and mature, so I wrote a love song that I thought people could relate to."

BaHamaDIa

◆ ◆ ◆

NEVER FORGET:
Bahamadia is featured on the open mic institution Lyricist Lounge's first compilation album, *Lyricist Lounge Volume One*, released in 1998.

WHO SHE IS:
Bahamadia (Antonia Reed) wrote poems and short stories as a kid and began rhyming over house tracks in the eighties. She took drum lessons at Settlement House of Music and went on to DJ house parties, block parties, and at community rec centers. Recorded in 1993, her single "Funk Vibe" caught the attention of artists like Kurupt and Sean Diddy Combs, but she eventually partnered with rapper/producer Guru after her sister's friend slid him a demo tape. *Kollage*, released in 1996, is her sole studio album.

LISTEN:
"Total Wreck" is one of those metallic, scratch-heavy records programmed to play in an underground rap dungeon.

When people think of Bahamadia, they might think of a feeling (chill) or a sound (jazz) more than a song. That sound is in many ways the sound of Philly: live, kinetic soul. The Roots. Everything Jill Scott does. In 1993, Bahamadia recorded a regional hit titled "Funk Vibe" that made its way to Guru, half of the legendary duo Gang Starr. Bahamadia's signature sound was soft and meditative but tough—a subtle style that complemented Guru's tone.

Kollage, her first and only major-label album, mirrored the cozy, even sensual, experience of an intimate lounge set, with double-timed raps tucked behind trumpets and downbeat keys, much of it created by the East Coast's greatest producers: Guru, Da Beatminerz, DJ Premier.

"Feminine energy is quiet in its movement, and it's more profound and more impactful when you're paced and you take a conversational approach. It feels regal, too," she says. "You mean what you say and you say what you mean. I never talk about things that don't resonate as being truthful."

The jazz and blues singers she followed—Nancy Wilson, Phoebe Snow—influenced her flow, along with rappers like Ultramagnetic MCs.

" **FEMININE ENERGY IS QUIET IN ITS MOVEMENT, AND IT'S MORE PROFOUND AND MORE IMPACTFUL WHEN YOU'RE PACED AND YOU TAKE A CONVERSATIONAL APPROACH.** "

The first thing Guru did was have her head to the studio. The single "Total Wreck" came from those initial sessions. She recorded all but one song ("Biggest Part of Me") for *Kollage* in one take. "Guru gave me one hundred percent creative control. I never had ghostwriters, none of that," she says—which allowed for looser sessions, the way she preferred. "I was always a fan of Gang Starr's music, and sonically I felt like it complemented my tone and what I was about in terms of rhyming and creating songs. The cadences. Jazz was just really cool [as a backdrop], and the soul movement is historically what Philadelphians are known for."

Guru connected jazz and hip-hop and released compilations of albums he dubbed the *Jazzmatazz* series, where he paired jazz musicians with artists like Angie Stone, Erykah Badu, and on *Vol. 2: The New Reality*. For that album, Bahamadia, who features on "Respect The Architect," once again appears as a quiet storm.

LIL' KIM

◆ ◆ ◆

NEVER FORGET:
Her 1996 debut album, *Hard Core*, was, at that point, the highest debut for a female rapper on the *Billboard* albums chart.

WHO SHE IS:
The Lil' Kim era began when she met the Notorious B.I.G. in Brooklyn and joined his crew, Junior M.A.F.I.A. Besides providing sex 101 for adolescents and adults, Kim set the template for glam styling in rap. Four more albums followed *Hard Core*: *The Notorious K.I.M.* (2000), *La Bella Mafia* (2003), *The Naked Truth* (2005), and *9* (2019).

LISTEN:
With Biggie's echoing voice in the background, "Suck My D**k" belongs on a list of top Lil' Kim songs, which would also include "Big Momma Thang" and every song on *Hard Core*.

The defining image of Lil' Kim's career is a portrait of her squatting in a leopard-print bikini, an outtake from the photo shoot for *Hard Core*. Her mentor, Notorious B.I.G., chose the photo for posters leading up to the album's 1996 release, knowing exactly which pose to use. "He threw the negatives on the table and pointed to the one with my legs open and said, 'That's the one right there,'" Kim told *XXL*, ten years later. Throughout the recording process, Biggie masterminded Kim's image and content, telling her to soften her voice, for example, to sound less masculine.

Kim, at some point, decided to own that persona, becoming a dream girl men envisioned, rap's ultimate sex symbol, praised for both her skills and her salesmanship of fucking. Before Kim, the top-selling women rappers—Queen Latifah, MC Lyte, Salt-N-Pepa—had been all about challenging sexism in hip-hop. Kim brought a raw sexual energy to the genre and became the model for a generation of female rappers caught in a battle between owning their sexuality and exploiting it. She made the new concept of a female rapper—with a sexy visual to go with their music—not a choice but a necessity.

Before *Hard Core* hit the streets, Kim ran with Junior M.A.F.I.A., the nine-deep Brooklyn crew assembled by Biggie. The first song she ever rapped on, 1995's "Player's Anthem," released when Kim was seventeen, established Junior M.A.F.I.A. as the latest formidable rap squad and set the tone for Kim as a soloist. Hardly anyone questioned her talent or ability. She raps so hard on the *Hard Core* track "Queen B@#$H" that she runs out of breath by the end of the verse: "Sippin' Zinfandels up in Chippendales / Shoppin' Bloomingdales for Prada bags, female Don Dada has . . ." Still, fans and critics wondered how much of Kim was really Biggie, which made it hard to talk about Lil' Kim without talking about him.

"Just being the girl in the group was majestic," says Kierna Mayo, the founding editor in chief of *Honey* (Kim covered the magazine twice). "Kim was four-eleven. She's tiny. It made her that much more profound, when you juxtapose the largeness of Big against Kim's small frame. He was a Svengali of sorts, and she was his loyal concubine. And it was dramatic and sometimes tragic to see." A week after *Hard Core*'s release, another rapper, Foxy Brown, released her own debut album, *Ill Na Na*, creating a double dilemma: Kim and Foxy's new blueprint for success liberated women's dirty thoughts, but it was all about male fantasy.

In 1996, Kim appeared on an episode of *BET Talk* with Tavis Smiley, alongside Luke Campbell of 2 Live Crew fame, to discuss the raunchiness of their lyrics. "It's my image. If people didn't see this on me, they probably would walk past me," Kim said on air. "A lot of men flock to me, they flock to my poster. They flock to my personality as well."

Kim's traumatic backstory played into her image. After her parents divorced, a move with her mother to New Rochelle begat a period of homelessness. One of Kim's favorite books was Alice Childress's novel *Rainbow Jordan*, because she related to the foster-child protagonist.

Kim later returned to live with her dad (and her brother) in Brooklyn, where her father, a former military member, ran a strict household. He spoiled her with designer Gucci threads, to the envy of her classmates. But she and her father argued constantly. (Kim once stabbed him with scissors.) Kim eventually left home, couch-surfing with friends and transporting drugs for dealers as her profession. Everything changed after she ran into Biggie on Fulton Street in Brooklyn and rapped for him. This was the man who, she later rapped, "swooped a young bitch off her knees" and served as her mentor and lover.

Jacob York, the former president of Kim's label, Undeas Entertainment, met her on St. James Place, Biggie's home base. "I remember she had black spandex on and these boots and she had a hat on her head, 'cause her hair was short, and she had a halter top on. She just started rapping, and it was this very deep voice," York says. "She wasn't as sexual on the Junior M.A.F.I.A. album as she ended up being on her album. What we kept presenting to her were ways to feminize herself more. By the time it got to *Hard Core,* she began to develop a sound."

Biggie heard the bass in her voice, too, and reshaped it. The goal for them was to soften her tone. They were building a perfect rap girl. "When I first met Lil' Kim, her aggression was Fredro from Onyx, and Big hated it," says Lance "Un" Rivera, who co-founded Undeas with Biggie. "When we were making the Junior M.A.F.I.A. album and she did 'Backstabbers,' he heard the tone in her voice and said, 'This is it.' He said, now you appeal to my manliness from a music standpoint."

Kim and Biggie's tense relationship is part of hip-hop lore. They fought in a recording studio elevator. She watched him marry R&B singer

Faith Evans and date Charli Baltimore. Kim became pregnant with Biggie's child and had an abortion while recording *Hard Core* at the same time that she was working on Junior M.A.F.I.A.'s debut album, *Conspiracy*. Her subject matter, as a result, skewed dark (she rapped a lot about death and drugs). York says they had to stop recording because the music was getting "darker and darker."

KIM'S COLLABORATORS HAVE ALL BUT CONFIRMED THAT WHILE BIGGIE COACHED HER ON CADENCE AND FLOW, SHE WROTE MOST OF HER OWN MATERIAL.

"It was kind of a sad album at that point, 'cause she was going through that personal relationship with Biggie," says York. "If you listen to the original [*Hard Core*] album, there's no Lil' Kim verse on ["Crush on You"]. It's just Cease. Because I just said, 'Fuck it, we putting this single on it, and we gonna use it to propel his career 'cause I'm not gonna get anymore music out of her."

Her image, through Biggie and Rivera, was all about the fulfillment of desire. "My strategy was [consistent] when it comes to Kim: She wasn't the wife. She was the high-end side chick to drug dealers," says Rivera. "We placed her in a world that we were living in, and it was: You wear all of the finest things because the number one drug dealer, you're his side chick, and he buys you everything. It's all driven by the male hormones, the male ego, the fantasy. It's not about love. It's about being nasty." This was an obvious issue, having a cast of men controlling her image, which only fueled the myth that Biggie was writing most of her lyrics.

Kim's collaborators have all but confirmed that while Biggie coached her on cadence and flow, she wrote most of her own material. Rivera says of *Hard Core*, "She wrote the majority of the album. Biggie wrote a few songs. All of the singles that she's ever been on that were hits, she wrote those verses herself."

The late rapper Prodigy said he saw Kim write the entirety of her verse for Mobb Deep's "Quiet Storm (Remix)" in the studio. Jacob York says he sat in on most of the studio sessions for *Hard Core*. It was hard for people to imagine that a woman with access to a gift like Biggie wouldn't have him writing all her lyrics. But that assumption was ultimately a sign of rap's low expectations for women.

"She wrote her singles. 'Get Money'—she wrote that motherfucker. She wrote 'No Time,'" says York. "It was more about her being taught how to rap. 'Cause Kim always understood what to write, but sometimes she would go places. She goes back to that girl on the block with that deep voice."

York breaks down the math. "She wrote another verse to 'Get Money,' and Big was like, 'That verse is trash,'" he remembers. "So what he did was, he rapped his verse, she studied it, and she came [up] with a verse. He helped her with the first, like, eight bars of that [and said], 'Yours should match mine.' That little part after 'You wanna get between my knees,' that was the Biggie influence. After that, you can tell that the flow completely changes. And that's Kim all at her own devices on that record."

"I REMEMBER THAT KIND OF LANGUAGE BEING LIBERATING AND EXHILARATING, AND IT KIND OF PUT ALL OF US ON BLAST."

York says he and Rivera wrote the porn star reference in Kim's verse on Junior M.A.F.I.A.'s "I Need You Tonight," where she name-drops Vanessa del Rio. But for "Big Momma Thang," he says Kim wrote the references to two famous black mid-nineties porn stars, Heather Hunter and Janet Jacme. "I don't think it was that we forced the words into her mouth as much as we emancipated what she felt she could and couldn't do. Kim is what you heard in those records."

But Kim was shaped by men who got to dictate how she would be marketed. If she was constantly being molded and if being any other way than sexy wasn't a viable choice, she couldn't have a complete sense of power. What's remarkable is how rappers like Kim and Salt-N-Pepa, despite being under the guidance of male producers, still used their voices as tools of liberation.

Although Biggie's involvement will always be a point of contention, he is a big reason her best album was her first one. What Kim accomplished on her own, despite his input, is still monumental. Her lyrics ("No licky licky, fuck the dicky dicky") became shameless mantras for women who were both discovering and engaging in sex. "If you look at the adult sex business from the beginning of time," says Heather Hunter, "the whole idea was to open the doors so our culture could embrace it and, as African American women, to be proud of your sexuality and be proud of your temple. To see Lil' Kim, the Wanda Dees of the world, the Foxy Browns, to see these people open these doors and embrace it and move forward, to me, was a beautiful thing."

When asked about control of her "hard-core" image, Kim told bell hooks in a *Paper* interview, "We all had a lot to do with my career; we all have our input. I would say that it was me who just started it, because I would have to do it and feel comfortable, you know what I mean? You can't really just make someone into something and it works all the time; that person has to be a natural."

Some of the control she might've lost elsewhere, she regained by crafting her own designer image as a black Barbie. Lil' Kim would wear anything anywhere to stand out: a red leather biker outfit with matching helmet, a sheer *I Dream of Jeannie* gown

IF KIM HAD NOT TAKEN THE RISKS IN MUSIC AND FASHION THAT SHE DID, FEMALE RAPPERS TODAY WOULD PROBABLY STILL BE UNDERPLAYING THEIR LOOKS JUST TO LEGITIMIZE THEIR MUSIC.

with a mask, full-on lingerie, mink wrist cuffs, a purple seashell pasty on one lonely breast. During photo shoots, she would *do* anything: dress like a blow-up doll; transform into a living, breathing Louis Vuitton accessory; and, yes, squat in a bikini made by designer Patricia Fields. She wore vibrant furs and 1950s-housewife wigs in the video for her single "Crush on You" (the theme of which was inspired by *The Wiz*). She rocked hot pants while riding a World Trade Center escalator in the video for "No Time."

"Everybody wanted to dress her, photograph her, put makeup on her. Annie Leibovitz, Bruce Weber," says Christina Murray, the head of black music publicity at Atlantic Records for Kim's first two albums. "You have artists that would say no, but Kim was not like that. 'Kim, they wanna do your hair like this.' Kim was never, like, 'No.' She saw what they saw in her, and she was open to all those things."

Kim's stylist, Misa Hylton Brim, made customized looks and gave Kim the shock value needed for fashion to embrace her as a pliable muse. (The furs and jewelry Kim wore in "No Time" came from Brim's personal collection.)

"Because Kim's lyrics were risqué and because at the time she was in a relationship with Big, Un's idea was to create her image as the mistress of rap. And he gave us the freedom to take that concept and run with it," says Hylton Brim, who saw Kim's style as a reflection of Kim's inner self, which said it was okay for women to *want to* dress like a doll, or drape themselves in rings and things. It was okay for women to create fantasy..

"If Kim had not taken the risks in music and fashion that she did, female rappers today would probably still be underplaying their looks just to legitimize their music," says Brim. "Kim created another lane, allowing women to shape their own images and express themselves in any way they want through style. We don't have to be just one way as women. We get to choose what we wear and how we wear it."

The press framed Kim's career with varying degrees of praise and concern. For its February 1997 magazine cover, *The Source* featured Lil' Kim and Foxy Brown back-to-back, with the cover line "Sex & Hip-Hop: Harlots or Heroines?" For its October 2000 issue, *Ebony* published a piece about Kim as an American sex symbol, asking, "Is Mainstream Ready for Lil' Kim?" *Essence* put Kim

on the cover that same month, with the line "The Big Problem with Lil' Kim."

There were women who found her image offensive; others felt freed by it. And both men and women wanted the fantasy. For women writing about hip-hop, discussing Lil' Kim was like deciphering a quantum entanglement. She seemed to exist solely as a topic for debate about hip-hop's worst traits, not just as a medium for sexual liberation; she was a subject to advance conversations about misogyny in rap and a reflection of black girls' insecurities. It wasn't just her image, but her physical exterior, which changed over the years; she has admitted to plastic surgery and once had a second nose job after her boyfriend assaulted her. These complexities made her fascinating and also contributed to making her a star. She wanted to be pretty, to be sexy, to be not Kimberly Jones, but Lil' Kim. And by being Lil' Kim, she looked to free herself and others.

Aliya S. King, a former staff writer for *The Source*, was in her early twenties and teaching history at a high school in East Orange, New Jersey, in 1996 when *Hard Core* dropped. She remembers the girls in her class dancing like Kim and wearing the same bright wigs. "They were definitely liberated in a way that I wasn't," says King.

"She reminded me of girls I grew up with who were all about the fashion, all about the boys, and those are the kind of girls who got talked about," says Karen Good, who interviewed Kim for the September 1997 edition of *Vibe*. "There were rumors, and they were called all kinds of 'hoes' and 'bitches,' and they were just, like, 'Well, I'll be the best bitch.'"

Hard Core dropped when I was thirteen years old, learning about sex ed through detailed anatomy books, YA novels, and Lil' Kim saying, "I used to be scared of the dick / Now I throw lips to the shit," which sounds like a coming-of-age story on its own. Kim's music helped girls feel comfortable talking about sex. Most impressive, she was the world's most tireless advocate of men eating pussy. She refused to settle for less and gave us Smithsonian-worthy lines about it:

"Lick up in my twat / Gotta hit the spot"

"No licky licky? Fuck ya dicky dicky and ya quickie"

"Got buffoons eatin' my pussy while I watch cartoons"

"You ain't lickin' this? You ain't stickin' this"

"Only way you seeing me is if you eatin' me"

"All I wanna do is get my pussy sucked"

Et cetera. This was language that changed the game; it was adult film refurbished as rap, which set a precedent for future artists like Khia and Trina.

"I remember that kind of language being liberating and exhilarating, and it kind of put all of us on blast, those of us who hadn't felt free enough, during that time, to have these contradictions in our public persona," says Kierna Mayo. "It just kind of blew everybody's mind."

After Biggie's death in 1997, Kim's subsequent albums became a litmus tests for her ability and whether she could rap on her own and still sell. She could and she did. Think of her pussy-eating manifesto "How Many Licks," featuring the thong man Sisqo and a music video that leans fully into Kim's manufactured-doll imagery. Think of her professing to be a "black Barbie dressed in Bulgari" and rapping about deep-throating on her spastic single "The Jumpoff," from her third album, 2003's *La Bella Mafia*. While the precision wasn't the same as with *Hard Core*, she could definitely rap on her own.

Kim's very public contradictions and the spectacle of sex around her allowed the rappers after her to take the most valuable parts of her blueprint and leave the rest. The fruits of her labor were seeded through rappers like Cardi B and Nicki Minaj, who modeled her colorful wigs after Kim's (Nicki also re-created Kim's squat pose early in her career, before they began beefing). Kim was, in every way, an experiment, a muse, and a sacrificial lamb.

THE SQUAT

PHOTOGRAPHER MICHAEL LAVINE ON CAPTURING THE SQUAT SHOT OF LIL' KIM THAT MADE MEN GO WILD

The only time I ever met Lil' Kim, she was really quiet. We found a cool location, which was a brownstone apartment on Fifteenth Street in the city, and rented it [for the shoot]. Biggie wasn't there. It was Un [Lance "Un" Rivera] in complete control of everything. Lil' Kim did not speak to me. No words [came] out of her mouth. Un just told her what to do. So it's always been really shocking to me to see Lil' Kim come out of her shell. She was very quiet and shy.

They had the idea—they wanted a bearskin rug. There was a scene with a bed, and there was this telephone, rose petals—those props on the bed were not my choices. I was the one that decided the angles, the lighting, position, and the look. I had a prop stylist who brought all those flowers. I don't remember who brought what. But some of that stuff is really cliché: a bearskin rug and a bottle of champagne.

That shot of her squatting was so in-your-face. That's the kind of thing that just happened by accident. It seemed right for that space. Not that crouching is some original position. It made sense for her to do it, and it made sense for the label to capitalize on the image and put it out there. It borders on: *Fuck you, I'm a strong woman, I'm gonna do this*. And that's where it crosses over from being sexualized to being like, *I own this*.

She was beautiful, and it was provocative, and she was interesting, and people were interested in her. And she was a good rapper. All the right elements came together to create a star.

The "Lady" Rappers

Lady B

On her hit single "To the Beat Y'all," Lady B flipped the story of Jack and Jill into a tale about Jill getting pregnant. She later became a popular radio DJ in her hometown of Philadelphia.

Lady Sovereign

Try to name all the British female rappers who successfully crossed over into the US market, and you'll probably think of Monie Love and Lady Sovereign, who rapped in a cockney accent and made a moderate splash on the American side of the pond with her single "Love Me or Hate Me" while signed to Island Records.

Lady Leshurr

The British grime rapper from Birmingham packs a ton of syllables and banter into her freestyles, the most popular being "Queen's Speech."

Lady May

Her 2002 single "Round Up" featured R&B singer Blu Cantrell, who was famous for her revenge single "Hit 'Em Up Style (Oops!)."

Lady Crush

She was around fourteen years old when she auditioned for a chance to appear on rapper Tim Greene's single "Facts of Life" and won. The spitfire raps on her single "MC Perpetrators" sound straight out of an eighties break-dancing movie and features Lady Crush laying out a challenge: "You wanna battle me, you betta eat ya Wheaties."

Big Lady K

While signed to Priority Records, she released an album of thoroughly eighties-style raps, *Bigger Than Life*, in 1989.

FOXY BROWN

NEVER FORGET:
Her sophomore album, *Chyna Doll*, was only the second album by a female rapper to debut at No. 1 on the *Billboard* Hot 100 chart, after Lauryn Hill's *The Miseducation of Lauryn Hill*.

WHO SHE IS:
Foxy Brown (Inga Marchand) was raised in Brooklyn as a child of well-off Trinidadian immigrants. By sixteen, she was going bar for bar with the likes of LL Cool J ("I Shot Ya Remix") and Jay-Z ("Ain't No Nigga") as the next big thing, having inspired a bidding war among record labels before she hit the legal drinking age. She was sick (in a good way) and sometimes shamelessly filthy on four albums: *Ill Na Na* (1996), *Chyna Doll* (1999), *Broken Silence* (2001), and *Brooklyn's Don Diva* (2008).

LISTEN:
On her dancehall single "Oh Yeah," a party record, Foxy raps about the dilemma of people thinking she's "too pretty to spit rhymes this gritty."

The Source magazine rarely put new rappers on its covers in the nineties. But Lil' Kim and Foxy Brown weren't just any new rappers. They were rumored rivals, and *The Source*, the hip-hop bible, was into making statements. The magazine's February 1997 issue featured both artists shoulder to shoulder against a chartreuse background—a show of unity for the friends who would later become foes. By elevating these two women in rap, *The Source* had predicted a shift in the genre, led partly by Foxy Brown.

The Source's cover line, "Sex in Hip-Hop: Harlots or Heroines?" set up the idea of women in rap being torn between two extremes. Foxy and Kim released their debut albums in the same month, November 1996, which placed them in constant competition. They were both young, talented, and explicit. "It felt like this savior-complex mentality that the culture was bestowing upon them, like, *Oh, my god, I've never heard a woman rap like this*," says Selywn Hinds, then editor in chief of *The Source*. "Also, neither of them was shy about notions of sexuality or letting themselves be pushed. We wanted to lean right into that provocation. That framing, the possibility, the contradiction, and the danger." Photographer Jordan Donner, who was mostly booking fashion editorials at the time, mediated the photo shoot. He remembers the friction in the room, which he felt both Kim's and Foxy's crews

perpetuated. "One of [the women] went into the bathroom for a while and didn't wanna come out," says Donner. "I sidebarred both of the girls at some point and said, 'Listen, you guys are so cool. You're so amazing. Your careers are on fire. Let's just have five minutes together, and we're gonna get a lot of great shots.' It was competitive: *Who's gonna have the look?*"

They were unicorns, celebrated for being beautiful and skilled. But even more so than Kim, Foxy was seen as one of the guys, simultaneously sexy and "nice for a girl." She was a dark-skinned vision to a teen rap fan like myself, and she would spit the type of filthy punch lines that drew enviable reactions and shock from men.

Foxy was sixteen years old, still in high school, when she wrote and recorded her verse for LL Cool J's single "I Shot Ya (Remix)." On a song with Ladies Love Cool James, Prodigy, Keith Murphy, and Fat Joe, she pulled off an incredible rookie exhibition, preceding LL Cool J with a verse about "sexing raw dog without protection, disease infested." Foxy's cousin, producer Clark Kent, set her up for the coronation, placing her in a session with established rappers and the Trackmasters production duo Tone and Poke.

"[People] really couldn't believe that she wrote every line of that song, right in the studio. They really think that Jay-Z wrote a lot of her stuff," says Foxy's brother Gavin Marchand. "I was there. She got that stigma because those guys are so great that they can't believe a female can write just like the men, which is unbelievably stupid."

The timing of "I Shot Ya" and "Ain't No Nigga," another scene-stealing moment for Foxy, was the cannonball of her career. While Jay-Z found the quippiest ways to dismiss one-night stands on the latter, Foxy Brown invoked the image of a dude "playing inside my pubic hairs." It blew people's minds.

"I lost my mind," says Kevin Liles, former Def Jam Recordings president. "You would think that she was a guy rapping on the record with Jay. That's how great her lyrics were. That's how great her delivery was. And when she performed it, that's how she came across: 'It's not just Jay's record; it's me and Jay's record.'"

While both Kim and Foxy appealed to men's desires, Foxy's style of rap made her a particular magnet for male fans. She exuded credibility and embraced it. When she teamed up with Nas, AZ, and Nature to form the mafia-style lyrical supergroup the Firm—which released one project, 1997's *The Album*—she came off like the femme fatale infiltrating the crew to beat them at their game. On her solo showcase "Fuck Somebody Else," she raps: "Niggas is my hoes, cop my dough, wanna lace me with some head after my shows . . . Fuck a man, bitch got the world in her hands."

Foxy Brown's debut album, *Ill Na Na*, despite having a title that refers to her pussy, is not all about sex. The album opens with a scene of Foxy setting up a guy for a crime, then enters a stage of betrayal, and ends with a blaxploitation-baritone preaching about her badness. Along with these catchy obscenities, Foxy also made soft, commercial records like "Get You Home," with Blackstreet, and appeared as a guest on Case's classic "Touch Me, Tease Me." For her third album, *Broken Silence*, she turned to dancehall music, tapping into her deep connection to reggae, and reggae's own connection with rap, which was clear since the era of Bob Marley (often considered an early rapper). Rappers like Queen Latifah had dropped patois into their rhymes. But Foxy made the best dancehall rap records in hiphop, as one of the most prominent to blend the genres so seamlessly on an album. (The trend continued with rappers like Eve, Nicki Minaj, and Drake whipping out their best or most embarrassing patois to incorporate Caribbean styles on wax.)

Ill Na Na positioned Foxy as a force and placed her and Kim in direct opposition. The former friends who once appeared together on the same record, R&B group Total's "No One Else (Remix)," in 1996, were separated through competition and, in a great loss for hip-hop, they never recorded together again.

Their labels, Def Jam and Atlantic Records, even killed a planned *Thelma and Louise*–inspired joint album, for which they paid Foxy and Kim at least $500,000 apiece, per reports. Neither showed up to the studio, while executives, producers, and peers awaited them. Notorious B.I.G., Jay-Z, Lyor Cohen, and Kevin Liles were among those who were stood up.

"All the beats and all that were done. Ready to go," says Gavin. "They both cut their phones off and never showed up. The record company had to eat that money." Few people knew the core of Lil' Kim's and Foxy Brown's conflict, which was rumored to be something as simple as a "Bitch Stole My Look" moment. (The two wore the same outfits in photos for their debut albums.) The beef then reached a violent boiling point in 2001, when Kim's and Foxy's camps got into a shootout outside the Hot 97 radio station. Kim, convicted for lying under oath about the incident, served ten months in prison.

Their beef seemed to confirm how much women in rap couldn't coexist. "The fact that they were positioned that way reinforced the idea of a scarcity model for female rappers," says former *Vibe* editor Elizabeth Méndez Berry. "I wish we could get to an abundance mindset, where we can have a spacious spectrum of female rappers that includes the Foxy and Kim types but isn't limited to them, and never presumes that they need to fight each other to shine. Imagine all the woman posse cuts we've been robbed of?"

Foxy's public reputation didn't help her. While Kim was likable on songs and played the charm game in interviews, Foxy was less forgiving. She appeared polite and businesslike in interviews. If Kim was the little sister, Foxy was a distant cousin.

"Whereas Foxy was already in star mode, Kim was kind of just a regular girl. She was really sweet and open," says writer Michael Gonzales, who interviewed the two for their dual cover of *The Source* and says he later became friends with Foxy. "Meanwhile, Foxy was middle-class, came from a hardworking family, grew up in a house, and she was just not nice. [*Laughs*] . . . Foxy was always Foxy. She was never Inga. She was always on. Kim, after she came out the studio, and after she came offstage, she was regular Kim."

Gavin remembers, "She was not a party person at all. I'm, like, 'You don't wanna hear your music in the club?' She's, like, 'No, for what?' Some people might've thought that her attitude was rude. But she had to learn how to be callous, business-wise. She had to learn how to think like a man and be tough about the situation so she could get what she deserved."

Maybe being standoffish was a tool of survival for a teenager who started her career off making very adult business decisions, facing high expectations.

In defending her image and content, Foxy would mention women like Josephine Baker or Bessie Smith, who played up their sexuality for the sake of business.

"What we didn't know back then was how their sexual freedom was going to change how women in rap are perceived and what the community is looking for in a female artist," says Kim Osorio, former editor in chief of *The Source*. "Lil' Kim, what she did, she did it so well that it was almost like every girl in hip-hop wanted to do that. And if you were Rah Digga, if you were Bahamadia, it was, like, Nah, that's not what the people . . . wanted to hear. . . . You had to do it in your panties in order for people to pay attention."

While aware of her physical power, Foxy was a teenager who was sexualized by men and created a whole new expectation for women in rap. Total control was largely an illusion. What started with Kim and Foxy reverberated for years.

DESIGNER RAPS:

FASHION BRANDS FOXY BROWN HAS PROMOTED IN SONGS, FROM A-TO-Z

A
ARMANI

B
BURBERRY

C
CARTIER
CESARE PACIOTTI
CHLOË
CHRISTIAN LOUBOUTIN

D
DIOR
DOLCE & GABANNA

E
ELLEN TRACY

F
FENDI

G
GUCCI

I
ISAAC MIZRAHI

m
MARC JACOBS
MOSCHINO

P
PRADA

V
VERSACE

Z
ZAC POSEN

NONCHALANT

The year of Lil' Kim's *Hard Core* and Foxy Brown's *Ill Na Na* was the same year that Nonchalant, then a twenty-six-year-old rapper from Washington, DC, released her first and only big single, "5 O'Clock," a smooth cautionary tale against selling crack. The hook should sound familiar to rap kids of the nineties: "5 o'clock in the morning / Where you gonna be? / (Outside on the corner)."

DC had a local rap scene—artists like Questionmark Asylum and DC Scorpio. But, "The most [people] heard from rap was [E.U.'s] 'Doin' the Butt,' " says Nonchalant. "That's all they knew about DC music, outside of go-go. So breaking ground with record sales that nobody else had done before was really, really great."

Nonchalant originally titled "5 O'Clock" instead "Brother Man," with a hook that went: "Brother man, come on . . ." Nonchalant rewrote the chorus after, yes, walking the streets at 5:00 a.m. At that hour, she noticed that the only people out and about in her neighborhood were service workers and drug dealers. As a post office employee, she was part of the former. "I had to get to work super early, and in the District, like a lot of places in the country, drugs were rampant. I would see young men outside, around the pay phones, and I remember saying to myself, 'I hope I never see one

◆ ◆

NEVER FORGET:
Her single "5 O'Clock" peaked at No. 24 on the *Billboard* Hot 100.

WHO SHE IS:
Nonchalant grew up in a middle-class family in Washington, DC, where the rap album that influenced her most was Slick Rick's *The Great Adventures of Slick Rick*. She briefly tried singing, before rapping. While working with a producer named Bam, she recorded a demo, "The Flow," in 1996, and, within two months, she signed to MCA Records.

LISTEN:
Her sole album, *Until the Day*, features the track "Lookin' Good to Me," where she raps about another activity that can go down at five in the morning.

◆ ◆

of my nephews out there at five o'clock in the morning.' It was their job. They were there on time, all day, reporting [in]. I switched the hook up, and that's where it came from: 'Five o'clock in the morning, where you gonna be, outside on the corner.' "

Because her vibe was mellow and her first single had a message about black men becoming statistics, Nonchalant got lumped in with "conscious rap." To help put her career in context: A 1999 *Los Angeles Times* article described her as a potential successor to Lauryn Hill. "5 O'Clock" became the lead single for her debut album, *Until the Day*, which came out during a turning point: the era of Bad Boy, luxury rap, and Lil' Kim.

Nonchalant remembers it as a time when female rappers went from emulating guys to feeling pressure to show more skin. "You weren't able to show your feminine side [at first]. You couldn't talk about how you liked sex. All the clothes were very big, so if you wore something tight, that was making a statement in itself. And if you were like a Foxy Brown or a Kim, when they came out, you were automatically categorized."

MISSY ELLIOTT

◆ ◆ ◆

NEVER FORGET:
She won the first and second (and only) Grammys for Best Female Rap Solo Performance before the Recording Academy cut the category.

WHO SHE IS:
Alone in her bedroom in Portsmouth, Virginia, Missy made the most of her solitude as an only child. She sang to an audience of dolls, followed *American Bandstand*, and wrote fan letters to Diana Ross and Janet Jackson. "I didn't have brothers and sisters to play with, so I created a world of my own. Everyone had imaginary friends. I had a whole imaginary world," she told *Billboard*. After a stint in the R&B group Sista, she went solo, and teamed up with producer Timbaland, producing, songwriting, and releasing six solo albums.

LISTEN:
"She's a Bitch," a song where Missy revels in being rich and intimidating, deserves a listen for its title alone.

◆ ◆ ◆

A garbage bag wasn't just a garbage bag in Missy Elliott's universe. It became a costume. Her first music video opens on a shot of her from a distance, distorted through a fish-eye lens. She's wearing what looks like a black garbage bag, puffed up so she appears cartoonish, almost cosmic, and full of volume. A reverse shot follows: Missy in a basic white tee, staring out at the viewer, smiling with all her teeth.

That 1997 video for "The Rain (Supa Dupa Fly)," the lead single from her debut album, *Supa Dupa Fly*, was the first of her many attempts to reimagine sound and vision. It wasn't just something new. Missy was a wellspring of oddball ideas who rapped, sang, produced, and created concepts that challenged the way fans experienced music videos and music itself. She's in a rare class of innovators, able to produce music and image from scratch and send it into space as art.

Hype Williams, the director behind some of the most iconic and weird, high-budget videos of the 1990s, had the idea to turn Missy into the Michelin Man for "The Rain" video (his directive for the visual treatment was, literally: "She's a Michelin Man"). Missy loved it. Her goal, inspired by Michael Jackson, was to make music videos on the scale of movies. Stylist June Ambrose's interpretation of the Michelin Man idea was to have a blow-up suit made from vinyl, with neoprene on the inside.

Ambrose inflated the suit (which wasn't a garbage bag), with Missy still in the thing, at a gas station a block from the soundstage in Queens, during filming. After an unexpected leak, Ambrose then had to continually re-inflate the suit every few minutes with a handheld bike pump on the set of the three-day shoot. "This was my version of a black Michelin Man," Ambrose told *Elle*. "I knew I wanted it to be a mock [turtle]neck, something that would really kind of consume her."

"The Rain" offered a bit of insight into Missy's world. All her music videos take place in a time and space beyond reality, with outsized costumes, textures, colors, and heavy on flamboyance and camp. In the video for "Sock It to Me," directed by Williams, she wears a Transformers-like robot uniform in space. In "She's a Bitch" (also Williams), she's bald with her face painted, donning a charcoal-colored costume that makes her look like a supersized fly. In "One Minute Man," she removes her own head and raps while holding it.

Hardly any rappers at all were that adventurous. Missy dreamt in moving pictures and allowed other innovators to exorcise her weird side. (Busta Rhymes, another visual mastermind, was one inspiration of hers.) The trash bag was part of her vision of the future. "We give our music a futuristic feel. I don't make music or videos for 1997—I do it for the year 2000," she told *The New Yorker*. Missy told the *Los Angeles Times*, "I want my videos to be different, to be cutting edge. I just got tired of seeing all these rappers in videos driving around in Mercedes and drinking champagne."

Missy and her soul mate, Tim Mosley, met through a mutual friend (the rapper Magoo) in Mosley's bedroom recording studio in Virginia Beach. He was known as the young, fresh producer with the magic touch. (This was before he became super producer Timbaland, whose alias

and popularity rivaled those of a major footwear company.) Missy was in a girl group called Fayze with her two friends Chonita Coleman and Radiah Scott. During her first meeting with Timbaland, she listened to a few of his tracks and sang over them, their chemistry instant. (He's compared their bond to that of "an old married couple.")

Fayze had been performing at local shows but didn't yet have a record deal in 1991. When they went to see Jodeci, the horniest R&B group of the time, in concert, they snuck backstage to audition for Jodeci member Donald "DeVante" DeGrate, who had his own imprint, Swing Mob, under Elektra Records. (He called his crew of artists Da Bassment.) DeVante signed Fayze and renamed them Sista, later adding LaShawn Freeman to the group. Timbaland served as their in-house producer.

Missy wrote most of their material, easily outpacing her group mates. "She could say some stuff that would make you stand there like a deer in headlights," says Freeman. "I remember DeVante was, like, 'All right, Missy's writing a whole album. I want y'all to start writing.' So we had this little competition, me and the other girls." On one of their songs, "It's Alright," Missy raps, "When I fart, I poops cash from my ass," and then it gets sexual: "Oh, daddy, is you ready / To slurp me in ya mouth like spaghetti?"

Sista had a memorable single, "Brand New," but their full album, *4 All da Sistas Around da World*, never came out. Once Jodeci broke up, Swing Mob shuttered, and Sista disbanded. The time spent with DeVante paid off, though. Sista, along with members of Da Bassment, served as apprentices, running errands and performing tasks for Jodeci. Timbaland described the experience as something of a boot camp where he learned to structure songs from watching DeVante. It was during this time, while

working craft services on the set of Jodeci's video for "Feenin'," that Missy met Hype Williams.

Sylvia Rhone, then chairperson and CEO of Elektra Records, was eager to sign Missy to her label as a solo artist. To sweeten the deal, she handed Missy her own imprint, the Goldmind Inc., so she could sign and develop artists, including herself. Missy's first major solo showcase (following Raven Symone's "That's What Little Girls Are Made Of" in 1993) was a guest verse on Gina Thompson's 1996 R&B single "The Things That You Do (Remix)," where Missy rapped a series of syllables within a verse that made everyone on Earth pause: "Hee-hee hee-hee haw / Hee-hee-hee-hee-hee-hee-haw."

Through the early to mid-nineties, she was writing hit R&B records for artists like 702 ("Steelo") and Ginuwine ("I'll Do Anything/I'm Sorry"). She also worked incognito as a writer/conductor for Sean "Puff Daddy" Combs at Bad Boy Records—for example, arranging the vocals for the Lox on "All About the Benjamins." Lox member Sheek Louch said during a Cipha Sounds improv show, "[Jadakiss] did a verse to it. And then [Missy] was, like, 'You gonna go here. You gonna go here. Y'all two, you and Kiss, gonna write Puff's verse.' I'm, like, 'What the fuck?' Then she just walked off, beatboxing . . . She put the whole 'Benjamins' together."

Missy and Timbaland stayed close and set themselves up as the production/writing duo behind the most radical R&B hits of the time. Missy's songwriting was key to their success, especially come 1996 when they met their muse, R&B singer Aaliyah, who was impressed with a demo track they produced titled "Sugar and Spice" and wanted to work with them.

Instead of shrinking, Missy amplified herself, treated her body as art, and framed sex as comical pleasure. She presented her sexuality as actively fun and funny at a time when the industry took sexual content from women seriously and, later, cynically, and didn't celebrate her body type. In Missy's eyes, there was no question that she was desirable, even if the business didn't see it, which made her casual, brazen use of sexuality hard for fans themselves not to embrace. She has an entire song about one-minute men and various raps about big dick energy.

Missy's writing made Aaliyah's sophomore album, *One in a Million*, sound like the product of a cool, sci-fi angel. Angelique Miles, the Warner Chappell executive who signed Missy and Timbaland to a publishing deal, told *Vibe*, "Missy's a poet. 'Baby, you don't know what you do to me . . .'—those first lines of 'One in a Million' are romantic." Missy and Timbaland invented new styles of R&B based on weird percussion and stop-and-start rhythms that played like irregular heartbeats. They excelled at making music that maximized negative space. "The Rain" is littered with dramatic pauses, making each line sound like slam poetry, except doper: "I feel the wind / Begin / Sit on hills like Lauryn." Likewise, *One in a Million*, produced and co-written by Timbaland and Missy, was an instant game-changer, with a sound that felt foreign and futuristic and inspired imitators.

When Timbaland played the sample for "The Rain"—Ann Peebles's "I Can't Stand the Rain"—in the studio, Missy, in true only-child fashion, disappeared to record her verse. She would often go off on her own. "I've never seen her record on the mic," Timbaland told *FADER*. "People wanna perfect their craft, and Missy . . . likes to be by herself when she does that—just her and the engineer," he said.

"The Rain" was a hit on terrestrial radio and in the real world but not on the charts. As a strategy to bait consumers into buying albums, labels would release a song from the album to radio as a promotional single instead of a physical release (yes, singles were once available on slim cassette tapes

"SHE COULD SAY SOME STUFF THAT WOULD MAKE YOU STAND THERE LIKE A DEER IN HEADLIGHTS."

and CD singles in physical stores). Elektra used this strategy with "The Rain," meaning the song wasn't eligible for the Hot 100 chart.

Pharrell Williams, a producer who grew up around Missy and Timbaland in Virginia, spoke of her in terms of science. "We came up in a time where we were always told no. Where we were always placed in a box. And she defied it. Over and over again," he told *Elle*. "She defied the physics that were dictated to us. She ignored the gravity of standards and prejudices and stereotypes."

There's one female rap producer widely known by name, and her name is . . . play along here . . . Missy Elliott. It might be that mixing, engineering, and beatmaking aren't encouraged as activities for girls when they're young. Even today, female producers are scarce across the board—a woman has never won a Grammy Award for Producer of the Year, Non-Classical, while superstar producers like Timbaland, Pharrell (who won Producer of the Year twice at the Grammys), Diplo, and Swizz Beatz are recognized by their signature sounds.

Much of Missy's production work—including songs she co-produced with Timbaland for herself and others—had gone unheralded. She told the Associated Press in 2016, "A lot of people don't know [about my work on] a lot of records that I've written or produced . . . I always said if a man would have done half the records that I've done, we would know about it."

Then in 2019, Missy became the first female rapper inducted into the Songwriters Hall of Fame, and only the third hip-hop artist, after Jay-Z and Jermaine Dupri. The honor was a long time coming. Her résumé includes co-producing the No. 1 hit "Lady Marmalade," featuring Christina Aguilera, Pink, Lil' Kim, and Mýa. The song won a Grammy for Best Pop Collaboration in 2002. Missy also co-produced and co-wrote Raven-Symoné's

chirpy anthem "That's What Little Girls Are Made Of." She co-produced and co-wrote an extensive list of R&B records, including:

- SWV's "Can We" and "Release Some Tension"
- Monica's "So Gone"
- Whitney Houston's "In My Business" and "Oh Yes"
- Destiny's Child's "Confessions"
- Beyoncé's "Signs"
- Mýa's "My Love Is Like Whoa"
- Jazmine Sullivan's "Need U Bad"
- Keyshia Cole's "Let It Go"
- Mariah Carey's "Babydoll"
- Tweet's "Oops (Oh My)"
- Ciara's "1, 2 Step"
- Fantasia's "Free Yourself"

After a decade-long hiatus without releasing an album, and while battling Graves' disease, Missy resurfaced in 2015. By then, there were artists like Nicki Minaj, Tierra Whack, and Tyler, The Creator filling the void of oddball rap, creating videos steeped in shock and surrealism. That year, in her video for "WTF (Where They From)," featuring Pharrell Williams, Missy wore a disco-ball suit and had dancing marionette figures of herself and Pharrell. It was time for her to return to being the queen of weird.

ALL UP IN THE VIDEOS

DIRECTOR DAVE MEYERS ON COLLABORATING WITH MISSY ELLIOTT ON HER OUT-OF-THE-BOX MUSIC VIDEOS

At the time I met Missy, I was struggling to make a mark in videos and stand out myself. I had done a Lil' Mo video, and Missy was like a godmother to Lil' Mo. I had heard that Missy was watching me on the Lil' Mo set, and about three months later, her A&R person arranged a meet, and she took me out for sushi in Westwood, Los Angeles.

After dinner, we got into her Lamborghini, and she played the song "Get Ur Freak On" for me. And then she drove me to see *Crouching Tiger, Hidden Dragon.* Most artists didn't take the time to vibe with me prior to [directing] a video, so I was swept away by her creative courtship. I felt compelled and excited to do something different [with Missy]. Sensing and understanding her ideology, I felt like, if I don't go far enough, then she's gonna not like it. So I went as far as I could.

The foundation of our friendship was that we both liked crazy stuff. [The video for] "Get Ur Freak On" was inspired by a Japanese book that I had about underworld architecture. I built as many sets as we could afford, with the steel girders and the weird underground textures. That was how the collaboration worked in the early days: me testing out weird stuff, like [her] swinging from the chandelier—seeing how far she'd let me go. And it just got weirder as the videos progressed. We spent on the high end of what rappers would spend, because her label president was a devout believer in her brand.

In "One Minute Man," I suggested she pull her "head" off, and she replied, "Okay, Dave." One problem with a lot of special-effects ideas is that they can be done really wrong [and look] cheesy. Her trust enabled me to grow as a filmmaker and be celebrated for standing out instead of fitting in. Back then, she was having to deal with a system that was relatively conformist, so she had to be really strong to push [beyond its limits]. That strength [of her convictions] was unique, because [while] a lot of artists . . . had suggestions . . . the general goal was to fit into MTV and assimilate—party videos and whatnot. Not only was she visually couture, she was also not [of] your typical mold.

ANGIE MARTINEZ

NEVER FORGET:
Like Jay-Z's, her interviews are hotter.

WHO SHE IS:
Angie Martinez became known as "The Voice of New York" after working hotline duties at the urban radio station WQHT. She's known for later conducting star interviews with a surgeon's precision on "Hot 97" and, later, Power 105.1. But she was also, briefly, a rapper.

LISTEN:
On the club record "Take You Home," Angie Martinez and singer Kelis shop for Mr. Right after-hours.

LADIES NIGHT

EVERYTHING YOU NEED TO KNOW ABOUT LIL' KIM'S "NOT TONIGHT (LADIES NIGHT REMIX)," FEATURING ANGIE MARTINEZ, LISA "LEFT EYE" LOPES, LIL' KIM, DA BRAT, AND MISSY ELLIOTT:

1 The song was released in 1997 as a remix of Lil' Kim's "Not Tonight," from her debut album, *Hard Core*.

2 But since the song didn't sound anything like the original, it came to be known as just "Ladies Night."

3 It's one of the greatest posse cuts and definitely the most fun one, featuring a suite of elite women: Lil' Kim, Left Eye, Da Brat, Missy Elliott, and Angie Martinez.

4 It samples Kool and the Gang's "Ladies Night."

5 When Angie Martinez rapped, "I just made this muthafucka up last night," it was true. The first time she rapped was a verse KRS-One wrote for her, for his song "Heartbeat." When the song's producer, Lance "Un" Rivera, asked her to be on Kim's all-star remix, Angie had trouble writing her verse. "I must have spent two days in my house with a pad and a pen, writing pages' worth of shit that was probably all terrible," Martinez wrote in her book, *My Voice: A Memoir*. "I wrote about one hundred bars, 'cause I didn't know what was good, what was wack. So I went in the booth, and I just started doing all of it, everything that I'd written. We did it a bunch of times, and Un picked the best eight bars."

6 "Not Tonight" came about because Atlantic Records wanted to show a different side of Kim. "When we came with that poster, the squat, they said, we don't want our name on this poster, 'cause you're gonna get so much backlash," says Rivera. "[Lil' Kim's] idea, 'Ladies Night,' was to unite women. Missy came in and took charge of the formatting of the record, and it became history."

7 It's featured on the soundtrack to Martin Lawrence's movie *Nothing to Lose*.

8 "Ladies Night" peaked at No. 6 on the *Billboard* Hot 100 chart.

9 It earned a Grammy nomination for Best Rap Song by a Duo or Group.

10 In the music video, directed by Un Rivera, the women ride Jet Skis, scuba dive, party on a boat, and have a group of buff men pamper them in West Palm Beach.

11 The concept, according to Rivera: "It was an exotic island that was secret to women. No one's ever seen it. Only women knew that it existed. You had to swim through these caves, and you ended up in this place that was all about catering to women."

12 The video features cameos from Queen Latifah, SWV, Mary J. Blige, Xscape, Total, Blaque, Maia Campbell, Big Lez, and Changing Faces.

13 Mary J. Blige's barefoot dancing in the video is iconic.

14 Missy Elliott was famous from the single "The Rain (Supa Dupa Fly)," but her debut album, *Supa Dupa Fly*, wasn't out yet at the time of the song's release.

15 All the women performed "Ladies Night" at the MTV Awards. You may remember the outfits, styled by June Ambrose. Angie Martinez wore a sateen pantsuit. Lil' Kim and Left Eye looked like Nefertiti. Missy Elliott had a gold sweat suit. Da Brat dressed as a full-on gladiator.

16 In 2017, Lil' Kim suggested a remake of "Ladies Night" featuring herself, Cardi B, and Remy Ma.

17 In 2018, on an episode of her *Queen Radio* show, Nicki Minaj said she would be open to recording a remake of the remix, because "Why not?"

18 As of 2020, neither Lil' Kim nor Nicki Minaj had recorded that remake.

CHARLI BALTIMORE

After the Notorious B.I.G. died in 1997, Charli Baltimore's career was at risk. The man she was dating was gone, and his business partner, Lance "Un" Rivera, wanted to fulfill the late rapper's wish of turning Charli into a star. As a posthumous favor to Biggie, Un inherited her as an artist and signed her to his new label, Untertainment Records, having never heard her rap. It didn't matter. Charli told Un she wrote her own rhymes, but his immediate plan was to hire ghostwriters for her album.

According to Un, it wasn't so much that he thought she *needed* men to write for her—"It was about whoever can give me a hit," he says. "I was paying anybody to write me a hit." He got the rap trio the Lox to write her first single, "Money," in 1997, for the soundtrack to the romantic comedy *Woo*, starring Jada Pinkett Smith. Another possibility as a potential ghostwriter was Charli's labelmate, Harlem rapper Cam'ron. Charli refused. She wasn't claiming to be rap's Charlotte Brontë. She just knew she could write and was adamant about letting people know it.

Pop icons like Whitney Houston, Madonna, and Aretha Franklin regularly worked with multiple songwriters. But rap had a stricter criteria: you either wrote or pretended to write your own shit, and using ghostwriters was seen as a crime. At the same time that men were ridiculed for not writing their raps, women were held to lower expectations—to fans, it seemed like a given that Lil' Kim and Foxy Brown had male ghostwriters, even when that wasn't true, and this was something Charli Baltimore resented.

Before Pharrell Williams became *Pharrell*, he offered to produce Charli's entire debut album, according to Un, who says Pharrell wanted to outsource the writing. Charli once again refused. "She was, like, 'Nah, I'm a writer. I can write my own shit,'" Un recalls.

Un eventually came around. "When Un saw that I could really write, he was fucked up, like, 'Shit, she really can write.' I never had another person write a single lyric again for me ever," says Charli. "But in the nineties, nobody cared. It was, like, 'Cam's writing her music.' Whatever guy was in the mix is the guy that's writing the girl's music. There are girls that can out-write dudes, so it always bothered me that I felt like a prop. And because I was so young, I didn't know any better."

Un and Charli clashed when it came to vision, too. She wanted hard-core records in line with her "Mobb Deep, Onyx flow," she says. Un wanted her to be "a rap Britney Spears," he says, partly because of her model looks. Charli wanted to market her strengths as a rapper. "I come from fucking Philly, from the hood," she says. "I had almost got in my mind that I couldn't even make a pop record. I was a hard-core street writer."

When Charli was around fourteen years old, Will Smith popped up in the Gallery Mall during her shift at Philadelphia Footwear. Charli ran out of the store to spit a rap for the Fresh Prince on the spot. He later called her and invited her to the studio, but the timing was off. She had an early curfew, and nothing materialized.

In the summer of 1995, Charli met another rapper, the Notorious B.I.G., at a concert of his in Philly. She'd just graduated from Pierce College and had her second daughter. After the show, she and her cousin waited outside the club for a potential photo op with Biggie. Biggie agreed, but the scene was too hectic. He asked her to follow him back to his hotel, where they exchanged numbers outside the building—the beginning of a friendship.

Biggie's notorious relationship web involved three famous women in hip-hop: his wife (R&B singer Faith Evans) and two rappers he dated (Lil' Kim and Charli Baltimore). They've all described their experiences with him in interviews, and Evans wrote a 2008 memoir. The events described here are how Charli remembers them.

Charli and Biggie talked on the phone for weeks, she says. He invited her to parties. They began dating. She even called out from her job once at a law firm to visit him at one of his tour stops. She spent a weekend with him in California when he was there to shoot a cameo for an episode of the sitcom *Martin*, and she describes Biggie as "the perfect gentleman" during that time. While he was still married to Faith Evans, he told Charli they had separated.

For a while, Charli kept a running list of the messages women left on Biggie's answering machine. After gathering enough material, she flipped the messages into a verse and rapped it for him, leaving Big with the takeaway that Charli had talent. She should try to write more, he said, and he challenged her to write daily.

Charli recalls: "He was, like, 'Can you do me a favor? Can you write a rap every day, and every day I want you to call me and rap for me.' I'm, like, okay, fucking Biggie Smalls wants me to write a rap and rap for him every day. I was, like,

He's bullshitting, he doesn't really think I can rap. But he really would stay on my ass. He would call me early in the morning or late at night: 'Are you writing? Are you writing?'"

Within a few months, she was in the studio so often that she had to quit her job at the law firm. Most rap fans discovered her in 1996, when she cosplayed as Faith Evans (wig and all) in Biggie's rap crew Junior M.A.F.I.A.'s video for "Get Money."

Before Biggie died, there were plans for a supergroup called the Commission comprised of Biggie, Charli, the artist formerly known as Puff Daddy, Junior M.A.F.I.A. member Lil Cease, and a young Brooklyn rapper named Jay-Z. "Big came up with the Commission idea, and that's eternally embedded in the 'What's Beef?' record when he shouts out the [names of the] whole Commission. He passed away, so we weren't able to record."

The ensuing drama about Biggie's relationships with Faith, Lil' Kim (who was an emotional wreck after his death), and Charli turned into hearsay. "I never cared about any of that. In my mind I'm, like, *Y'all are focused on the wrong thing. We just lost a legend,*" says Charli. "Everybody's, like, staking their claim to this man, and I'm, like, he's not here. I never read Faith's book, but she does acknowledge that I was his girl . . . It was hard, because, with Un, they wanted to ride on 'This was Big's girl.' I never wanted to do that. I was comfortable enough in my talent. Me talking about Big—that was everybody's main question, and I was, like, this doesn't have anything to do with my music."

Biggie had an idea to market Charli to the people by concealing her face on posters so everyone would focus on her rapping. Once Charli signed with Un, he and Jacob York ran an ad campaign along similar lines, with posters that showed Charli facing backward with the tagline: "Who is Charli Baltimore?" The idea came from a Looney Tunes commercial.

Two years of drills under Big had improved Charli's writing. But her relationship with Un was still strained, and her album was shelved before its scheduled release, along with about sixty songs she'd written and recorded. Un lost his deal due to a regime change and what he calls "the dysfunction of Epic Records."

Charli's debut album, *Cold As Ice*, scheduled for release in June 1999, was never formally released. She admits the material was subpar. "Stand Up," a track featuring Wu-Tang Clan's Ghostface Killah, remains her favorite record and the best showcase of her writing. "I swallow rhymes, making bitches swallow nines," she raps. Most of the other tracks, she hates, especially the pop single "Feel It," produced by Teddy Riley. (No offense to Teddy.) To prep for its music video, she trained with a choreographer who'd worked with Michael Jackson, but she forgot all the moves by the day of the shoot.

This, clearly, wasn't her forte. Again, she was pigeonholed by her looks. "Our mistake was that we judged Charli by her image and said, 'Here's the female Mase.' But Charli was more of a Nas than a Mase," says York. (Mase, signed to Bad Boy Records, had made a living with their signature glossy rap, and Nas was, in contrast, a lyrical prodigy.) "If you put her on a beat with Ghostface, she delivered, 'cause she was lyrically and metaphorically great. We made the mistake of trying to take this image and popify it, when we should've taken this image and ghettofied it."

Around 2000, Charli met Irv Gotti, head of Murder Inc Records, home of the gravel-voiced Queens rapper Ja Rule. The first thing Irv asked, Charli remembers, was: "Who be writin' your shit?" She told him *she* be writing her shit. "Get the fuck outta here," he said. (He may have even laughed.) And the cycle continued.

With Irv, she entered another round of intense training—what she refers to as Irv Gotti Boot Camp, which involved spending forty-eight hours in an LA studio. Irv would cue beat after beat and have her write so he could see her process in real time. He invited her to a studio session with a roomful of men and challenged her to "smoke 'em." She did, and he ate it up.

Under Def Jam, Murder Inc had a lawless streak when it came to hitmaking. Every song they put out became a hit, including their remixes with Jennifer Lopez ("I'm Real," "Ain't It Funny"). Ja Rule, operating at peak Ja Rule, brought the most mellifluous street rap to radio since Nelly two years earlier. Ashanti meanwhile blossomed into the highest-selling R&B singer-songwriter of the early 2000s, off her No. 1 record "Foolish." Having both Vita and Charli Baltimore on the roster at once, even for a fleeting moment, was rare. (Irv had

HE INVITED HER TO A STUDIO SESSION WITH A ROOMFUL OF MEN AND CHALLENGED HER TO "SMOKE 'EM."

Irv, who wanted Murder Inc to be an empire of songwriters, encouraged internal battles between his artists, giving beats to whoever could write the freshest hook. When the label's breadwinner, Ja Rule, began moonlighting as a gruff-voiced singer, he also wrote R&B records like Jennifer Lopez's "I'm Real (Remix)" and Mary J. Blige's "Rainy Dayz."

Ja Rule welcomed Charli into the fold after Irv played him a song she'd written for one of his acts. A year later, Ja Rule commissioned her for "Down Ass Bitch," a song for his third album, *Pain Is Love*. The Bonnie and Clyde–style video stars Charli as the eponymous "down ass bitch" who chooses prison over snitching. The guest feature with Ja was something of a reinvention, after fans thought Charli had disappeared from the scene.

promised to instead help Charli find a label deal elsewhere. Then after "Down Ass Bitch," the offers flew in, and he changed his mind.)

That era of success simmered after the Feds raided Irv and his brother Chris Gotti's offices and charged them with money laundering in 2003. The case against them (a judge acquitted them in 2005 after a highly publicized trial) threw off their label's mojo. Ja Rule had meanwhile fallen victim to his enemy 50 Cent's incessant assaults against his career and character.

Before the trial even started, Charli requested out of her contract. Rapper The Game tried to woo her to his imprint, Black Wall Street, at one point, but in 2006, Charli found another hustle, writing with super producer Scott Storch in Miami for about a year. She did a reality show, released mixtapes, and continued writing.

FACTOIDS

PRINCESS NOKIA, formerly known as **WAVY SPICE,** showed her dreamy and angsty side on two projects she released on the same day in 2020: *Everything Is Beautiful* and *Everything Sucks.*

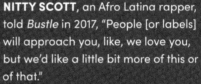

NITTY SCOTT, an Afro Latina rapper, told *Bustle* in 2017, "People [or labels] will approach you, like, we love you, but we'd like a little bit more of this or of that."

KID SISTER signed to A-Trak's and Nick Catchdub's label Fools Gold, released her single "Pro Nails," a chopped-and-screwed beauty-shop anthem.

South Central, Los Angeles, rapper **AK'SENT** went from performing in dance classes with Debbie Allen to krumping and rapping.

In 1992, **SISTER SOULJAH,** known foremost as an author, provoked Bill Clinton, then governor of Arkansas, after she said, "If black people kill black people every day, why not have a week killing white people?" Clinton described it as hate speech, drawing a comparison to the Ku Klux Klan's David Duke.

Canadian rapper **MICHIE MEE** raps about being "overworked and underpaid for days" on her song "Don't Wanna Be Your Slave," featuring Esthero.

MEDUSA

NEVER FORGET:
She produced the spoken-word record "Life Is a Traffic Jam" for the soundtrack to the 1997 film *Gridlock'd*, 2Pac's penultimate acting role before his death. Actor Thandie Newton performs the song with 2Pac in the movie.

WHO SHE IS:
Medusa (Mone Smith) grew up in the Altadena section of Los Angeles and learned about music from spending time around her famous aunt, singer-songwriter Billie Rae Calvin. Among the most respected figures in LA's underground rap scene, Medusa released her album *Whrs The DJ Booth?* in 2012.

LISTEN:
On "Power of the P" (featuring S.I.N.), Medusa raps about the mystique of pussy.

A fun fact about *Moesha*, the 1990s sitcom starring R&B singer Brandy as an angsty suburban teen, is that it's set in the Leimert Park section of Los Angeles. There's an episode in season six (the final season) that finds Moesha and her crew attending an open-mic night called Poetry Night at the Pendulum. Playing the role of a poet named Lady Lunatic, LA rapper Medusa delivers two minutes of spoken word about the dangers of assimilation.

The setting, the cameo, and the subject of the poem were no coincidence. *Moesha* centered around a group of high schoolers living in a middle-class black community and popular arts district that has since been gentrified. In the nineties, Leimert Park was home to the Good Life Cafe, a health food store that transformed into a performance hub and communal space for poets and lyricists seeking an alternative to the gangsta rap that came out of the West. "It was the only spot that would offer an all-ages open mic," says Medusa. "In addition to that, it introduced you to soul food and a vegetarian way of living that you may not have gotten at home."

Medusa's biggest influence growing up was her aunt Billie Rae Calvin, a singer-songwriter who was a member of the Motown group Undisputed Truth. When Calvin toured with the Jackson 5, Medusa tagged along for the West Coast leg at seven years old. She would sit in on her aunt's studio sessions and watch her write songs and play piano—Calvin famously wrote the hit song "Wishing on a Star," performed by the group Rose Royce. "That whole energy, being backstage, the celebration and meeting those musicians—all of that inspired me," says Medusa.

Medusa's introduction to hip-hop was not rapping but pop-locking. In tenth grade, she joined a crew of dancers called the Groove-A-Trons, who would all ditch school to battle other groups at Venice Beach, in Westwood, at parades, and at roller-skating rinks. "I made sure my hit and my kick were on the same level as the guys'," she says. "It kept me on my toes."

After spending a year in jail for possession of forged documents, Medusa and her cousin Koko (aka S.I.N.) went straight to the recording studio, where they wrote the song "Diva's Den." They later recorded "Power of the P," a dedication to, well, pussy, and decided to try performing at Good Life, because, "Every time we passed it, the crowd was thick in the parking lot," she says. "We knew we couldn't cuss. We knew there were rules." The Good Life owners soon caught on to the explicit content and shut their performance down. "I always keep it on a power tip when it comes to women, because we get our power stripped from us so easy, or we get caught up in an empowerment that may not belong to us."

In her stage shows, Medusa also performed a song titled "This Pussy's a Gangsta," which she never turned into an official record.

SHOUTOUTS!

MONIE LOVE

NEVER FORGET:
She was a teenager when she rapped with Queen Latifah on "Ladies First."

WHO SHE IS:
The first Brit rapper most hip-hop fans fell in love with was Monie Love (Simone Johnson), who already had a fan base in the UK before moving to the States. She introduced herself to US fans when she demonstrated master breath control alongside Queen Latifah on "Ladies First" and as an affiliate of Native Tongues, the conscious-rap clique that A Tribe Called Quest and De La Soul called home. After two albums, Monie transitioned to becoming a radio personality based in Atlanta.

LISTEN:
Her record about being a choosey lover, "Monie in the Middle," from her 1990 debut album *Down to Earth*, is based on the true story of her sidestepping rapper Big Daddy Kane to talk to his friend instead.

CHOICE

NEVER FORGET:
She dissed N.W.A, Too $hort, and Geto Boys on her single "The Big Payback."

WHO SHE IS:
You might only remember the rapper Choice if you lived in or around Houston when she released her debut album, 1990's *The Big Payback*, one of the crassest albums ever recorded, years before Lil' Kim's *Hard Core*. On the album itself, released through Rap-A-Lot Records (the label J. Prince launched that was home to Geto Boys), Choice raps extensively about being a self-sufficient "badass bitch," little dicks, and the danger of gold digging. But her claim to fame was the title track, "Payback," where she tried to emasculate members of N.W.A, as well as Too $hort and Geto Boys. She released two albums (the second, *Stick-N-Moove*, in 1992).

LISTEN:
On her record with Geto Boys member Willie D, "I Need Some Pussy," a song that's basically about having a case of blue balls, Choice raps, "I got a pussy 'bout the size of Bolivia," a country the CIA website describes as "slightly less than three times the size of the state of Montana," for what it's worth.

LADYBUG MECCA

NEVER FORGET:
Her group Digable Planets won a Grammy in 1994 for Best Rap Performance by a Duo or Group for their single "Rebirth of Slick (Cool Like That)."

WHO SHE IS:
Born and raised in Maryland, Ladybug Mecca (Mary Ann Vieira) developed her mellow rap style from listening to Brazilian singers and jazz staples like Billie Holiday. In the tradition of acts like A Tribe Called Quest and De La Soul, her group Digable Planets—herself, rapper/producer Ishmael Butler (Butterfly), and Craig Irving (Doodlebug)—made music that infused rap with jazz, the type of low-end songs that could soundtrack a black romantic comedy. "We created a whole separate world, where people could escape to, but it was still dealing with real life," Mecca says.

LISTEN:
The lead single from Digable Planet's debut album, *Reachin' (A New Refutation of Time and Space)*, was "Rebirth of Slick (Cool Like Dat)," a smooth voyage that went to No. 15 on the *Billboard* Hot 100 singles chart. The song soundtracks a Tide commercial.

QUEEN PEN

NEVER FORGET:
Her single "All My Love" sampled Luther Vandross's "Never Too Much" and became a Top 40 hit.

WHO SHE IS:
Soon after debuting on the R&B group Blackstreet's 1996 hit "No Diggity," Queen Pen (born Lynise Walters) signed to producer Teddy Riley's label, Lil Man, and released her debut album, *My Melody*, in 1997. She broke new ground when she rapped about stealing a man's woman on her song "Girlfriend," which sampled an openly gay artist—Meshell Ndegeocello's 1993 single "If That's Your Boyfriend (He Wasn't Last Night)"—and drew speculation about Queen Pen's own sexuality. The *New York Times* described Queen Pen in 1998 as "perhaps the first recording artist to use rap, a genre known for the misogyny and homophobia of its lyrics, to depict lesbian life." While Queen Pen may have rapped about being with a woman, she didn't openly identify as queer.

LISTEN:
"Party Ain't a Party," a party anthem that insists the party doesn't start until you get there; it should play in your head before you walk into any party.

Eve

NEVER FORGET:
With *Let There Be Eve . . . Ruff Ryder's First Lady* in 1999, Eve became only the third female rapper (behind Lauryn Hill and Foxy Brown) to have a No. 1 album on the *Billboard* Hot 100 chart.

WHO SHE IS:
Raised by a single mother in the Mill Creek projects of West Philadelphia, Eve was battling in lunchroom rap cyphers at age fifteen and was part of the high school girl group EDGP (pronounced "EGYPT"). In 1998, after a deal with Dr. Dre went sour, she became the First Lady of Ruff Ryders and released four albums. In 2017, she landed a job as co-host of the CBS day-time show *The Talk*.

LISTEN:
"Let's Talk About," a back-and-forth with her labelmate Drag-On, on which Eve slanders "little dick niggas" and fair-weather friends.

The element of style was always crucial in hip-hop. But by 1999, rap had become the world's most profitable, influential genre, and rappers were self-made millionaires, ready to look the part. Lil' Kim and Foxy Brown made high fashion look so good that a decadent sense of style became essential to the image of the female rapper, whose value was inevitably tied to her looks. And then came Eve, the First Lady of Ruff Ryders, a crew whose spiritual core was an extremely spirited rapper named DMX. That summer, Eve's first single, "What Y'all Want," a salsa-inspired song of the season, set her up as a future star, which meant she would be performing at one of the biggest showcases in hip-hop, the 1999 Source Awards.

Eve's labelmate Drag-On took the stage first at the show, followed by the Lox, and then Eve, who cruised in on *an ATV bike*, dressed in a Batgirl-inspired ensemble: leather pants, a cut-out top, and over that, a cape.

Viewers weren't likely to even register the cape (let alone its then-little-known designer, Raf Simons), which Eve quickly doffed. Kithe Brewster, a fashion editor with connections in

Europe, and Eve's new stylist at the time, chose the outfit, using his access to designers like Tom Ford and Karl Lagerfeld (then head of Chanel) to slowly reinvent—or renovate—Eve's look. When she returned to accept the Source Award for Solo Artist of the Year in 2000, she wore Fendi. (In a sign of the times, Beyoncé, presenting with Nelly, read Eve's name off a T-Mobile Sidekick.)

Eve's style was part of a strategic group effort. "We targeted the fashion world from the very beginning. We were all collectively able to elevate how she saw herself and separate her from the pack," says Eve's former manager Marc Byers. "The fashion world didn't invite her right off, but when the hits started happening and the fashion was going hand in hand, they saw how we were moving culture and had to let her in."

Luxury designers weren't lending clothing to rappers, forcing stylists like Misa Hylton-Brim, who worked with Lil' Kim and Mary J. Blige, to DIY outfits. "Fashion houses were still trying to understand the music and the culture," says Chris Chambers, the former VP of Publicity at Interscope Records who connected Eve to Kithe Brewster. "Eve was a very instrumental part of the relationship between hip-hop and the fashion community growing. She was high fashion without being overtly [sexualized]."

One of the earliest unofficial unions between hip-hop and designer brands was through Daniel Day, aka Dapper Dan, a tailor famous for stitching fake Gucci and Louis Vuitton logos into his clothing. When his DIY operation launched in Harlem in 1982, everyone from Salt-N-Pepa to LL Cool J wore his creations. Dapper Dan received cease-and-desist letters, and Fendi seized some of his goods in 1988. But the fashion world soon went from snubbing the culture to stealing its cool.

Chanel launched a hip-hop-inspired 1991 collection, and Tommy Hilfiger built a kingdom selling oversized urban attire. (Gucci hired Dapper Dan as an ambassador in 2018.) Lil' Kim became a Marc Jacobs muse and a fixture at New York Fashion Week in the nineties. Foxy Brown, the self-proclaimed "poster girl" for Christian Dior, further bridged the gap between the streets and high fashion, boasting that she could jump "out the Range in Iceberg tights," as she once rapped, and remain fresh. Artists like Kanye West and Pharrell Williams get credit for crashing Balmain, but Eve was one of rap's earliest high-fashion influencers.

It helped that Eve's fans and clientele found her accessible. While Kim and Foxy made music that unapologetically catered to men and became avatars of male fantasies, Eve made songs that focused on love, crew loyalty, and being a dope rapper. On her album skit "My Bitches" (a companion piece to DMX's "My Niggas"), Eve applauds women who pay their own bills and care for their kids while dealing with men. On "Love Is Blind," she raps directly to abused women and their abusers ("How would you feel if she held you down and raped you?"), a song that's both cautionary tale and revenge fantasy, in which Eve's character gets to murder the abuser at the end. The story was based on the real-life experience of her friend Andrea, who appeared with Eve on an episode of Queen Latifah's talk show that aired in April 2000. Eve paired her message with a sense of couture. "My first time looking at Eve, it was like, oh my God, this lady is just super sexy," says rapper Megan Thee Stallion. "She was smooth, sensual. Like her little body movements. I just felt like that was my vibe."

When Eve began her career at Dr. Dre's label, Aftermath Entertainment, it was a unique opportunity for an East Coast rookie (even more rare, a female rapper) to partner with a West Coast legend; Dre even put Eve up in an apartment he paid for in Los Angeles.

The union was brief. The sole musical product of their partnership is a song Eve recorded for the *Bulworth* soundtrack in 1998 titled "Eve of Destruction," her rap moniker at the time. "Baby girl from Illadel here to enhance your lives / Doubted my skills, bet you mad now, should'a snatched me up / I'm in LA now with Dre now, ain't comin' back 'cause I'm stuck," she raps. Dre eventually dropped her from Aftermath. Eve told *Newsweek* in 2001, "Dre did not know what to do with me." Although Dre seemed clueless about many of the artists on his roster (remember King Tee, RBX, et al.?), lack of direction was and still is an issue that's especially dooming for female rappers.

Eve's management team introduced her to another popular Interscope imprint, Ruff Ryders, founded by siblings Darrin "Dee" Dean, Joaquin "Waah" Dean, and Chivon Dean. Eve freestyled with two rappers from the label, Drag-On and Infra-Red, in what was more a formality than an audition. Dee wanted to sign her right away. She joined Ruff Ryders in the fall of 1998 and was dubbed the First Lady of Ruff Ryders. Eve stood out as the lone woman in the crew with the paw print tattoos on her breasts and a First Lady title that reflected her street sophistication.

By the turn of the century, Lauryn Hill had all but retreated to her Batcave after her debut album. Every rap crew and/or label in America fulfilled their female-rapper quotas. And there was Missy Elliott on the side, dressed in the finest dystopian space suits. Eve and Trina were the type of women rappers who seemed to be more in control of their image. Still, labels were in the image business, devoting bigger budgets to stylists and beauty teams until signing female rappers was deemed a financial burden and therefore bad business. The same labels that wanted women to look good decided maybe it costs too much money.

By her second album, 2001's *Scorpion*, Eve had pop-rap appeal, thanks to her single "Who's That Girl?" And her biggest song, "Let Me Blow Ya Mind," produced by Dr. Dre and featuring Gwen Stefani, went to No. 2 on the *Billboard* Hot 100. Alexander Allen, Eve's stylist at the time, continued to push her high-fashion agenda. For the 2002 VH1 Vogue Fashion Awards, he dressed her in DSquared2, when the brand launched. Eve, he says, was the first woman with a custom red-carpet outfit by DSquared2. Eve summed up her style on the track "Gangsta Bitches": "Pretty with the heels on, or shitty with the Tim boots."

It was only a matter of time before Eve joined the long line of rappers who launched their own clothing labels. (There was Diddy's Sean John, Jay-Z's Rocawear, and Bushi Sport by Busta Rhymes.) Eve followed suit in 2003 with a line called Fetish, then extended her career beyond rap, starring in her own UPN show, *Eve*, as (what else?) a Miami-based fashion designer named Shelly Williams. By 2009, her clothing line had shuttered, but she'd become a fixture in fashion circles, in an era when a rapper's presence at fashion shows was a coup for the designers.

PRETTY & GRITTY

STYLIST KITHE BREWSTER ON MAKING EVE HIGH FASHION

Foxy and Lil' Kim would rap about bringing fashion to the game, and Kim did change it a lot. But it was a different time, where the big fashion houses—especially in Europe—were not working so closely with rappers, per se. Eve only had that kind of access because of my access. If you look at the way, for example, Nicki Minaj or Cardi B is supported by the fashion houses [it's because] Eve [created] that mold. Her first album cover, if you look at the [outfits], it's Tom Ford, Gucci, the brand-new collection before it was on the streets. "Before it's on the streets" is the distinction, because the clothes were not allowed to be put on these kinds of girls yet—rappers, hip-hop artists.

It was different for me to take on a rapper [as a client], because I'd spent most of my career in Europe. I started my career working part-time in a fashion showroom owned by my uncle. From there I moved to Paris at age nineteen. After years in Paris, I moved to London. I worked with Bewitched, a post–Spice Girls group—and Finley Quaye, at the same time working [for magazines]. Because I was established with the fashion houses, it was easier for me to get access to these editorial and runway looks. I fought the [fashion brands'] press offices. I had big clients like Julianne Moore and would say to these houses, "If you don't loan me for Eve, then I'm going to remember that when you want me to place your clothes on my Hollywood girls."

If you look closely at the first video, you can see where Eve could go somewhere, because she had an incredible presence. [I dressed her in] Raf Simons and pushing Alexander McQueen— very, very edgy designers like that as well, and not just the big names. I remember Naomi Campbell and [other] models all saying to me, "We wanna look like Eve." When you need her [to be], she's androgynous. She was tomboyish and tough in a way, and that toughness was what I was trying to relay, without it being compromised by the glamour. I knew there was a way to mix [the two].

SOLÉ

One of the artifacts of Solé's time as a rapper is the February 21, 2000, cover of *Jet* magazine, a black-owned publication that was popular in barbershops and beauty salons. The image is a composite of Eve, Lil' Kim, Foxy Brown, and Solé. The cover line: "The Hottest Females in Rap Music." Lil' Kim and Foxy Brown were onto their sophomore albums by then. Eve was the First Lady of Ruff Ryders. And Solé landed the cover because of "Who Dat," her hit collaboration with rapper JT Money.

The early to mid-2000s brought a flash of prosperity to female rappers. In terms of numbers, it was an era sandwiched by surplus and mediocrity; as NPR noted, "Whereas in the late 1980s and early 1990s there were more than 40 women signed to major labels, in 2010 there were just three."

Inspired by Foxy and Kim, Solé went from making party songs in her teens to inhabiting a "semi-hard-core persona," she says. The video for her single "4, 5, 6" finds her role-playing in costumes at a strip club: as a cowboy, a nurse, etc. "I did it in a kitschy, burlesque way as opposed to [wearing] actual stripper outfits. It was playing into that but not promoting it, in my twenty-something-year-old head," she says. (As an artist who got her first break at twenty-six, Solé says she was considered "old" at that point and told to lie about her age.)

Tricky Stewart, the super producer behind Beyoncé's "Single Ladies" and Justin Bieber's "Baby," met Solé in LA. As one of the first artists signed to his production company, Red Zone Entertainment, she started out contributing background vocals to R&B singer Tamar Braxton's debut album. Solé wrote her verse for JT Money's "Who Dat," and the song became one of Stewart's earliest produced hits, which helped Solé land her own solo deal.

"She was just as commanding in her delivery as Foxy and Eve, but I also thought she had her own cadence," says Stewart. "The way that she rapped and the speed in which she rapped, being from Kansas City, she had a little tongue twisting, maybe a little Bone Thugs."

But so many rap artists of the pre-internet era were only in hip-hop for a season. After her 1999 debut album, *Skin Deep*, her follow-up, titled *Fly Away*, had a lead single ready to go. Overwhelmed by the pomp of the music business, she backed out of her deal and stopped the album's release. (The album never came out.) She asked to be released from her contract with DreamWorks Records and got her wish. She loved the creative aspects but not the lifestyle of hip-hop. She hated clubs, didn't drink or do drugs, and never even smoked. On tour, she would carry a bag of books and read in her hotel room. So once she left the company, she completely disconnected from the industry. When asked what her proudest career achievement is, she says: "Walking away."

Solé then embarked on a second life as a yoga teacher, trained in everything from Jivamukti to tantric, pelvic-floor, and prenatal yoga, along with other therapies like Reiki and chakra-balancing

under her company Devi Tribe Wellness. Yes, the woman who once rapped, "Ya ex-bitch can't fuck with this," became a spiritual healer.

"Even though I was in the [rap] industry, I was never *of* the industry, which is part of the reason I ultimately left. I never liked somebody telling me what to do, who I needed to be. I never liked the smoke and mirrors," she says. "I love show business and entertainment, but I don't like the fakeness of it." Plus, she says, "I was warring with what I was writing and the images I was putting out. I didn't feel like if I did something more positive and enlightening that it would be accepted, but that's what my heart was pulling me towards."

WHEN ASKED WHAT HER PROUDEST CAREER ACHIEVEMENT IS, SHE SAYS: "WALKING AWAY."

LaDY LUCK

NEVER FORGET:
She was recruited to Def Jam at seventeen years old.

WHO SHE IS:
A native of Englewood, New Jersey, Lady Luck (Shanell Jones) performed her first rap (which her mom wrote for her) at the impressive age of five. Luck's great aunt was Sylvia Robinson, founder of the pioneering hip-hop label Sugarhill Records. Her mom was a radio promoter for the label. Lady Luck became one of the youngest rap prospects of the 1990s, and though she never released an album, her rap battle with Remy Ma gave her lifelong acclaim.

LISTEN:
On EPMD's operatic club banger "Symphony 2000," Luck brags that other rappers will have to switch their flows to keep up with her.

At seventeen years old, Lady Luck joined the biggest label in hip-hop, Def Jam Recordings, in a deal worth north of half a million dollars. As soon as she signed her contract, she left her lawyer's office in New York City and hopped on a bus for the New Jersey stop on the *Hard Knock Life* tour, which featured a goliath set of headliners all at their peak—Jay-Z, DMX, Ja Rule, and Method Man & Redman.

The same year she signed to Def Jam, Seagram's Universal Music Group, which already owned 60 percent of the company, bought out the rest of the label from its heads Russell Simmons and Lyor Cohen. (Def Jam founder Rick Rubin had left in 1988.) The label was at its most profitable, after $176 million in sales in 1998, which meant Def Jam had money to blow.

Lady Luck's big break happened in February 1999, when she called in to New York's Hot 97 for host Ed Lover's morning show series "Check the Rhyme," a segment where aspiring rappers battled live on air. Luck won five times that week and one morning earned a visit to the station. Kevin Liles, who was newly promoted to Def Jam president, heard her rapping on the radio on his way to work and was interested in signing her immediately; he called Hot 97 and told the hosts, "Yo, tell the girl and her parents to come directly to my office." Lady Luck jokes, "Kevin Liles promised me

explains in retrospect, "If he had vision, he would understand that there were millions of girls. Look at all the rappers that are Lady Luck today."

Luck signed to Def Jam in March 1999 and began her senior year at Teaneck High School that fall with a record deal—a prodigy at seventeen. By her first day of school, she had a song on the radio—a verse on rapper Pharoahe Monch's single "Simon Says (Remix)," featuring Method Man & Redman, Busta Rhymes, and Shabaam Sahdeeq—and was also the subject of a column, "Diary of a New Jack," in the rap magazine *The Source*, chronicling three up-and-coming rappers. From her dispatch in the December 1999 issue, she said: "I can't front. I'm scared. I got so many things I wanna do. I want to put my friends on. But first I have to finish my album. And I don't want to finish this album and feel like I could have done better."

"With Luck, it was about lyrics. It was about her competing. You throw her into a pit of rap lions, she's coming out," says Liles. In an October 1999 profile in *The New Yorker*, he explained Lady Luck's appeal with an analogy. "When you think about Eve, if Eve's man was in a gunfight and he got shot, she would pick up his gun and start shooting at the other guy," he told the mag. "Lil' Kim would fuck that other man. Rah Digga would stab that other man. Luck would have a great time with that man, and then hit him in the head with a bat."

This was a bit of an overstatement. "I'm, like, I'm not hitting nobody with a fucking bat, Kevin!" says Luck. "At the time, what everybody loved about Luck was that I rapped like a boy," she says. "They didn't know what to do with me, 'cause I was an overweight pretty tomboy. I don't know what the fuck to do, 'cause I just got here. So it was [like] a really [well-paid] college internship."

everything. I was, like, 'I just want [a copy of] the Foxy Brown CD.'"

The Hot 97 freestyles kicked off a bidding war among the era's top record companies, including Def Jam. While selling mixtapes in Teaneck, New Jersey, Luck had befriended a crew of barbers to the stars who at this point introduced her to some of their famous clients. She rapped for Puff Daddy at Bad Boy Records. (In the meantime, Liles gifted her roses for Valentine's Day to woo her to Def Jam.) She also rapped at the office of Loud Records. Another barber took her to Roc-A-Fella Records, where the label's co-founder Dame Dash told her, while in the middle of getting a haircut, "Lady Luck, I know people who wanna be Jay-Z, but who would wanna be Lady Luck?" She

"THEY DIDN'T KNOW WHAT TO DO WITH me, 'cause I was an OVERWEIGHT PRETTY TOMBOY."

For months, she worked with a series of mentors, including her labelmate EPMD at one point (she appeared on their single "Symphony 2000"). Kevin Liles wanted to A&R her project, but he was busy being president of a label. In stepped another Def Jam executive, DJ Enuff. "That was a mess," Luck recalls.

While at Def Jam, Luck collaborated with Missy Elliott and Lil Mo. But there was no album to show for it, for a few reasons. Labels began to see female rappers as divas who ate up budgets because of the glam teams they needed to keep up the image that the label executives had themselves enforced. Luck, who wore baggy clothes and a fitted cap, was neither selling sex nor the First Lady of a crew. She didn't need a team of stylists, and she became stymied by expectations as the industry transitioned to marketing sex as the standard. Def Jam never quite nailed the formula.

In other words, for once Luck's timing was bad. "Although people loved her, we didn't have the right song," says Liles, who admits that signing a young prodigy had its setbacks. It required more attention and grooming. "That experiment didn't work at that particular time. It didn't mean that it wouldn't work later," he says. "It didn't mean it wouldn't work for somebody else. But I thought it was the best thing for her to do something else."

A subsequent rap battle with Remy Ma in 2004 preserved Luck's legacy. After hearing around New York that Remy Ma had been asking about Lady Luck, Luck stepped up to the challenge of going bar for bar with New York's newest rap sensation. The pair faced off for several rounds and for more than twenty minutes in a battle at the Fight Klub in New York City. The showdown became legend. Remy won the $20,000 pot and later defeated Luck in a separate rematch. Luck went down swinging but believes real rap heads know who won that day.

"I'm not a battle rapper," she says, rejecting the label that brought her notoriety. "[But] I wanted to be better than everybody else. I had to rap better than these boys around here, or they gonna clown the little girl trying to rap."

In 2018, she released a sexually suggestive music video that played off Nicki Minaj's song "Barbie Dreams." In the video, Luck gets it on in bed with a Nicki Minaj doppelganger. By then, Luck had reinvented herself, shedding baggy jeans for bikinis as a new selling point, in hopes of revamping her image.

Lauryn Hill

NEVER FORGET:
The Miseducation of Lauryn Hill won five Grammys, including Album of the Year, and was the first No. 1 rap album by a female rapper.

WHO SHE IS:
Lauryn Hill was six years old when she started raiding her parents' vinyl collection in South Orange, New Jersey. Ten years before *Miseducation*, at thirteen, a young Hill performed Smokey Robinson's "Who's Lovin' You" during Amateur Night for *Showtime at the Apollo.* An overachiever at Columbia High School, she took part in cheerleading, track, and choir, when she met Pras Michel. They formed a trio called Tyme and when Pras's cousin Wyclef Jean stepped in to replace their friend, the Fugees were born. (Their original name was Tranzlator Crew.) Her brief solo career and singular debut album, *The Miseducation of Lauryn Hill*, solidified her as one of the greatest rappers ever.

LISTEN:
An all-time top-10 R&B duet, Lauryn Hill and D'Angelo's "Nothing Even Matters" sounds exactly like the title: soothing, soulful, and focused on momentary bliss.

Lauryn Hill dropped a simple cautionary tale in the summer of 1998: "Doo Wop (That Thing)." Over a harmonized intro, she starts off singing in Arabic ("aṣ-Ṣirāṭ al-mustaqīm," meaning "straight path"), then offers a quick anecdote: A woman—a *Jezebel*—let a man hit it three weeks ago, and he hasn't called since. She follows with what feels like the start of a thesis—"To begin, how you think you really gon' pretend?"—and raps about wanting guys to stop being toxic and for women to avoid violent men and weaves.

"Doo Wop (That Thing)," the catchiest judgmental song of all time, made Lauryn Hill the first woman rapper to top the *Billboard* Hot 100, when the chart itself was forty years old. By then, she was clearly the most skilled and elastic member of the Fugees, as masterful at singing as she was at rapping. Instead of sex, she sold skill and enlightenment, an aesthetic much different than Kim's or Foxy's.

Two years after their debut album, *Blunted on Reality*, the Fugees (Hill, Wyclef Jean, and Pras Michel) effervesced into global superstars with the follow-up, *The Score*, a salve of boom bap rap with heavy Caribbean influence. On their biggest hit, "Fu-Gee La," Wyclef cites *American Bandstand*, raps the word "ichiban" (Japanese for "number one"), and references

dancehall in one clean verse. Lauryn Hill sings the hook and ends her verse with a flourish: "Find me in my Mitsubishi, eating sushi, bumping Fugees." She bodied the remix, too, a smooth, super-lyrical exhibition featuring Nappy Heads. "I never fear the Ku Klux / My own clan is acting up," she raps.

The Score sold more than six million copies, won a Grammy Award for Best Rap Album, and primed Lauryn Hill for stardom. She was an obvious rap phenom and a potential triple-threat (rapper/singer/actor), then known as the fearless choir star singing gospel in the 1993 movie *Sister Act 2: Back in the Habit*, starring Whoopi Goldberg. (Or if you went back further, you might recognize her as the teenage elevator operator, Aretha, in Steven Soderbergh's Great Depression film *King of the Hill*.)

Two Fugees records showed off Lauryn's range: "Ready or Not" saw her switching from arrogant wordplay to soulful harmonizing over the hum of a dark drumbeat. On a cover of "Killing Me Softly," she matches Roberta Flack's sky-high vocals flawlessly. Hill told *The Source*, "I know this sounds crazy, but sometimes I treat rapping like singing, and other times I treat singing like rapping. But still, it's all done within the context of hip-hop." Executives at Columbia Records—namely, Sony head Tommy Mottola—rejected Lauryn's blend of soul and hip-hop, which they, for odd reasons, saw as a divergence from the success of the Fugees' straight hip-hop sound.

But the beauty of *Miseducation* is this hybrid that hypnotized a future generation of singing rappers. Nicki Minaj called Lauryn Hill a "goddess." Drake sampled "Ex-Factor" for his 2018 ladies' anthem "Nice For What" and is never not singing. And Cardi B interpreted "Ex-Factor" on her single "Be Careful," where she, while rapping, sings of disappointment, playing off Hill's concept of

romantic loss. While people instinctually credit Kanye West and Drake as the inventors of singing in rap, there's a long, commercial history of predecessors, including Ja Rule, Nelly, Lauryn Hill, and Missy Elliott, who long harmonized so that others could Autotune, and when it wasn't part of every commercial rapper's repertoire. Rappers had been singing before (Queen Latifah, Salt-N-Pepa), but Hill was basically an elite gymnast in two different sports.

But the first promotional release from Hill's solo debut, *The Miseducation of Lauryn Hill*, was a straight-up rap record, "Lost Ones," the subject of which is a rapper, a lover, or both. Fans recognized it specifically as a Wyclef diss song. "Doo Wop (That Thing)" and its smooth, barbershop-quartet production was the commercial hit that followed. Hill became the fun type of *problematic* artist. In the music video for "Doo Wop," she appears in split screen: on the left (set in New York City, 1967), wearing a wig with straight hair, and on the right (New York City, 1998), her signature faux locs. The song is something of a timeless think piece, as gorgeous and self-righteous decades later as it was in 1998. She told the Associated Press in 1996, "It became popular to be stupid, to be violent, to be unintelligent, and that's bad. When people stop being who they are naturally and start pretending to be something negative or not real, that's what's wack." In 2015, a writer for *San Francisco Weekly* described "Doo Wop" as "an exercise in respectability politics" and "one long concern troll."

Of course, it's not that simple. While Lauryn did sound like a hip-hop preacher, she also faced the burden of being The One at a still-naive age of twenty-four, while living a conflicted life, which she sang and rapped about with a rare vulnerability. Joan Morgan wrote about "Doo Wop" in her book, *She Begat This: 20 Years of The Miseducation*

THE BEAUTY OF *MISEDUCATION* IS THIS HYBRID THAT HYPNOTIZED A FUTURE GENERATION OF SINGING RAPPERS.

of Lauryn Hill, "Dismissing Lauryn here as purely judge-y and hypocritical is too flat of a read. When Hill rhymed that she was only human, she was advocating for her right to be complicated and beautifully contradictory—and ours, too, whether she realized it or not."

Hill's personal demons came wrapped in scandal. She wore her hair in dreads, later discovered to be faux locs. And she sang about heartbreak but didn't reveal she was likely rapping and singing about her bandmate Wyclef Jean. She released only one album and opened herself up, which made people both want more from her and paint her as something of an unreliable narrator.

"More than a judgment on her, I feel like it exposes a lot more about us, about how we create these categories and rally behind them, and then we assign scripts to people," Morgan told me during a Jezebel interview in 2018. Hill herself recalled to *Essence* in 2009, "I was a young woman with an evolved mind who was not afraid of her beauty or her sexuality. For some people that's uncomfortable. They didn't understand how female and strong work together. Or young and wise. Or Black and divine."

Few rap albums, let alone debuts, have earned the "classic" label, and Hill was a genius both in rap circles (with a solo album that was anticipated in a way that Nas's 1994 debut *Illmatic* was) and among music elites. On *Miseducation*, recorded while she was pregnant with her first child (by Bob Marley's son Rohan), she took on multiple roles: a miserable lover, the other woman, a mother, and a teacher. "I think every woman goes through a relationship which is a great lesson in love," she told *Vibe* in 1998. "I had gone through one earlier, and it was kinda like my therapy to write about it. I made peace when I created these songs." Nas told *XXL* in 2013, "We were like, yo . . . we're about to embark on a journey with this young woman, and we're just gonna allow her to take us anywhere we want to go." While rappers like Mos Def and Talib Kweli gained mass critical success by selling a brand of social awareness and no-frills rap (in part, to a legion of white indie-rap fans)—turning their underground style mainstream—their counterparts like Jean Grae weren't nearly as elevated. These women, respected lyricists in the purest sense and with their own cult followings, weren't exactly a marketable prototype.

"There have always been talented independent women rappers, but the question is how much traction were they able to get?" says former *Vibe* editor Elizabeth Méndez Berry. "Will they ever get radio play? Do great producers work with them? Whatever is the metric for hotness now, do they have access to it? Can they cross over? Indie men do, but indie women much less so because the female rapper archetype is not a regular person who raps brilliantly. It's a surgically enhanced amazon who happens to rap brilliantly. These women are not 'regular.' The men are."

At the same time that Lauryn was being praised, she was penalized. Plenty of musicians chose to pause their careers to focus on motherhood, sometimes ending their professions in an industry that viewed pregnancy as a hindrance, but none rapped about it. There had never been a rapper whose decision to simply have a baby was so public, a pressure Lauryn sang about on her album cut "Zion," a beautiful rap lullaby. It's weird to think about in retrospect, considering how rappers like Cardi B and Nicki Minaj maintained relevancy while having babies during the primes of their careers. They were able to openly celebrate motherhood, though even Cardi had to defend the timing of her pregnancy.

Lauryn stood at a comfortable distance from her fans and kept her love life private, though it didn't stop rumors that songs on *Miseducation* secretly addressed the dissolution of her relationship with her bandmate Wyclef Jean; namely on "Ex-Factor," she mourns a tragic separation: "I keep letting you back in / How can I explain myself ?"

Wyclef told his version of the story in his 2012 memoir: "I was married, and Lauryn and I were having an affair, but she had led me to believe that the baby was mine, and I couldn't forgive that," he wrote. "This killed our trust in my mind, and it caused us to start drifting apart."

Whoever inspired Lauryn's vulnerability, it remained unspoken. Pras told *Rolling Stone*, "The album emotionally grabs you, because it was her true feelings of things that happened during that period of her life."

Miseducation was a work clouded in folklore once fans realized that the odds of Lauryn Hill releasing another solo album were low. Her sole follow-up, *MTV Unplugged No. 2.0*, recorded in summer 2001 and released in 2002 as part of MTV's series of live studio releases, featured erratic acoustic meditations that went over people's heads, including mine.

So acclaimed was Lauryn that in the absence of a sophomore album from her, mainstream and hip-hop fans were foaming at the mouth to find a successor—somebody, anybody—be it Nonchalant (of "5 O'Clock" fame) or, many years later, Noname, who debuted with her 2016 mixtape *Telefone* and drew early comparisons to Lauryn. Similarly, Noname was treated as if her role was to save hip-hop from the clutches of women like Cardi B who sold sex appeal. "I still see people tweeting me sometimes like I'm this generation's Lauryn Hill or I'm like the conscious version of different female rappers who don't make the type of music that I make," Noname told *FADER* in 2018. "I don't really believe in that at all. I'm not trying to be the anti-something or pro-something else."

Hill was originally listed as the sole producer and composer on the album's liner notes but then famously found herself in a legal battle with four producers (Rasheem Pugh, Vada Nobles, Tejumold Newton, and Johari Newton) who claimed they worked on the album and didn't receive proper credit. She settled in court in 2001.

The confusion over the extent of her contribution to her own album tarnished her reputation, as did a habit of lateness to her own concerts later in her career, which became a punch line. "I don't show up late to shows because I don't care. And I have nothing but Love and respect for my fans. The challenge is aligning my energy with the time, taking something that isn't easily classified or contained, and trying to make it available for others," she said in 2016. Something only Lauryn Hill would say.

Whether people remember her for her undoing as much as for her genius, her aura was that of mystique, idolatry, and a little lingering disappointment that we could only get a piece of her and nothing more.

MISEDUCATION WAS A WORK CLOUDED IN FOLKLORE ONCE FANS REALIZED THAT THE ODDS OF LAURYN HILL RELEASING ANOTHER SOLO ALBUM WERE LOW.

VITA

◆ ◆ ◆

NEVER FORGET:
She's remembered for appearing on melodic anthems with Ja Rule, like his hit "Put It On Me," which peaked at No. 8 on the *Billboard* Hot 100.

WHO SHE IS:
As a teen, Vita (LaVita Raynor) opened shows for acts like Queen Latifah in her hometown of Plainfield, New Jersey. Though she had a portal to the music industry through the success of her sister, Kima, of the R&B trio Total, Vita wound up breaking into rap through acting. After a supporting role in the 1998 film *Belly*, she met producer Irv Gotti and Ja Rule and signed to Murder Inc Records when the label was at its peak.

LISTEN:
On the Murder Inc remix with Ja Rule, "Down 4 U," Vita pledges, in her babylike Vita voice, "Vita thighs only divide / If you inside."

◆ ◆ ◆

The 1998 movie *Belly* is legendary in hip-hop for several reasons, because of and despite its flaws: a messy plot, bad acting (hey, Nas), and an over-shot budget, among other things. Visually, it's remarkable. In the opening scene, DMX, playing the drug-dealer protagonist Tommy, and Nas (his partner, Sincere), stroll through a New York City strip club lit in glossy sapphire lighting that makes them look like the subjects of an oil painting. The scene, soundtracked to an a cappella version of Soul II Soul's "Back to Life," is the first thing many people mention when they talk about *Belly*. For his feature film debut (and only movie), director Hype Williams took his flashy music-video aesthetic to classic extreme. In the process, the world met Vita.

Then around twenty-one years old, Vita auditioned for *Belly* three times after initially meeting Williams when she was an extra on a Sears commercial that he directed. She signed to his management company, Big Dog Films, and Williams cast her in the role of Kionna, a sixteen-year-old Tommy has sex with despite having a girlfriend and also despite her being sixteen.

(While her character's age should have been a major problem in the movie, in the world of *Belly*, this fact went unchecked.) "I recall that when she came in, [the response] was almost immediately, 'This is the person,'" says *Belly*'s casting director Winsome Sinclair. "She brought the energy to the character that Hype was looking for."

Belly was the first occasion for people to not only see but also hear Vita. She recorded her first song, "Two Sides," for the motion picture soundtrack under her original stage name Hot Totti (because, she explains, "I was just that hot cup of coffee with that spice of rum in it; my family's from Bermuda"), rapping from the perspective of a wife on one verse and a mistress on another, and sounding like she'd taken a slight drag of helium. What was originally supposed to be just a guest spot on a Murder Inc compilation album, *Irv Gotti Presents: The Murderers*, turned into a full-blown deal.

Vita became part of the soundtrack of the early 2000s while on team Murder Inc Records, the home of rapper Ja Rule back when his melodic thug-love ballads overpopulated the top 10. You could hear him—and, by association, Vita—every day on the radio, and she appeared in videos as his petite loyal sidekick on songs like "Holla Holla (Remix)" and "Down 4 U." On their biggest collaboration, "Put It On Me," Vita complements Ja's ode to commitment and elongated syllables with her own verse about faithfulness. On a label with double and triple threats like Ja Rule and Ashanti, Vita was a spirited accomplice.

"The first song I ever wrote—it took me two weeks—was 'Two Sides.' So I knew it had it in me to write, but when I went to Murder Inc, it was [a] little more hard-core," says Vita. "There were certain formulas, so I [wrote] with Cadillac Tah, and he was like how Biggie was to Kim. We would teach each other, so it wasn't like he was giving me the plays.

I also wrote on the Murder Inc album. I've always been open to working with writers 'cause I feel like its enough money for everybody."

The Murder Inc roster as a whole, from Ja to Vita to Charli Baltimore, sounded like the voices cast for a rap cartoon. "We had the formula that a lot of people ran with, as far as melodies and Ja's cadence," says Vita. "'Pac did it, but Ja took it to another level." Vita was a cool little sister, tiny and with a pipsqueak voice that was unmistakable. "I never felt pressure to sell sex, and I never felt pressure to be sexy," she says. "I felt like anything that I did was always me."

Vita was working on her solo debut, *La Dolce Vita*. Hype Williams agreed to handle the visuals while Irv Gotti covered production, but Hype and Irv bumped heads on direction, she says, and she never completed the album.

When Murder Inc's co-founders Irv Gotti and his brother, Chris Gotti, became embroiled in a federal investigation, it put a damper on everyone's plans. Vita left Murder Inc before the trial and quit rapping, focusing on acting and developing other artists.

SHOUTOUTS!

M.I.A.

NEVER FORGET:
M.I.A. performed in a sheer, belly-exposing polka-dot dress at the 2009 Grammy Awards, while nine months pregnant.

WHO SHE IS:
When M.I.A. (Maya Arulpragasam) dropped her debut single, "Galang," in 2007, it sounded like someone was literally kicking the door down. The person who entered (M.I.A.) had a colorful swag and a gift for mixing genres. She took a documentarian's approach to rap and drew parallels between the struggles of minority Americans ("paranoid youth blazing through the hood") and what she experienced as a Sri Lankan Tamil refugee who'd moved to London with her mother at age eight. M.I.A. released five albums, including 2005's *Arular* and 2016's *AIM*.

LISTEN:
Her hit single "Paper Planes," which features the sounds of gun-cocking and cash registers in its chorus, peaked at No. 3 on the *Billboard* Hot 100 chart, aided by key placement in the Seth Rogen movie *Pineapple Express*.

LIL MAMA

NEVER FORGET:
Her role as Left Eye in VH1's biopic of TLC, *CrazySexyCool*, should've won some version of an Oscar.

WHO SHE IS:
A mini Harlem Renaissance happened around the summer of 2006, when the duo DJ Webstar and Young B dropped their viral party song "Chicken Noodle Soup," ushering in the era of dance rap. In 2007, a tiny energetic rapper from Harlem named Lil Mama (Niatia Kirkland) released her single "Lip Gloss" and her debut album, *Voice of the Young People*. She moved from rap to television, working as a co-host on *America's Best Dance Crew* and on the cast of the reality show *Growing Up Hip-Hop*.

LISTEN:
"Lip Gloss" is a young-adult bop about boys who like kissable lips.

RAPSODY

NEVER FORGET:
Rapsody was only the fifth female rap act nominated for a Grammy in the Best Rap Album category for her 2017 album, *Laila's Wisdom*.

WHO SHE IS:
Some rap fans discovered North Carolina rapper Rapsody (Marlanna Evans) through Kendrick Lamar (the two meditate on skin color on his song "Complexion [A Zulu Love]", from *To Pimp a Butterfly*). Before that, though, Rapsody had established herself as a workhorse and a rap scholar through a series of mixtapes and EPs while signed to producer 9th Wonder's label, It's a Wonderful World Music Group. Rapsody went from underrated to decorated when she earned a 2018 Grammy nomination in 2018. She made her third album, 2016's *Eve*, an ode to influential black women, naming each track after a legend (Nina Simone, Oprah Winfrey, etc.).

LISTEN:
On "OooWee" (featuring Anderson .Paak), a mellow thought exercise, Rapsody embraces her role as a speaker box for millennials.

DEJ LOAF

NEVER FORGET:
She got her rap name from sporting loafers on her feet in high school.

WHO SHE IS:
Raised on the East side of Detroit, Dej Loaf blew up in 2014 with her single "Try Me," and signed to Columbia Records that same year. Dej had obvious street appeal, not to mention an enviable fur-centric fashion sense that earned her coverage in rags like *Vogue* and *Elle*. Though as of 2020, Dej had yet to release a major-label debut album, she offered a steady supply of singles, mixtapes, and two EPs, . . . *And See That's the Thing* (2015) and *Go DeJ Go (Vol. 1)* (2018). In an interview with me for *FADER* in 2016, she said, "My voice was always different so even though I'm not, like, Mike or Whitney with the vocals, I have a distinct sound and voice, too, so it's like, I could be great within myself. I could figure out how to make this work."

LISTEN:
"Try Me," a threatening street record with a sweet melody, sounds as if Tommy from *Rugrats* were talking tough.

KHIA

NEVER FORGET:
She debuted her unforgettable song
"R-E-S-P-E-C- Me" (As in, "respect me")
on the VH1 reality series *Ego Trip's Miss
Rap Supreme*.

WHO SHE IS:
At fourteen, Khia (Khia Chambers) ran
away from home and into the West
Tampa Projects to make it on her own. In
high school, she got pregnant with her
second child, a daughter (whose name is,
remarkably, Khia). She started out singing
before switching to rapping and recorded
her 2002 debut album, *Thug Misses*, while
bartending at Club Excess in Tampa. It
bears mentioning that Khia was chosen
to rap on Janet Jackson's 2006 song "So
Excited."

LISTEN:
Obviously "My Neck, My Back," but also
"Jealous Girls," a steely 808 dance record
about deflecting envious women.

◆ ◆ ◆

Verse one of Khia's biggest contribution to rap, "My Neck, My Back (Lick It)," contains the single greatest instructional line of the greatest ever—and likely only—song about cunnilingus and anilingus combined: "First you gotta put your neck into it . . ." And then, as Khia instructs, "just lick it right and good."

When the song dropped in 2002 as the lead single from her album *Thug Misses*, it was on the heels of a sexual revolution, engineered by Lil' Kim and Foxy Brown in the late nineties. Oral sex had a shining moment in rap when Kim professed, "I used to be scared of the dick / Now I throw lips to the shit," which was the first line on the first full song of her debut album—so, as first impressions go, it was like the Kool-Aid Man bursting through the door. It's also what opened the door for more freak expressions from the likes of Khia.

"We've been sucking and slobbing and doing everything. I need to let you know how I want to be pleased," she told me for an *XXL* profile in 2006. Despite only reaching No. 42 on the *Billboard* Hot 100 chart, "My Neck, My Back" was an instant rap classic. What's remarkable about the song—besides the idea to pair "neck and back" with "my pussy and my crack"—is the ease with which Khia makes her demands, as if she's listing them as bullet points: "Lick it good," "Get on your knees," and so on.

The American version of the music video, directed by Diane Martel, envisions Khia and the women beside her in party settings: at a barbecue, on a pool float. Visually it's barely raunchy. "I was in my video getting my toes polished. I was in my video with my hair wrapped up, being natural, being a queen," Khia said to me. "Wasn't no butt-naked girls clapping or booty-shaking or Buffy the Bodies in my video." (Buffy the Body was a famous model during the era of the video vixens, a nickname for the women featured in rap videos.)

"My Neck" is Khia at her best: blunt, dirty, and authoritative. Post–"My Neck," she developed more of a reputation for shit-talking than music—namely, a near-Grecian feud between her and Miami rapper Trina. Khia once said of Trina, "Bitch, you do not have more hit singles than me," which was untrue, but she will always have her song about necks and backs.

A SELECTION OF LEWD LYRICS

◆◆◆

"You can li-li-li-lick me from my ass to my clit / Ru-ru-ru-rub up on my tits while I nut on ya lips."

FOXY BROWN,
"What's Your Fantasy (Remix)"

◆◆◆

"I like a dick with a little bit of curve / Hit this pussy with an uppercut."

MEGAN THEE STALLION,
"Captain Hook"

◆◆◆

"Put yo tongue in and out the back end / Put it in deep, watch this pussy start snappin."

KHIA,
"Lick Me Dry"

◆◆◆

"Hold on for a second while I lay on the floor / When I wrap this pussy around your goddam chin."

H.W.A.,
"Eat This"

◆◆◆

"Real bossy bitch, Pyrex on my tits / Make him lick my clit, then I get up and dip."

J.T./CITY GIRLS,
"Millionaire Dick"

◆◆◆

"I know you like the way I bounce that, strip that, flip back / Make the pussy drip back."

TRINA,
"Off Glass"

TRINA

NEVER FORGET:
Her ability to cram an obscene number of vulgar lyrics into a single verse.

WHO SHE IS:
Trina was raised in Liberty City, Miami, where she met rapper Trick Daddy and recorded their dirty duet, "Nann Nigga," which put both Trina and Miami on the map. She ended her real estate pursuits to sign with Slip-N-Slide Records. It wasn't until her sixth album, *The One*, released in 2019 under her imprint, Rockstar Music Group, that she felt independent.

LISTEN:
"Pull Over," a celebratory record about an ass so impressive, it's almost illegal and warrants a ticket.

Trina's greatest strength as a rapper was her obsession with sex and money and how well she rapped about getting them. Much of her catalog features songs about money: earning it, taking it, controlling it—everything short of having sex with it—all for the sake of independence and for gaining wealth and pleasure.

Consider her introduction to rap in 1998, a collaboration with fellow Miami rapper Trick Daddy titled "Nann Nigga," the premise of which is: You don't know anyone like me. Trick Daddy makes his case first: You don't know anyone who sells dope like him or balls better in the club. But then all of that is forgotten once Trina opens her verse and rattles off a list of shameless achievements: "You don't know nann ho / Done been the places I been / Who could spend the grands that I spend / Fuck 'bout five or six best friends." She follows that up with a mad lib of dirty phrases: "make you cum," "deep throat a dick," "let another bitch straight lick the clit." And this was the first time that people heard her rap.

Trina spent five albums in the span of a decade instructing women how to financially climb and how to manipulate men in a capitalist system. She titled her first album *Da Baddest Bitch* (2000) and used it as a platform to profess a love for all types of sex, to promote responsible scamming, and to prove inadequate men were expendable. "I'm getting paid, yelling fuck a man!" she rapped, managing to dismiss (fuck him) and entice (fuck him) a man in one line. "Everybody fucks. Yo mama fucked. That's how you got here. So I feel like it's nothing to be ashamed of," she once said to *Vibe*. Still, whenever she softened up and pivoted to songs about breakdowns and breakups ("Here We Go," featuring Kelly Rowland), it was like Trina, the Diamond Princess, needed a hug.

"When I was introduced to the world in 1998, I did not realize that there were so many women who needed that raw voice and motivation," Trina says. "Female rappers from Miami were not viewed too seriously until [my] introduction."

In her home city of Miami, the king of raunchy rap was Luther Campbell, aka Luke Skyywalker, aka Uncle Luke, the club owner and brains behind the nastiest squad in hip-hop, 2 Live Crew. Through the better part of the nineties, they set both conservative and liberal heads spinning into oblivion with borderline-porn raps and visuals. In high school, Trina would frequent Luke's club, Pac Jam, which was known for playing the uncensored rap songs and explicit music that formed the bedrock of Miami bass. The club also held regular dance contests.

Trina was around fifteen when a friend who danced at Pac Jam invited her to the studio with Luke, who was recording his single "It's Your Birthday." During the session, Trina got to say her name on the record as part of Luke's roll call of birthday shout-outs. She also got a two-second cameo in the music video, where you'll find her in bangs and a little black dress.

Trina first met Trick Daddy in Liberty City, a black neighborhood (also Luke's hometown) where all three lived and attended Miami Northwestern High School. Her mother was a well-known beautician in the area, which meant life was a little like *Cheers*. "In high school, she was the star, the pretty,

bowlegged girl everybody was talking about," says Ted Lucas, founder of Slip-N-Slide Records. "She always had an entourage. Her mom had a beauty salon on Fifteenth Avenue, so she came from a family of successful people."

Local strip clubs were literal hotbeds of Miami bass, which was foremost about the bass—Roland TR-808, sustained kick drum, and heavy bass that shattered sound systems—as well as the pursuit of money and fun. "New York got that intelligent rap," Luke said to *Spin* in 1990. "Miami got the kinda rap you wanna have fun to and get loose to. We leave that 'Long live the old school' bullshit to New York. We're 'Long live the almighty dollar.'"

Trina got the memo. In her twenties, she made $1,000 a week at the popular strip club Rolexxx but later realized that stripping was not for her. Trick Daddy, meanwhile, was in and out of prison, trying to find his footing in rap. When he started recording his second album, *www.thug.com* (an excellent, prescient title before the internet age), he called on his old friend Trina, who was rapping as a hobby, to spit a verse for "Nann Nigga." The single was one of those back-and-forth trash-talking records, and he intentionally wanted her to dominate him on the song.

Trina spent about a month writing her verse, some of which Trick Daddy rewrote to make it even dirtier. The song took off in Miami and everywhere else because a woman was rapping about sex in a way that was somehow even more graphic than what Lil' Kim did. "We put that record out, and less than two weeks later, people were paying her $10,000 to do a part on their song," says Ted Lucas. After months of calls and emails from Lucas, Trina signed to Slip-N-Slide, alongside Trick Daddy.

"Nann" reached No. 3 on the *Billboard* rap singles chart and made Trina an empress of explicit

"WHEN I WAS INTRODUCED TO THE WORLD IN 1998, I DID NOT REALIZE THAT THERE WERE SO MANY WOMEN WHO NEEDED THAT RAW VOICE AND MOTIVATION."

lyrics. She was either doing the fucking, demanding it, or explaining how she wanted it in her songs, which read like correctives to X-rated lyrics by men. Trina legitimized filthier sexual expression and made discussions of sex shameless in a way that was freeing for black women. Hannah Giorgis wrote for *Pitchfork*, "In a world where we are imagined only as bodies to be acted upon and not active agents in our own sexual fulfillment, every syllable spent celebrating our own eroticism, our right to not just safety but also pleasure, is its own revolution."

The music was Trina's own interpretation of the up-tempo raunchiness that had bloomed in Miami. "You had JT Money. You had 2 Live Crew, all these guys representing that nasty take from the male perspective," says Lucas. "Sex talk, nasty talk—that was Miami. It was raw, uncut, and she was saying stuff other women wouldn't say. She put it out there publicly." Trina came from an extensive line of provocateurs in the Miami bass scene. "Trina got that torch from Anquette and brought that street edge," says Ernest Foxx of Black Mob Group. His production partner, Tone, adds, "When Trina said she was the baddest bitch, she was already that. It wasn't like they had to mold her into a persona. She got that from her mama. She really is who she is."

"Nann" came out during a time of nouveau opulence in rap. Hip-hop was well on its way to a mainstream takeover and clinching the record of highest-selling genre in the country (away from country music). In 1999, *Time* published its famous "Hip-Hop Nation" cover, along with a story about hip-hop's surge, and in the article Christopher John Farley wrote that "hip-hop is perhaps the only art form that celebrates capitalism openly."

While rap had a history of worshipping money (Eric & Rakim had to be "Paid in Full"), the focus shifted from coveting it to rappers finally having it. Aspirational hip-hop, the ultimate forum for escapism in the mid- to late- nineties, grew as rappers became millionaires and the economic power of hip-hop grew wildly. That era was the start of what writer Scott Poulson Bryant had predicted in *Vibe* as hip-hop's "mad dash toward the finishing line of capitalism."

WHEN TRINA SAID SHE WAS THE BADDEST BITCH, SHE WAS ALREADY THAT. IT WASN'T LIKE THEY HAD TO MOLD HER INTO A PERSONA. SHE GOT THAT FROM HER MAMA. SHE REALLY IS WHO SHE IS.

TRINA'S PURSUIT OF RICHES WASN'T ABOUT THE JOY OF OBTAINING MONEY ALONE, THOUGH SHE WANTED THE BENEFITS AND PRIVILEGE THAT CAME WITH WEALTH.

(The purveyor of this style was Sean "Puffy" Combs, who's credited for kicking off a money-obsessed era of hip-hop. In 1998, Jay-Z and producer Jermaine Dupri's "Money Ain't a Thing" became a hit and an ethos. A year later, Lil Wayne invented the concept of "bling bling.")

On the one hand, this was rampant materialism, a move away from the counterculture of the poor; on the other hand, hip-hop's financial dominance meant black artists were finally accessing a part of what was sold as the American dream that had for so long felt unattainable. Trina's pursuit of riches wasn't about the joy of obtaining money alone, though she wanted the benefits and privilege that came with wealth. More important, her songs made women feel not just powerful but hypothetically rich. "Da Baddest Bitch" is the type of music you listen to before job interviews for motivation. "Shit, it pays to be the boss, ho" is more effective than any TED Talk. As Joan Morgan wrote in *Chickenheads Come Home to Roost*, "At its essence, trickin' is a woman's ability to use her looks, femininity, and flirtation to gain advantage in an inarguably sexist world."

Lil' Kim had by then created a whole new dictionary of graphic descriptions like "I'm drinkin' babies" on her first album, *Hard Core*. This was the language that set women like Trina free. On "Da Baddest Bitch" alone, Trina raps: "I'll make him eat it while my period on," "I'd probably fuck ya daddy if ya mammy wasn't playa hating," and, "If I had a chance to be a virgin again, I'd be fuckin' by the time I'm ten."

You can hear Trina's influence in acts like Megan Thee Stallion and Miami duo City Girls, who rap on their breakout single "Act Up," "If his money right, he can eat it like a Snicker."

Beyoncé

◆◆◆

When Beyoncé released "Bow Down" as a teaser single in 2013, it made people who didn't already know that Beyoncé was an excellent rapper realize she was an excellent rapper. The second half of the track is where she goes off, cascading onto the track with cocky lyrics over opera wails, vocals dramatically slowed down. Whenever she whipped out the talk-rap flow or the Houston swagger-drawl, rapping on Megan Thee Stallion's "Savage" remix, DJ Khaled's "Shining," or "Formation," it was seen as a national emergency.

A BRIEF HISTORY OF WOMEN

◆◆◆

"Fucks, no, I see half of that dough / Made you into a star, pushing hundred-thousand-dollar cars."

**FOXY BROWN,
"AIN'T NO NIGGA," 1996**

◆◆◆

"Creeping on the come up on the mission to get, paid / Haters want to stunt up / But they run up in my, face."

**MIA X,
"MISSION 2 GET PAID," 1995**

◆◆◆

"I'ma throw shade if I can't get paid / Blow you up to your girl like the Army grenade."

**LIL' KIM,
"CRUSH ON YOU (REMIX)," 1996**

◆◆◆

"Fuck being broke for days / Ladies gots to get paid."

**GANGSTA BOO,
"WHERE DEM DOLLAS AT," 1998**

◆◆◆

"You ready? Huh, it's time to pay up / The capital S gonna spot."

**SALT-N-PEPA,
"LET'S GET PAID," 1988**

DEMANDING MONEY IN SONGS

♦♦♦

*"Nothing in this world /
that I like more than checks."*

**CARDI B,
"MONEY," 2019**

♦♦♦

"Betta come break me off a fee /
Keep yo' girl on yo' bankroll."

**LA CHAT,
"BABY MAMA," 2001**

♦♦♦

*"Fuck me, blame me, fuck
you, pay me / This is what
you made me, where my
money at?"*

**NICKI MINAJ, WYCLEF JEAN, "SWEETEST GIRL
REMIX," 2007**

♦♦♦

*"I don't lift a finger 'less I'm
getting paid."*

**SAWEETIE,
"TOO MANY," 2018**

♦♦♦

*"Give me all your money and
give me all your residuals."*

**NICKI MINAJ,
"DANCE (A$$) (REMIX)," 2011**

La CHAT

The actor and writer Issa Rae once hosted a YouTube vlog series called *Ratchetpiece Theater*, featuring highlights of her favorite "ratchet" rap songs, which were always unapologetic, often crass, and often Southern party rap with beats that were timed to the precise BPM that bumps in a strip club. She explained in one of her videos, "This show is about appreciating the finest of the gutter. It's about finding the diamond in the roughneck." That rowdy style of rap was a way of life for fans and artists down south.

"Some people might call it ratchet, but I call it real. I call it street. I call it gangsta. Ain't nothing made up, nothing sugarcoated," says La Chat. "I try to speak for the struggle, especially struggling women. Everything can't be star shit." La Chat was not about star shit—she has a song called "Yeah, I Rob," which is pretty straightforward.

Before the mid to late nineties, much of mainstream rap was centralized to New York City and Los Angeles, forcing regions in the South to bubble up on their own, often independently. The advantage shifted once rappers and CEOs from the cornerstone cities of Houston (J. Prince), Miami (Luke Campbell), Atlanta (Jermaine Dupri), and New Orleans (Master P) proved their movements (bounce, screw, crunk)

SOME PEOPLE MIGHT CALL IT RATCHET, BUT I CALL IT REAL. I CALL IT STREET.

could attract major-label attention—and sales. These movements uprooted the rap world, forcing stubborn East Coast fans to recognize the influence of other regions and spread the wealth around.

La Chat was fourteen or fifteen years old and a regular at talent shows around Memphis (she once lip-synched to MC Lyte's "Lyte As a Rock"), when Three 6 Mafia's Juicy J, who'd heard about her through a mutual friend, Lil Noid, called her and asked her to rap for him.

Juicy J convinced her to stop wasting her time in the drug world and get into the music business. It quickly became clear that doing so was the right career move. Three 6 Mafia landed a deal with Relativity Records for their imprint, Hypnotized Minds, and blew up with party tracks like "Tear Da Club Up"; La Chat officially joined Hypnotize Minds (which re-released her album *Ultimate Revenge*) and collaborated with them often on posse cuts. For "Chickenhead," a duet she did with Three 6 Mafia member Project Pat, La Chat says she suggested they trade verses back and forth, like a lovers' spat. She wrote her lines, he wrote his, and they compared notes. The woop woop chorus builds into a call-and-response, which rapper Cardi B recycled for her 2018 song "Bickenhead."

As the South took over in the early aughts, turning regional acclaim into a nonstop wave of success, entities like No Limit and Cash Money Records enjoyed the gold rush. In Memphis, Three 6 Mafia became kings of party and horror-core, while the women in their crew, La Chat and Gangsta Boo, gave voice to a breadth of everyday women from the South who were strip club workers, mothers, and hustlers themselves.

In 2001, when La Chat released her major-label debut, *Murder She Spoke*, she says she never made a dime from it, despite selling more than 100,000 copies. "No one could tell me where the money was at that was due to me. I was, like, I gotta break loose and get my money," she says. La Chat detached from Three 6 Mafia, left Hypnotized Minds, and like a lot of rappers in her region, she went independent.

AMIL

NEVER FORGET:
One of Beyoncé's earliest collaborations as a solo artist was a record with Amil.

WHO SHE IS:
As the story goes, Amil met Jay-Z through her friends Liz Leite and Monique (the three of them called themselves Major Coins, but the group existed mostly in theory). Jay-Z needed a woman to complement his verse on "Can I Get A . . ." and had both Amil and Liz audition. The rest is Roc history. Amil landed a guest verse on the single "Can I Get A . . ." along with a record deal on Jay-Z and Damon Dash's boutique Def Jam label Roc-A-Fella Records. Amil released her only major-label album, *A.M.I.L.: All Money Is Legal*, in 2000 before bowing out of the music industry.

LISTEN:
Jay-Z's dizzying (in an enjoyable way) club record "Do It Again (featuring Amil and Beanie Sigel)" finds Amil bagging a guy at the club who ends up underperforming.

If you watched TV in the 1990s, chances are you saw a rapper or two hawking Sprite. In a series of commercials based on the kung fu film *Five Deadly Venoms*, five women were chosen to rap while dressed as martial arts characters who loved to fight and drink soda: Eve (as Blond Bee), Roxanne Shanté (Black Widow), Angie Martinez (Firefly), Mia X (Ladybug), and Amil (Praying Mantis). Rapper Kool Keith played the villain in the story, and R&B legend Millie Jackson popped up in the final sequence to declare, "My ladies got lyrics, ya heard me?"

The commercial sounds wild in retrospect, but it's telling that Sprite was banking on female rappers to sell their refreshing soft drink. It meant there were *five* prominent female rappers at the same time. It also meant Amil was popular enough to pitch in; at the time, the only woman signed to Roc-A-Fella Records, the label that Jay-Z and Damon Dash founded and transformed into a dynasty. Amil relied on the cachet of the biggest rapper on the planet, who began selling millions of records and turned a song from a Broadway musical about an orphan named Annie into a hit single.

Amil was easy to I.D. by sound. Her voice sounded as if a *Rugrats* character got hold of a mic and started rapping profanely. "Her voice was so distinct," says Jon-John Robinson, who produced the track "Get Down" on her album, *All Money Is Legal*. "She had that high, soft voice, but she was super cerebral." Her first memorable appearance was in 1998 on Jay-Z's "Can I Get A . . . ," a song featured on both the *Rush Hour* soundtrack and his album, *Vol. 2 . . . Hard Knock Life*.

Note that this is a song on which two men consider if they're rich enough (in character) to impress a woman. "If I was broke, would you want me?" Jay-Z wonders. Amil raps about having ambitious standards yet low expectations: "You ain't gotta be rich, but fuck that / How we gon' get around on ya bus pass." She gets off on ambition and says that only after seeing an engagement ring will she introduce the man to her parents.

Amil appeared on a handful of records during the Roc-A-Fella era, proving herself as the crew's go-to female voice. Hip-hop was then a monster of a genre—the highest-selling musicians in the country were rappers—and rap crews had taken to recruiting every single one of their friends to their boutique labels to maximize profits in their circles. There was always one woman in the clique who would stand out visually and musically, but without ever eclipsing the head/mentor of the crew. "Coming off *Hard Knock Life* and Volume 3, [Jay-Z is] on top of the world, so pretty much anybody he brings into the game has a real shot, just off the strength of his cosign," says Just Blaze, who produced Amil's album and raised his production profile through Roc-A-Fella. "You gotta remember, this is the era where your cousin's sister's dog walker's doctor's daughter could get a record deal because they knew you. And you might mess around and sell 500,000 copies, and if you sold 500,000 copies, you were considered a flop back then. Like, oh, you only went gold? You might get dropped."

Once women made it into the crew, they often existed as accessories in the lineup or the token ride-or-die chick. In Roc-A-Fella's league of former-hustlers-turned-businessmen, Amil was a "Joanne the Scammer" of her time, rapping about money, survival, and swindling men. "She was the type to hustle a dude for his money and make him think he was gonna hit it just to get some jewelry out of it," says Just Blaze.

Amil rapped about earning her own money, too. In the video for "I Got That," the lead single from Amil's album, *All Money Is Legal*, she and Beyoncé (three years before she went solo) go on a shopping spree at stores like René Lezard, while Amil raps, "I don't need a man to / Do for Amil what Amil can do." (Eve makes a cameo in the video as well.) The album houses a top-10 Roc-A-Fella posse track, "4 Da Fam," a regal swagger record featuring Jay-Z, Beanie Sigel, and Memphis Bleek; and it was because of Just Blaze's work on Amil's album (specifically, a song with her and Bathgate that Jay-Z repossessed) that he became one of Jay-Z's go-to producers.

The Amil era of Roc-A-Fella came and went, as she quickly became disillusioned with the industry (clubs, tours, politics) and left the label after releasing her sole album. "I wasn't the artist that was doing everything to be No. 1. I wasn't doing anything to make myself bigger than what I was," she told *Billboard*. "I rebelled against the industry, because it's not what I wanted." Jay-Z went on to un-knight her on several occasions, including "The Ruler's Back," the intro to his 2001 album *The Blueprint*, where he not-so-subtly name-checked Amil, rapping, "Fuckin' with me, you gotta drop *a mill*," though it's a compliment to be dissed by Jay-Z. Amil's exit may have been unceremonious, but her voice remains on a handful of Roc-A-Fella tracks and in our hearts.

SHAWNNA

NEVER FORGET:
She's one of only eight female rappers to have a No. 1 song on the *Billboard* Hot 100, thanks to her verse on Ludacris's "Stand Up" in 2003.

WHO SHE IS:
Shawnna (Rashawnna Guy) was born and raised in Southside Chicago, the daughter of blues legend Buddy Guy. Shawnna and her friend Lateefa Harland Young formed a rap duo called Infamous Syndicate and went around Chicago promoting their demos at barbershops before earning a local hit ("Jenny Jonez"); they briefly signed to Relativity Records and released one album. Shawnna met Ludacris on the Lyricist Lounge tour and joined his crew, Disturbing tha Peace, releasing her debut solo album, *Worth the Weight*, in 2004 and *Block Music* in 2006.

LISTEN:
Shawnna's greatest single, "Gettin' Some"—the "some" in question being "head"—takes its chorus from a line in Too $hort's 1993 song "Blowjob Betty."

Ludacris's debut single, "What's Your Fantasy," welcomed Shawnna to the rap world in 2000 in obscene fashion, although Shawnna appears only on the hook. Ludacris spends three verses listing unusual places (and places *within* places) where he'd like to fuck: the Georgia Dome ("on the fifty-yard line"), in the club ("in the DJ booth"), on a beach ("with black sand"), as well as a public bathroom, a classroom, the library, and the White House. It's a great song. An impressive tour de sex in the spirit of Uncle Luke.

But the remix improves heavily on the original. Ludacris raps only the chorus this time and cedes the floor to Shawnna, Trina, and Foxy Brown for an all-time dirty posse cut. Trina kicks it off with lyrics about her quest for a clit-licker. Shawnna fantasizes about being "on top of the projects getting head." And Foxy Brown drops a verse more X-rated than most of her catalog: "Ass in his face / Cock spread out." Whatever "cock spread out" means, it sounds nasty, and "you gotta su-suck the pussy / While I sit on your dick," as she raps, seems physically impossible.

Shawnna, then a new rapper out of the Chi, was on a record with two women who'd built their names and images off being lewd. "What's Your Fantasy" set Shawnna up as a successor to the Lil' Kims and Trinas of the world, too. Along with the onset of trap music (Southern-bred hustlers' anthems), this was the dawn of Crunk (by way of Lil Jon) and a proliferation of songs meant to play in the hottest strip clubs. "This was a time where you start to see, at the turn of the century, the music that was rising to the top," says Kim Osorio, former editor in chief of *The Source*. "Strip club culture was about to become a dominant thing in hip-hop, and the South was really pushing that heavy . . . In order to be respected, [your music] had to be at the strip clubs."

Signed to Ludacris's Disturbing tha Peace imprint, Shawnna guested on some of his most uncensored tracks, including "P-Poppin," a song about the difficult act of "popping pussy on a handstand." Shawnna wasn't as much of a raunchy artist as people envisioned, but this was an industry that made it seem like being technically skilled and sexy were opposite ends of the spectrum instead of potentially two aspects of one being. Shawnna rapped about and exuded sex, though not as much as her peers, and she was also a classic lyricist who earned the nickname Shorty Two Mics for rapping into two mics at once onstage.

"I always thought she was the hardest female ever," says John Monopoly, Shawnna's former manager. "She had the sex appeal but had the lyrical ability and the voice as well, so it was like the perfect storm. She's probably one of the most underrated MCs, period."

Out of the few legendary odes to oral sex (Khia's "My Neck, My Back," Akinyele's "Put It In Your Mouth"), Shawnna's greatest single, "Gettin' Some," is tame in comparison. Even so, Monopoly says, "Everybody was, like, 'It's never gonna get on the radio. It's too dirty.'" Despite being her claim to fame, much to her chagrin, the song was just the tip of the iceberg, in terms of her skill.

Remy Ma

Life could've gone a few ways for Remy Ma after she got out of prison in 2014 following a six-year sentence for assault: one, she celebrates and collaborates with the most popular rapper at the time, Nicki Minaj, and for good measure throws Lil' Kim, Foxy Brown, Trina, Eve, and Missy Elliott onto a song, realizing life is short, so why not use her powers for good? Or she could make a new enemy.

As she reacclimated to rap, Remy seemed to be going the peaceful route. She reconnected with her estranged rap partner Fat Joe and modernized her brand by starring with her husband, rapper Papoose (the couple married in 2008 while Remy was in prison), in the VH1 reality show *Love & Hip Hop*. Things were all good and well. Then in 2017, Remy Ma went into (lyrical) MMA fighter mode and set her sights on Nicki Minaj, who, as Remy heard through sources, was using her influence to block Remy from potentially lucrative business opportunities.

"ShETHER" was instantly one of the most important records in hip-hop. First, the idea to take Nas's classic diss track about Jay-Z ("Ether") and simply put "She" in front of it was too clever to be true. Based on her record of leaving bloodbaths on tracks, rap fans knew that Remy was down to go bar for bar with men, women, and babies. She'd previously devastated Lady Luck in a rap battle, and she once

rapped, "A pregnant bitch talk shit, I'ma destroy her fetus."

On "ShETHER," Remy rapped a barrage of painful insults about Nicki's ex-boyfriend and alleged plastic surgery and made allegations of drug use, and in the process she jacked the crown for "queen of rap." It was nice: The return of healthy competition between two women in rap meant

track too soon after, titled "Another One"; Minaj returned with three singles at once, one featuring two of her friends, Lil Wayne and Drake ("No Frauds")—there, Minaj dissed Remy Ma with vigor: "Heard your pussy on yuck, I guess you needed a Pap," Minaj raps, referencing Remy's husband, Papoose, and . . . a Pap smear in one. Anyway, the point is that "ShETHER" was everything that

THE RETURN OF HEALTHY COMPETITION BETWEEN TWO WOMEN IN RAP MEANT THERE WERE TWO WOMEN IN RAP IMPACTFUL ENOUGH TO MAKE THE FACE-OFF INTERESTING.

there were two women in rap impactful enough to make the faceoff interesting. There were legitimate career stakes. Judnick Mayard wrote for *FADER* that year, "The greatness of Nicki Minaj and Remy Ma's rap battle is in proving that we've reached levels where women in rap both have metrics and PR machines to boost their numbers."

It was a battle of wits and dimensions: On one side was a rapper viewed as a purist who never lost her underdog spirit (Remy) and, on the other, a former mixtape assassin who'd blossomed into a pop star and entrepreneur (Nicki). The beef triggered an age-old conversation about female rappers being forced into competition, which tends to ignore that it was a woman, Roxanne Shanté, who popularized the public sport of battling on record with "Roxanne's Revenge."

Remy Ma had Minaj cornered with "ShETHER" but then blew her load by dropping a second diss

was good about Remy: She was tenacious and tactical, all true to her roots.

Start in the Bronx in 1999, a time when Big Pun, a six-hundred-plus-pound Latin rapper, was the biggest star to emerge from the borough since KRS-One a decade earlier. Revered for his mile-a-minute delivery, Pun had a boxer's finesse on street records and a smooth R&B sensibility on commercial singles like "Still Not a Player" (featuring R&B singer Joe) and "It's So Hard" (featuring Donell Jones). He had an ear for talent, too.

Remy Ma rapped for Big Pun for the first time in late 1999, when his debut album, *Capital Punishment*, was in steady rotation on the radio. Her mother chaperoned her to a meeting at Pun's house in the Bronx, and, at Pun's request, Remy later recycled the same verse she had rapped for him the day she met him.

At the beginning of "Ms. Martin," a Big Pun song that really belongs to Remy, Pun states: "Sometimes you gotta send a woman to do a man's job." This was unusual. The track, which comes at the tail end of his posthumously released April 2000 album, *Yeeeah Baby*, finds one of the greatest rappers ever introducing his female mentee as his gifted, more aggressive peer who'd go on to become a great. The song was entirely devoted to crowning Remy Ma as one of New York's most leathery rappers, stylistically.

Remy began quietly shadowing Pun in the studio and on music video sets, up until his death in February 2000. The science of rap was important to her. Producer Sean C told *Complex* in 2017, "Being a rapper was a big deal to Remy. Being the *best* rapper was a big deal to her. It wasn't about being the best female rapper." Remy Ma said to *Nylon* in 2016, "I don't even like the terminology 'female rapper' . . . If you're a rapper, you're just a rapper. If you're a doctor, you're not a female doctor, you're a doctor."

When Remy reteamed with Pun's friend and mentor Fat Joe, they were the rare tandem in hip-hop where the woman in the crew (Fat Joe's Terror Squad) was the superior MC. Remy proved her prowess relentlessly. On M.O.P.'s 2000 stickup anthem "Ante Up (Remix)," she rapped about outsmarting metal detectors, and she came across charmingly grimy on radio hits like "Whuteva" (2005) and "Conceited" (2005).

A steward for hip-hop traditionalists, Remy ascended around the same time that Southern rap was digging its heels in, and right as another New York rapper, 50 Cent, was harmonizing his way to platinum sales to the detriment of his rival Ja Rule. "Everybody is bouncing up and down with the Dirty South," Fat Joe told *Vibe* in 2004. "We love the South and the West Coast to death, but New York has lost its sound and presence in hip-hop. Now we're bringing back that old grab-your-dick hip-hop." It's safe to say Remy helped preserve that "grab-your-dick hip-hop," as well as New York rap.

Conflicts with Fat Joe over the promotion of her debut album, *There's Something About Remy: Based on a True Story*, put Remy in a difficult space, though. The two cut ties, and he dropped her from the label, but she had more serious problems to contend with, when she was convicted in 2008 for shooting a friend in the stomach. The six years she spent in prison allowed Nicki Minaj enough time to occupy the throne without contest, setting Remy on the path to the aforementioned "ShETHER."

After prison, she quickly made up for lost time, reconnected with Fat Joe, and collaborated with him on an album, *Plata O Plomo*, including the single "All the Way Up," which earned them a Grammy nomination. Just like that, Remy was settling back into a rap game with new women and new rules, but she was ready to let everyone in her radius know not to get too comfortable.

NICKI MINAJ

Nicki Minaj referenced her verse on Kanye West's 2010 single "Monster" no fewer than six times in her own songs. She called herself a monster on "Save Me" ("I'm a bitch, I'm a monster," she raps), then reminded listeners twice more on "Win Again" and "Automatic"—"I am a monster / This is ambition," she raps. And: "I'm a monster on the floor." On "Massive Attack," she embedded the word into the chorus ("We got Tom Toms over here bigger than a monster"). She also wasn't above mentioning the record as a houseguest: She teased "Monster Nicki" on Beyoncé's "Flawless (Remix)" and conjured the "Loch Ness monster" on Ciara's "Livin' It Up." This was the opposite of subliminal messaging.

But "Monster" was major, in terms of launching Nicki's career. The song took off mainly because she was a woman rapping well. On top of that, she was a woman outshining men on a major rap song with such precision—and not just any guys. Rick Ross starts the record off with an opening so abrupt, it's forgettable (just ten seconds). West impressively uses the word "sarcophagus" in relation to pussy. Jay-Z says his Achilles' heel is *love*, sounding so odd, it paralyzes the listener for the same ten seconds Rick Ross just wasted. And Nicki gets the last word, the edge, and the glory, and torches them all in terms of lyrics, flow, wit, and delivery, masterfully changing her pitch throughout.

When she raps about eating brains, she raises her voice a touch, makes it shaky, then grunts to remind people her money isn't fake—a whiplash expedition in the lineage of Ol' Dirty Bastard. It was the moment people realized Nicki Minaj could be a superstar.

Initially a surrogate sister to rapper Lil Wayne, as a member of his Young Money crew and imprint, Nicki soon eclipsed him, in part because of her many musical personalities. "I had so many people over the years tell me that I should sound a certain way," she told *FADER* in 2010. "[M]y rap style now reflects my true personality. Because I am so weird."

She told *Vibe*, "I like playing dress up. When I do my voices and faces, I don't think about anything. My mind stops."

From the time between Lil' Kim and Foxy Brown's heyday and Nicki Minaj's arrival, rap was increasingly a ghost town for women. The drought led to a streak of essays about the extinction of female MCs and set the stage for the coronation of Nicki Minaj, who had to go through pop to take her career past even Lil' Kim in her prime, as far as broad-scope acclaim. Releasing music that was bubbly and more youth-appropriate helped Nicki pass the bar without rapping as explicitly about sex. By dominating every guest verse imaginable, she became the new barometer for women and the next big rap mogul. This was a rapping Betsey Johnson who was melodic, versatile, and able to gather a broad range of fans—men, women, and children—while being a magnet for friction, beefing with everyone from Lil' Kim, Remy Ma, and Cardi B to her own labelmates. She had versatility.

On the bubblier end of the spectrum, a bookend to "Monster," was the ultra-girly ballad "Super Bass," the sound of a bright pink wad of gum popping against your lips in the summertime. Nicki balloons her vocals and punches consonants. "He just gotta gimme that look / When he gimme that look, then the panties coming off," she raps, this time over a twirling sparkler of a beat.

The song dropped a few months after her debut album, *Pink Friday*, as a bonus track on its deluxe version and became her biggest single (reaching No. 3 on the *Billboard* Hot 100), one of a series of statistical wins that ensured Nicki Minaj would be the first name mentioned whenever anyone brought up women in rap and sales. (Oftentimes, it was Nicki Minaj bringing it up.) Strangely enough, she didn't have a No. 1 single until 2020 when she earned two as a featured act—on Doja Cat's "Say So (Remix)" and on Tekashi 6ix9ine's "Trolls"—though "Super Bass" should've been one.

Nicki sang and rapped and became the ideal final form of a post-Lauryn MC: talented, autonomous, and highly sellable. Also, polarizing.

"I 'REINTRODUCED' the 'successful' female rapper back to POP CULTURE. Showed big business we were major players in the game just like the boys were," Minaj wrote on Instagram in 2017 (caps-lock emphasis hers), to clear up a misconception that she'd bragged about making female rappers mainstream. But in an effort to protect her position, Nicki fell into the habit of separating herself from other women and potential competition. "Nicki didn't rap like the rest of the female rappers," says Lady Luck. "She was a mix between, like, a Missy Elliott and something else. [She wore] a lot of colors. It was like the bitch who gets in the palace and then turns and looks at everybody else like ah-ha. 'Cause everything was 'you bitches is my sons.' 'Fuck you bitches, I'm the only one popping.'" (Luck makes sure to note that she loves Nicki.)

THIS WAS A RAPPING BETSEY JOHNSON WHO WAS MELODIC, VERSATILE, AND ABLE TO GATHER A BROAD RANGE OF FANS— MEN, WOMEN, AND CHILDREN.

Other than being theatrical, Nicki's famous "characters" served a purpose. She continually switched up her voice: a baby-like trill one second, animated or a playful baritone voice the next. And she rapped with a distinct New York—specifically, Queens—accent (pronouncing "off" like "awf") but avoided the conventional hardened style typical of New York rappers. By shape-shifting as an artist, she effectively neutered her accent. Similar to Drake, Minaj was able to, as Anupa Mistry wrote about the Toronto rapper, "become the kind of pop star that can code switch on a global level."

In her hometown of Queens, Nicki boosted her rep as a member of the group the Hoodstars, at a time when rappers were dropping mixtapes to jockey for label deals. Nicki's successive mixtapes (*Playtime Is Over* in 2007, *Sucka Free* in 2008, and *Beam Me Up Scotty* in 2009) served as her precursor to fame. In a rap world deprived of women, the mixtape rite of passage made her a hero.

Nicki had a memorable cameo on the street DVD *The Come Up, Vol. 2*, after a guy named Fendi found her on MySpace and recruited her for his independent label Dirty Money. On the DVD, you could find her fresh-faced, rocking bangs, rapping about a threatening other woman over the Notorious B.I.G.'s "Warning." Everyone in the rap world heard the shot, including Lil Wayne. He appeared on *Beam Me Up Scotty*, and Nicki appeared on his mixtape *Da Drought 3* before joining his Young Money imprint in 2009.

Nicki was the frenzied flash of lightning on songs like Young Money's "Bedrock," Usher's "Lil Freak," Robin Thicke's "Shakin' It 4 Daddy," Ludacris's "My Chick Bad," and Mariah Carey's "Up Out My Face." This quickly increased her exposure. An alum of New York City's renowned Fiorello H. LaGuardia High School of Music & Performing Arts, known as the *Fame* school, she, in the spirit of Lady Gaga, knew how to embody characters that

begot personas that begot superstars. A theater kid through and through.

Nicki was making the industry workable for women again, and so much was riding on her that she had little room to flop. So when her lead single, "Massive Attack," failed, the setback hurt, but her debut album, *Pink Friday*, still became the first album by a female rapper to top the chart since Eve's debut album in 1999. "I felt like I had something to prove to everyone who said a female rapper could not make an album unless she was talking about her pussy," she told me for a *Vibe* cover story in 2012. "And so I went above and beyond to prove that I could not talk about sex and not talk about my genitalia and still have a successful album. And I proved that. And now my time for proving things to my critics is over. I don't really need to prove anything to anyone else anymore."

The fact that Nicki's music left fans so divided made for a fascinating case study. Her dip into a sound and style blatantly designed for mass consumption (electronic pop beats and *singing*) challenged archaic beliefs of what a rap star sounded like. One of her biggest singles, "Starships," caused a ripple. Hours before she was supposed to perform at Hot 97's major concert, Summer Jam, in 2012, one of the station's personalities, Peter Rosenberg, made an errant comment about "Starships" not representing "real hip-hop." The public met Rosenberg with a collective boot because his argument was stupid and wrong. All the genres were intermingling. He, however, went from shitting on Nicki's music to calling her "potentially the greatest female MC of all time."

After re-creating Lil' Kim's famous squat pose in 1996, early in her career, Nicki took the focus off sex in her music and image. She used humor and caricature and opened a world of possibilities for other women. "I remember when she first came out, people wanted to make her stuff about sex so much.

But the music she was putting out was, like, so not that," says rapper Rico Nasty. "Like, *Pink Friday* was not that. It was so refreshing. It was different as fuck, so I think that's why it was crazy for all of us." But she didn't avoid sexuality altogether, as you know if you heard her song "Anaconda" in 2014 or saw the video, where Nicki creates a twerking women's paradise, reclaiming the power of the black ass and curvy body that white pop culture tried to steal.

The video went viral and inspired tons of essays and attention, including an ABC News segment titled "Nicki Minaj's 'Anaconda' Video: An Ode to Feminism?" Nicki played the ultimate balancing act of objectifying herself and being in control, and while those two ideas can coexist, it makes for some soul-searching. The way she sold sex on her own terms was a sign of progress. The female rappers who came after her saw a new road to success that revolved around personality, theater, and like Jay-Z, a desire to be in the boardroom, in control. "Nicki is beyond that puppet shit," writer Karen Good says. "She can do what she wants to do. She wants to be sexy. She wants a big ass. . . . They're not dissimilar, Nicki and Kim. They said 'we're gonna use [our sexuality],' and they had a crew of boys that encouraged this. On one hand, we're empowered sexually. On the other hand, in becoming objects, we objectified ourselves."

Nicki may have marketed eccentricity, but sex appeal was still a major factor for any woman rapper seeking mainstream success. "And that's not just in hip-hop—that's in music in general," says former *Vibe* editor Elizabeth Méndez Berry. "It's very rare to see a woman who doesn't fit the conventional idea of beauty become a massive pop star."

Nicki had plenty of fans to defend her against attacks and criticism. One of her smartest moves was grooming a battalion online to bend to her will. The timing of her success helped. When Twitter launched in July 2006, suddenly there were new social identities and a new language around fandom. Normal people had followers, and fan bases migrated online and turned into super fans and stans. Just as Nicki was becoming a star, so was Twitter, a blossoming community where these fanatics could exchange praise and criticism about their faves and their enemies. Tech sites like Mashable declared 2009 the year "Twitter conquered the world."

Online fan groups earned titles: Beyoncé's BeyHive, Lady Gaga's Monsters, Rihanna's Navy, Justin Bieber's Beliebers—and they were all devoted and, frankly, wild enough to garner many written articles about the thrill and danger of internet celebrity fandom. Nicki Minaj had her Barbies, or Barbs, an army of fans she could easily deploy when she had friction with other rappers: Lil' Kim (who claimed Nicki hadn't paid her proper homage), Remy Ma (see: the "ShETHER" era), and Cardi B (a beef that began with rumors of a disagreement over their Migos collaboration "MotorSport"). It's not unusual that Nicki would use the Barbs as a (sometimes toxic) force field against criticism. Or even as a defense mechanism to make up for the lack of protection around women in hip-hop who often feel unguarded.

It'd been a long time—the mid-2000s—since rap had not one, but two successful women on top. And the tension behind the scenes provided a prime opportunity for the new blood (Cardi) to go against the seasoned star (Nicki), and so the two of them did, even facing off in a physical encounter while dressed in couture in 2018 during New York Fashion Week. Women were back in the sport of rap.

NICKI MINAJ INVENTED COLOR

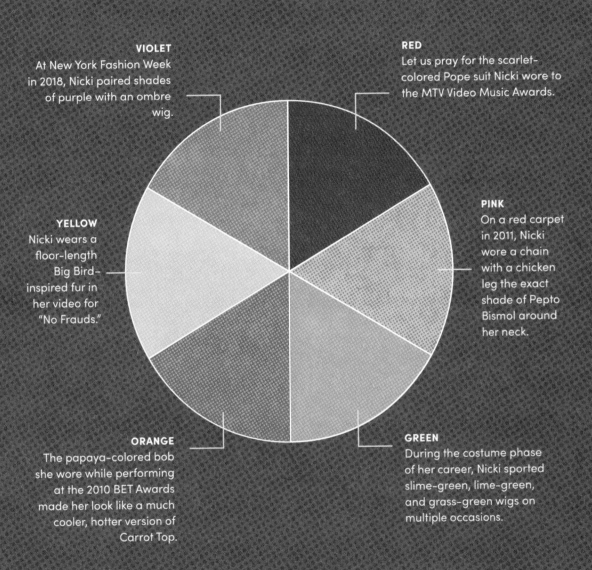

VIOLET
At New York Fashion Week in 2018, Nicki paired shades of purple with an ombre wig.

RED
Let us pray for the scarlet-colored Pope suit Nicki wore to the MTV Video Music Awards.

PINK
On a red carpet in 2011, Nicki wore a chain with a chicken leg the exact shade of Pepto Bismol around her neck.

YELLOW
Nicki wears a floor-length Big Bird–inspired fur in her video for "No Frauds."

GREEN
During the costume phase of her career, Nicki sported slime-green, lime-green, and grass-green wigs on multiple occasions.

ORANGE
The papaya-colored bob she wore while performing at the 2010 BET Awards made her look like a much cooler, hotter version of Carrot Top.

AZeALIA BANKS

Once Nicki Minaj proved female rappers could sell again, women were suddenly back in vogue, and labels were thirsty for the next big thing. In 2011, it was Azealia Banks, a rapper from Harlem and a glorious loudmouth who attempted to manifest her own destiny on her debut single, "212," where she offered herself as tribute in the opening line, rapping: "Hey [*pause*] / I can be the answer."

In the black-and-white music video, a close-up shot locks in on her lips rapping the lyrics. This was a twenty-year-old club savant who had the look of a fashion queen and fit the template set by Nicki: rap, sing, be stylish and a little bit weird (and crass). Banks was a lot weird artistically and gifted, and no one had ever rapped, "I guess that cunt gettin' eaten," on a record. But her coronation was so short-lived that it became a cautionary tale.

Banks used the early social network site MySpace (under the alias Miss Bank$) to talk her way into the business, reaching out to producers like Diplo to collaborate. "I was like my own little A&R street team, my little press machine on the internet," she told MTV News. Her songs, like "Supplier," were daring enough to earn her a budding development deal with the British music label XL Recordings, home of Adele and M.I.A., but the deal quickly soured over creative differences.

SHE PERFORMED AT KARL LAGERFELD'S HOUSE AT A DINNER PARTY FOR THE LAUNCH OF HIS LINE. SHE HIT UP PARIS AND NEW YORK FASHION WEEKS. SHE ATTENDED THE MET GALA WEARING ALEXANDER WANG. HER MUSIC WAS HEAVY ON THE RUNWAYS.

Banks took off artistically after she rapped over producer Lazy Jay's 2009 track "Float My Boat," and released it in 2011 as her single "212." With just one hit single and an EP titled *1991*, full of dance-rap crossbred gems, Azealia Banks was in demand. She became known as the "foul-mouthed" new rap sensation, with unlikely fans like Gwyneth Paltrow. (Paltrow tweeted, "Azealia Banks . . . Obsessed. Wow," on December 15, 2011.) After a long hiatus, the *Vogues* of the world understood the editorial value of Nicki Minaj and fresh faces like Banks and another counterpart, Australian rapper Iggy Azalea, who could all market high fashion.

A blitz of exclusive invites followed in 2012, as Banks's air of downtown cool had fashion elites ready to crown her their new rap muse. She performed at Karl Lagerfeld's house at a dinner party for the launch of his line. She hit up Paris and New York Fashion Weeks. She attended the Met Gala wearing Alexander Wang. And her music was heavy on the runways. The *New York Times* reported, "Fashion designers, in particular, seem to be drawn to her street-meets-chic look." A long way from when high-fashion brands wouldn't even lend clothing to rappers.

Producer Travis Stewart, aka Machinedrum, collaborated with Banks in the late 2000s after a popular young chef, Dante Gonzales, sent him her demos. "What impressed me was the fact that she sounded so seasoned. She sounded like a master already," says Stewart. "I was also blown away by the diversity. She was rapping over indie rock, house music, dancehall. I had been living in New York for about five years, and I felt like I knew everybody that was doing their thing. She came out of nowhere."

Banks was in and out of the recording booth in one or two takes, easily switching between singing and rapping. It was something special. "When you really listen to my music, you hear a girl who's . . . experiencing men, having money, not having money, people who are trying to tell her she's not cute, people telling her she can't rap, she can't dance," she told *Vibe* in 2012. "It's a young Black girl doing this for herself, by herself."

In January 2012, she landed yet another label deal, with Interscope Records. But while working on her debut album, *Broke with Expensive Taste*, she said she clashed with the white men in charge at Interscope over creative direction and song choices. That same year, she dropped her mixtape *Fantasea*, which again showed her ability to juggle rap and dance while also appealing to fans of ball culture (dramatic shows that feature drag performances), and offering drama—the aesthetic of the mixtape was aquamarine mermaid garb. She told *Rolling Stone* in 2014, "It felt like they were playing some sort of head game. And you know I love conspiracy theories. I was, like, 'They're trying to brainwash me! Fuck these guys!'" Per her request, Interscope released her from the label in July 2014.

Banks released the long-delayed *Broke with Expensive Taste* in 2014, through her then-manager Jeff Kwatinetz's label Prospect Park Records, and dropped another mixtape, *Slay Z*, in 2016. Critics praised her music—it was like a soundtrack to a glitter-bombed trap music ball. But at a point, it was too much drama. She became less of a top-draft prospect and more an example of squandered potential.

Lists of her sometimes one-sided beefs were more prominent online than her actual music, at a volume that was both impressive and tragic. Azealia dissented with anyone you could imagine: Russell Crowe (because he spit on her at a party in his home), Zayn Malik from the boy band One Direction (she called him "a white boy pretending to be black"), Iggy Azalea (Azealia took issue with Iggy's cultural appropriation), T.I. (they argued about Iggy's cultural appropriation). These dust-ups crept into politics (Sarah Palin) and tech (Elon Musk), and there were too many to keep up with, which, at the very least, means Azealia Banks succeeded in becoming a household name. She would occasionally make valid points (maybe Action Bronson was a "bootleg Ghostface"?), but then followed it up with something offensive. But her ongoing battle with what she described as mental illness complicated these bouts of controversy, and most times people weren't giving Banks the benefit of the doubt. Morgan Jerkins wrote for Pitchfork in 2017, "Banks did not introduce herself as the latest competitor for the female token that mainstream rap allows, but rather, someone who had already succeeded by her own metrics . . . Whether fabricated or real, this no-fucks-given persona was necessary armor for Banks."

It was easy to believe in her—she was bold and made energetic dance music that appealed to sweaty club environments. Banks was the beginning of a new school of rap stars, post-Nicki, who were similarly brash, in a less exasperating way. In spite of scandal, she persisted because of her talent but became a classic case of antics trumping art and when keeping it real goes wrong. To her credit, no other artist made mermaids look cooler.

CaRDI B

◆◆◆

NEVER FORGET:
She was the first female rapper to have two (and then three and then four) No. 1 hits on the *Billboard* Hot 100 and the first solo female rapper to win the Grammy Award for Best Rap Album (2019, for her debut album, *Invasion of Privacy*).

WHO SHE IS:
Cardi B (Belcalis Almánzar) grew up with her mother and younger sister as a "regular degular" girl from the Bronx who performed in high school talent shows. At nineteen, she quit a cashier job at the Amish Market in Tribeca to generate income faster as a dancer at strip clubs, including New York Dolls and Sue's Rendezvous in Mount Vernon. She soon flipped her social media fame into a reality TV job and a lucrative rap career.

LISTEN:
On "Bickenhead," a reboot of the classic Project Pat and La Chat duet, Cardi raps about different, impractical ways to "pop a pussy"—"Pop that pussy up in church / Pop that pussy on a pole / Pop that pussy on the stove"—proving variety is the spice of life.

Instagram launched a simple yet radical feature in June 2013: the ability to upload videos in addition to photos. Finally, users could bombard their followers with fifteen-second snippets of their lives, which was a bad omen for Vine, the six-second video app made popular by teens. (Vine died three years later.) But it was life-changing for people like Cardi B.

Back then, Cardi was a little-known stripper from the Bronx who quickly became famous through Instagram. Her videos, shot in the style of ad hoc tutorials, featured practical advice—about men, love, and money—based on her own life experiences. "That ain't no way to live, hatin' on hoes," she would say (more likely, scream) into a front-facing camera. "When ya man don't call you . . . you call his side bitch, like *deep-deep-deep*, hello?!" And so on.

She was open about everything: her daily moods, sexuality, financial ambitions, butt and breast augmentations. People loved her honesty, plus her comedy lent itself to the speed and flash of social media (her videos spread to places like Tumblr, Twitter, and Vine), which she understood as a space for persona-building.

Cardi's personality became a bright spot amid all the artifice, and her following grew into the millions, then in 2015, internet fame got her cast on the VH1 reality show *Love &*

Hip Hop. Her appeal was instant and infectious. "Hey, Amurrica, what's poppin'? My name is Cardi B," she said in her TV debut. "You might know me as that annoying dancer on social media that be talkin' hella shit, with the long nails and the big ol' titties."

The gap between *Love & Hip-Hop* and Cardi's becoming the wittiest rapper alive was astonishingly brief. The speed and intensity of her run was impressive and meticulously documented. Not only did she come out of nowhere, but she seemed to be getting really good, really fast. Rawiya Kameir wrote for *FADER*, "Cardi is not the first person to translate social media fame into a lucrative career, but I challenge you to name anyone who's leveled up as much, and as quickly."

Cardi went from releasing *okay music* to *good music*. In 2017, she dropped two mixtapes: *Gangsta Bitch Music Vol. 1* and *Gangsta Bitch Music Vol. 2*. The latter featured a skit titled "Leave That Bitch Alone," where she checks her man for "taking bitches to Outback," when he knows it's her favorite restaurant. (This was after she essentially turned Instagram commentary into a rap song with 2015's "Cheap Ass Weave.") These earlier mixtapes showed a rapper with room for growth. Step by step, people witnessed Cardi transform from internet icon to reality-TV personality to superstar in real time. Partnering with rapper Pardison Fontaine—who she met at the strip club Sue's Rendezvous when both were green—helped her get sharp. Fontaine said to *GQ*, "I knew she was a personality on Instagram and that people already liked her. I knew there had to be something there."

Traditionally, most rappers get exiled for openly using ghostwriters or other songwriters. Cardi admitted she needed help. Fontaine coached her through rapping and co-wrote her lyrics. "Yeah, I co-wrote, bitch," she said onstage at a show once.

"I don't give a fuck. All these rappers out here got writers. Even the ones that say they don't. They lying, bitch. They do. I don't give a fuck . . . I'm still gonna get paid, hoe." And so she did.

By the following summer, she had a surprise hit: "Bodak Yellow." The song's harsh, metallic beat was distinctly New York and aesthetically Cardi—charming yet threatening—and the lyrics were thoroughly quotable.

You could neither fuck with nor avoid Cardi B at that point. "Bodak Yellow" made her only the second female rapper to have a No. 1 song on the *Billboard* Hot 100 chart without a featured guest, after Lauryn Hill in 1998. She rapped on G-Eazy's "No Limit," on Migos' "MotorSport," on Bruno Mars's "Finesse (Remix)." Then her debut album, *Invasion of Privacy*, released in April 2018, went to No. 1. And her Latin-trap single, "I Like It," later topped the Hot 100, making Cardi the first and only female rapper to have two No. 1 records on the chart.

Cardi found herself in rare company again, becoming just the third female rapper to score a Grammy nomination for Album of the Year, next to Lauryn Hill and Missy Elliott. While Nicki Minaj managed to walk that fine line between street and corporate rap, Cardi was the embodiment of authenticity.

"You got Cardi, she's a stripper, and she's, like, 'What? I don't have the best grammar, and I'm not trying to be anybody's role model, by the way. All I really need is money,'" says Karen Good. "She's not part of a straight-up boy clique. She's just kind of self-actualizing, but she comes out of strip clubs, which is a male-dominated environment." As a former stripper, Cardi understood the nature of control, which probably helped her navigate a music business where control has to often be earned. "I think Kim took those lumps so that these women can be a little bit more in the driver's seat. They're not putting

STEP BY STEP, PEOPLE WITNESSED CARDI TRANSFORM FROM INTERNET ICON TO REALITY-TV PERSONALITY TO SUPERSTAR IN REAL TIME.

themselves in a box, and they're not letting other people do it," says Good.

Historically, there've been limited ways for female rappers to climb up the chain. More often, opportunity knocked through gatekeeping men, both in front of and behind the scenes. History implies that women in rap need a man backing them to rise to the level of a superstar. But the odds were in Cardi's favor by the time she blew up. There were many more entry points into fame (reality TV, social media) and a lot more measures of popularity, compared to what the women before her had. There was also a shift from radio, to mixtapes, to internet and streaming, which changed the narrative of stardom.

Whereas the street mixtape economy boosted Nicki Minaj's career early on, the streaming explosion, paired with the reach of social media, gave a generation of internet rappers an advantage; for example, Soulja Boy becoming famous via YouTube, and Belcalis becoming Cardi B through Instagram. *The New Yorker*'s Briana Younger wrote in 2018, "Thanks to platforms such as YouTube, Twitter, SoundCloud, and Instagram, along with the pseudo-democracy of streaming services, women can tap into their audiences directly and find measurable success."

Cardi was part of a big trend: Instagram and Twitter as brand extensions for average citizens and brilliant animals, not just celebrities. She refined her image on social media, but she was always a star. In 2015, when she went from stripping to making money through hosting and paid appearances, opportunities afforded to her because of her local celebrity and cult status on the internet, she quit the strip-club gigs altogether. And if there was anywhere she could go, it was toward rap.

"For someone like Cardi, what were her options to amplify her larger than lifeness?" says former *Vibe* editor Elizabeth Méndez Berry. "She's like, what format can I compress myself into that maximizes my personality? She does that with her Instagram posts and in her songs. Hip-hop gives you that density of language, that vividness that is perfect for her because nobody else talks like her. When you hear it, you feel like, *Oh my God this woman is able to bring us into her life with a proximity and detail and comedy.* She's literally built for this."

Cardi was honest about her motives with rap—and that her goal was to make hits that could make her money. "I'm a hoe. I'm a stripper hoe. I'm about this shmoney," she said in an early Instagram video. She said to *FADER*, "At the end of the day, you need to be with what sells . . . I have a passion for music, I love music. But I also have a passion for money and paying my bills."

Aspiring rappers on *Love & Hip Hop* try to use the show as a fast-track career boost, a place to promote their bad music, to invent caricatures and story lines for marginal amounts of fame. But most of them fail. Cardi B is the franchise's biggest success story—a social media personality who became more famous on TV and then again through the medium of rap. On camera, she played to the drama, getting caught up in a love triangle, and constantly name-dropped her then-boyfriend, who was in prison.

Cardi could've run into the same reality-TV fate as her castmates. But she was not like the others. After two seasons, she made her smartest move yet and quit the show to pursue a real-world career—the "and Hip-Hop" part—instead of just talking about it on television. She quickly went from invading everyone's living rooms to becoming a rap star. She didn't have years of tutelage with a male rapper or super producer—she barely knew how to rap at first. And she didn't come from the underground or debut with a popular crew. Instead, she offered a new bootstrap model for success created in her own image, ingeniously through social media.

The trifecta of Nicki, Azealia, and Cardi begat a new generation of women who would find success by building their own appealing personas and forcing heads to tun in their direction. "Labels were signing female rappers and putting them in a shelf and not focusing on them," Cardi tweeted in 2019. "Bitches been rapping, bitches been have talent, but the music industry wasn't believing."

Social media is often about synthesizing thoughts and moments into bursts of comedy. Vine was all about making people laugh, and Cardi had comedic delivery and timing and knew how to sell charm. Her Instagram videos featured countless messages of erotic advice, and her Twitter account was a constant source of truth. Sample: "Type of sex that when we finish I got one eyelash missing . . . that's what I want right now." When she got a new set of veneer teeth and went on an interview to show them off, she joked, "I even smile when I'm mad [now]." On her debut album, *Invasion of Privacy*, she threatens to "make a bowl of cereal with a teaspoon of bleach" as revenge against a cheater on one song, "Thru Your Phone."

When stamping a debut album as a classic, rap fans tend to rely on metrics of perfection. The length of the album is considered. No skips. Great production. Nas's *Illmatic*, Jay-Z's *Reasonable Doubt*, and Lauryn Hill's *The Miseducation of Lauryn Hill* all make the cut, but few albums by female rappers get on people's lists. *Invasion of Privacy* was the best rap debut in years and belongs in the canon along with Lil' Kim's *Hard Core* and *Miseducation*. It isn't as perfect as other classic debuts, but it is highly listenable; it represents a seismic moment in rap and the fully actualized version of Cardi B.

Invasion of Privacy jump-started a new era for women rappers in which success felt much more tangible. When Cardi collaborated with a then-blossoming star, Megan Thee Stallion, on "WAP"—a perfectly crafted duet about the slipperiness of their vaginas—it was a symbol of dominance. The music video, released in the middle of the pandemic of 2020, showed the two of them prancing through bright hallways in tandem and doing full splits with bare, oiled derrières. Not only were two women in peak position in rap syncing their skills effortlessly and tension-free, but also symbolically, this was the culmination of decades of work from their predecessors who set the stage for raunchy rap by black women to be shamelessly lauded. Like Salt-N-Pepa, like Lil' Kim, like Trina, like Foxy Brown, both Cardi and Megan were the centers of a provocative universe, but instead of men laying the dominos, it was about women making music for women's enjoyment, reclaiming the object gaze and the vision of sexuality that men had monopolized.

After years of debates about the lack of female rappers, Nicki Minaj updated the blueprint for success and Cardi multiplied the wealth of talent and resurrected the idea that numerous women who controlled their own stories could dominate rap at once. Never again would there only be one.

THE BOOK OF CARDI B: A FEW OF HER WISE QUOTABLES

"Dick-sucking contest, I'm winning."

"If a girl have beef with me, she gon' have beef with me forever."

"I think us bad bitches is a gift from God."

"I don't need no punishment by Christ. I need all the blessings."

"Uncle Sam, I want to know what you doing with my fucking tax money."

"I'm never gon' change. I'ma always be a ho."

"Don't be a 'why her and not me' type-a bitch. Be a 'how can I get next to that bitch' type-a bitch."

"Leave his texts on read, leave his balls on blue."

"I'm just a regular degular smegular girl from the Bronx."

THE FUTURE

Hip-hop was a lonely place for women right before Nicki Minaj released her debut album, *Pink Friday*, in 2010. In a sign of things to come, she very quickly outworked her male peers and sent multiple offshoots into the universe over the course of a decade, replenishing the landscape for women in rap.

It took years for rap to repopulate, but then Cardi B came in and perfected the art of ingenuity in the digital age. It was mostly due to her and Nicki's success that a cult of twentysomething women rappers emerged, with a range of personalities and skill sets, fueled by their own internet notoriety and versatility. For the first time in a long time, there was a surplus of women in 2019, so much so that the year ended with a record high for the entire decade—in the summer of 2019, Saweetie became the seventh female rapper to grace the *Billboard* Hot 100 chart for her single "My Type," along with three new acts that year: Lizzo, the flautist who makes intoxicating pop-rap; Megan Thee Stallion, the parent of the "Hot Girl Summer" slogan, and Miami duo City Girls, featuring Yung Miami and JT.

But even as the new generation has made their fanbases feel powerful, Lizzo still received the same crossover criticisms as J.J. Fad, and Jermaine Dupri reductively called Cardi B's music "stripper rap," proving how men in hip-hop like to create and then denigrate their very creations. There's still a disproportionate amount of men in high industry positions. Fans, insiders, and media participate in myths about sex and competition. Hip-hop is still a misogynist game, and as the #MeToo movement continued to expose gaps across various industries that led to violence against women, hip-hop was slow to reckon with a system that places women in unprotected positions.

Still, the boom continued in 2020, when Doja Cat, Nicki Minaj, and Megan Thee Stallion became the first black women to occupy the top three spots on the *Billboard* Hot 100. For many of these women, the internet meant a sustainable career could be achieved through their own ingenuity. They didn't have to be beholden to record labels if they didn't want to—they could build their own community online. They could be weirdos. Suddenly, women are all around, whether on a major label or DIY, and it's hard to imagine hip-hop going back to a place without at least a few of them owning their own lanes in rap.

Here are some shout-outs to the new era.

Shoutouts!

◆

Megan Thee Stallion

There's no beat Megan Thee Stallion can't ride. The Houston-bred rapper who cites Pimp C and Three 6 Mafia among her many influences freestyles with the confidence and precision of a veteran artist. Whether she's issuing cheeky threats over Memphis legend Juicy J's bouncing production, as she does on her 2019 major-label debut, *Fever*, or slowing things down with sensual lyrics over the classic "Still Tippin" instrumental, Megan is always on her "hot girl shit."

HANNAH GIORGIS

Quay Dash

Whether Quay Dash is rapping over brooding pianos or slick synths, the effect is consistent: She's incisive, thunderous, and massively clever. It's hard not to revere a woman who knows exactly what she wants, and from whom. The New York rapper has released just a handful of songs—enough to intrigue but not fully satiate.

RAWIYA KAMEIR

Saweetie

Since 2017's viral flex anthem "ICY GRL," Saweetie's frosty bars balances her self-proclaimed "pretty bitch music" with dream-chasing spirituals. The Bay Area MC's knack for plucking nostalgic samples (see: "My Type" and "Tap In") as a queen-sized soundbed for luxury rap keeps her catalog—a surefire soundtrack for women hustlers—as crisp as the white toes in her Tory flip flops.

ADELLE PLATON

Lizzo

Lizzo is a triple threat. She raps, sings, and plays the flute—all while twerking and celebrating all bodies, especially the "thick bitch." The aforementioned also make Lizzo one of those artists you have to experience live to really "get." And while I'd love to avoid comparing one woman to another—especially with Lizzo being such a standout among a long line of rappers who have often sounded or looked pretty similar—lyrically Lizzo leans more school of Missy Elliott, more pop than true hip-hop, but I welcome her digression from the sometimes crowded field.

TRACEY FORD

Shoutouts!

Doja Cat

Doja Cat is a fuckin' unicorn. Dripping in ridiculously colorful and raunchy metaphors, the multihyphenate's quirky, genre-blending bars give the game the spunky, Lisa Frank–style fun it deserves. Her music manifesto—a defiantly shit-talking stance on love, agency, and cunnilingus you can't avoid eating up—bridges humor and playfulness into every infectious punch line. She's a memeable darling of the internet era: a streaming dream with, most important, authentic music chops. And I, as we all should, stan.

NIKI MCGLOSTER

Junglepussy

As is true of so many of those artists featured in this book, there is no title that can encompass all of Junglepussy's talents. From her self-assured and smart-mouthed lyrics—delivered in that Brooklyn-girl growl—to her acting chops and flawless bright wigs (which are accompanied by hilarious comedic characters), her ability to captivate the audience is directly tied to her confident presence, exquisite rapping style, and long-standing belief that she pops for nobody but herself.

JUDNICK MAYARD

Tierra Wack

When Tierra Whack's *Whack World* arrived, it felt like an invitation to exorcise the weird, anxious part of our brains where high drama can live in a passing thought. Then twenty-two, the Philly-based rapper's string of minute-long songs measured the short distance between difficult realities and existential absurdity with a turn of phrase—"All dogs go to heaven," she raps on a cheery song about the loss of a friend. Whack may be an introvert by self-proclamation, but her style is brash, versatile, and incisively intimate. She reminds us to embrace the fun of lunacy and give credence to the voices in our heads.

PUJA PATEL

Leikeli47

Artists' gimmicks can sometimes elicit groans and side-eyes, but Leikeli47's colorful music makes listeners forget that they actually haven't seen her face at all. While the masked Brooklyn MC has chosen to make her physical appearance almost tertiary, the confidence of her slick, playful bars is unmistakable. With a voice that pairs well with popped bubble gum, flashy acrylics, and beauty supply store hoops, her brand of black-girls-first rap is plucked directly from the Missy Elliott family tree. From "Girl Blunt" to "Money" to "Attitude"—pretty much the sonic archetype of an Issa Rae playlist—Leikeli47's personality-spiked songs underscore all the ways you can still have hella fun with rap.

STACY-ANN ELLIS

Flo Milli

In the summer of 2020, Flo Milli released a hot debut mixtape with a self-explanatory title: *Ho, Why Is You Here?* The first verse on her breakout song "Beef FloMix" (which earned her a record deal with RCA) features lines like "I like cash," "fuck the fame," and "pussy put a spell on him," which says it all. The fact that Flo Milli ascended in hip-hop through the power of virality (namely on the wonderful, distracting video app TikTok)—and by making rap aimed squarely at rebuffing men—was a sign that women of her generation had found a new viable blueprint for success.

CLOVER HOPE

Young M.A.

On her debut single, "OOOUUU," which made her one of the few big New York prospects in forever, Young M.A. casually refers to oral sex with a woman in the opening verse. By 2018, queer female MCs had some success (Yo Majesty, Brooke Candy), but mainstream rap had yet to embrace an out black lesbian. *FADER* described Young M.A. as "without clear precedent, the first openly gay rapper to have not only cut through the mainstream of rap, but to do so while describing herself in an outright sex act." She released her debut album, *Herstory in the Making*, in 2019.

CLOVER HOPE

Rico Nasty

In a congested industry, individuality is a treasured anomaly. There's no denying Rico Nasty has it. She's unstoppable, unapologetically unveiling all versions of herself with every bar. Seven mixtapes in and with the single "Smack a Bitch," Rico Nasty turned heads with her boldness and unmatched style.

ERIKA RAMIREZ

Sydanie

Unlike America, and Britain's versions, a culturally distinct form of Canadian rap remains elusive. But, individually, the best rappers from Canada—or Toronto, at least—have managed to synthesize the city's intoxicatingly hybrid culture into their music. Sydanie, a young rapper of Jamaican descent (also a mother and community worker), improves on the template developed by O.G.'s like Kardinal Offishall and Michie Mee. As young Canadians become more conscious of the ways their identities diverge (along ethnic, religious, sexual lines) and converge (as immigrant-settlers, underemployed millennials, etc.), Sydanie provides a soundtrack that's raw, empathetic, funny—and deeply ethical.

ANUPA MISTRY

Noname

It is a serious thing, when a girl decides to live in this world with no name. What I love most about Noname, the young poet and rapper from Chicago, is how elegantly she stands astride a difficult line: the tension between wanting to be observed and wanting to be left unseen. "No name for people to call me small or colonize, optimism / No name for inmate registries if they put me in prison." Isn't that what so many women want nowadays, to be a little bit invisible?

DOREEN ST. FELIX

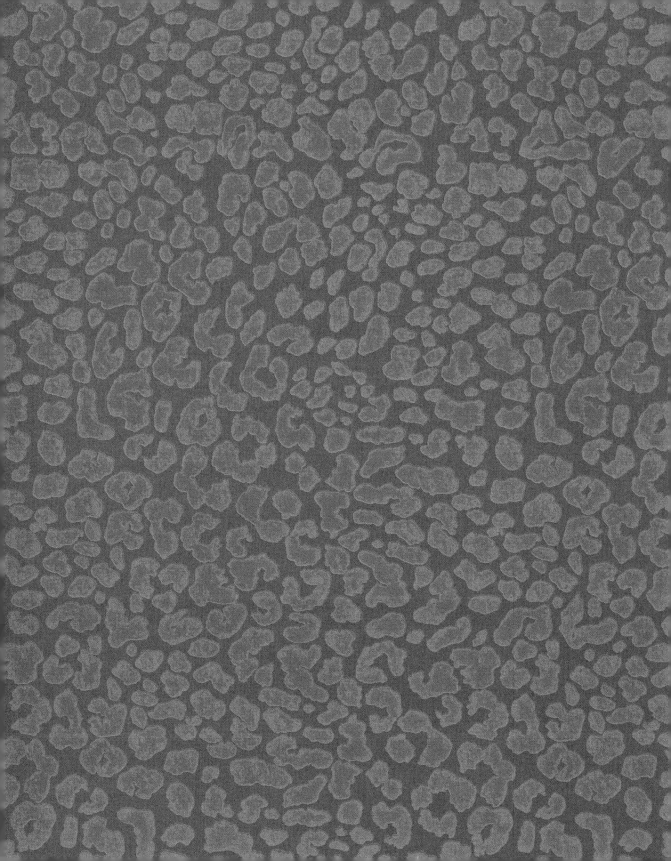

ACKNOWLEDGMENTS

To Rachelle Baker, thank you immensely. Your talent is a gift, and I'm so grateful we found each other and got to collaborate on this project. You're a brilliant treasure, and your art speaks volumes about your passion.

Thank you to my editor, Samantha Weiner, for guiding me and enduring my neuroticism since 2018, when this book was just an idea, and to art director Diane Shaw for her serenity and expertise. Many, many thanks to researcher Laura Bullard for her thoroughness.

I'm grateful to my mom for bringing me and my older sister into this world and then moving us from Guyana to New York to pursue her immigrant dreams. Thank you to both my parents for introducing me to libraries. It was through their love of learning that I fell in love with books and words that could take me through fantasy worlds.

To my father, who planted the seeds of my love for soul and R&B by playing Sam Cooke and Percy Sledge in the house, thank you. To Ellis, my second dad, who was patient during my worst teenage years. To my siblings: Samantha, Natasha, Roshan, and Dustin, for making me a better, slightly less rude person, as well as my nieces and nephew, who keep me young.

As a teenager, I would read *Seventeen* and *YM*, desperately wanting them to cover black girls. I lost myself in fiction and learned the limits of reality through print. I found myself better reflected in magazines like *Essence* and *Ebony* and *Jet*. Most of all, I fell in love with *Vibe*.

Vibe reflected the music, the culture, and the people I loved, from its covers to its writers to its artwork. Its spirit was young, its ambition strong. Thank you to the staff of *Vibe* over the years, print and digital. To Angie Romero, Hyun Kim, and Andrew Simon for hiring me as an intern during my senior year at NYU. And thank you to my earliest editors Rondell Conway, Noah Callahan-Bever, Erik Parker, and Benjamin Meadows-Ingram for entertaining my pitches and taking me to new places. I'll never forget talking to Keyshia Cole about tattoos or flying out to St. Louis to interview Penelope for a "Next" profile, thinking, *What a life!*

Thank you, Laura Checkoway for hiring me as a freelance fact-checker at *Vibe* and listening to my raw ideas, and to the magazine's then editor in chief Mimi Valdés and others who ran the masthead early: Jonathan Van Meter, Kevin Powell, Danyel Smith, Emil Wilbekin, Alan Light. I'm forever grateful for the ways you all endeavored to preserve black music.

Thank you to all the black publications.

To my NYU professors, Gary Belsky, Vivien Orbach-Smith, and Pamela Newkirk, thank you for making me feel like I could be a real writer.

To my editors at *Amsterdam News* and *New York Newsday* who taught me the importance of newsrooms, it's through your teachings that the wisdom and spirit of newspapers will never die.

I'm grateful to my bosses and friends at AllHipHop.com who cultivated my digital self. Chuck Creekmur and Grouchy Greg. Dove, Jake Paine, Jayson Rodriguez. Thank you, Benzino, for telling me I had to "get out that Internet world Clover." I never did.

Sending an eternal shout-out to Jermaine Hall and Datwon Thomas for nurturing my career as a writer and editor at *Vibe*. To my *Vibe* gang-gang: The Ratchets and the Rolodex, I love y'all.

To Elliott Wilson and Vanessa Satten for seeing the spark. To the staffs at *XXL* and *Billboard*. Jack Erwin, Anslem Samuel, B. Dot, Brendan Frederick, Taiia Smart-Young, Rob Markman, Carl Chery, wattup.

Thank you to the entire staff at Jezebel, where I got to be my smartest and weirdest self. Special thanks to my blog moms Emma Carmichael and Julianne Escobedo Shepherd.

Endless props to Shea Serrano for the book hook-up.

Thank you to all the incredible writers who contributed blurbs for this book: Doreen St. Felix, Judnick Maynard, Hannah Giorgis, Rawiya Kamier, Stacy-Ann Ellis, Adelle Platon, Niki McGloster, Puja Patel (thank you for witnessing me brainstorm titles!), Anupa Mistry, and my ace Tracey Ford.

To all who gave me feedback and edit notes and friends who endured my angsty updates about "my book!" Katie Hintz-Zambrano, Michael Arceneaux, Jia Tolentino, Thomas Golianopolous, Kyle Wagner, Clio Chang, Estelle Tang, John Kennedy, Qimmah Saafir, Megan Reynolds, Anne Branagin, Ashley Reese. To all my group chats (the Travel crew, the Hive, Pun Pals) for keeping me sane and laughing. To Travis Jones for loving and challenging me handsomely throughout the years.

To Beyoncé, for giving me work and inspiration and because she's Beyoncé. Thank you.

Many thanks to the publicists who helped with interviews, I appreciate your time and consideration toward this project.

Finally, thank you to all the women in this book who decided to make culture from scratch and transmit it through the ages and for all eternity. All the MCs, DJs, break-dancers, and graffiti artists who never got their dues. I wish this book could name a hundred more names. To those who made time for interviews and follow-ups and fact-checking, thank you. I'm grateful for previous books like *Vibe's Hip-Hop Divas* and Kathy Iandoli's *God Save the Queens*.

As a music writer for more than fifteen years, I've worked predominantly with men, but I recognized early on that women tell the best rap stories. To Dream Hampton, Danyel Smith, Kim Osorio, Aliya S. King, Lola Oguinnaike, Kierna Mayo, Akiba Solomon, Ayana Byrd, Erica Kennedy, Joan Morgan, Elizabeth Méndez Berry, Julia Beverly, Karen R. Good, and many, many more, I'm indebted to you and your work and your love. Thank you for making sure there could be no history of hip-hop without us.

To hip-hop media, my life force, thank you. All my love to hip-hop for helping a quiet girl speak.

AUTHOR BIO

◆◆◆◆◆◆◆◆◆◆◆◆◆◆◆◆◆◆◆◆◆◆◆◆◆◆◆

CLOVER HOPE is a writer and editor based in Brooklyn. She has worked as a music journalist since 2005, when she graduated from NYU and held an internship with her dream magazine, *Vibe*. She moved on to jobs at *Billboard* and *XXL* before returning to *Vibe* as an editor.

In the span of fifteen years, Hope has written for publications like *Vogue, Elle, Billboard, Wired, Harper's Bazaar, W*, the *New York Times, ESPN The Magazine, XXL, GQ, Cosmopolitan, Essence, Nylon*, and the *Village Voice*, among others. She has interviewed hundreds of rappers and kept the transcripts and audio files, and written cover stories on everyone from Beyoncé to Janet Jackson to Lil Wayne, Nicki Minaj, Usher, Ludacris, and Rick Ross.

Hope is a former Jezebel editor and an adjunct professor teaching culture writing at NYU. This is her first book.

◆◆◆◆◆◆◆◆◆◆◆◆◆◆◆◆◆◆◆◆◆◆◆◆◆◆◆

Editor: Samantha Weiner
Designer: Diane Shaw
Production Manager: Rachael Marks

Library of Congress Control Number: 2019939884

ISBN: 978-1-4197-4296-5
eISBN: 978-1-68335-805-3

Printed and bound in the United States
10 9 8 7 6 5 4 3 2 1

Abrams Image books are available at special discounts when
purchased in quantity for premiums and promotions as well as
fundraising or educational use. Special editions can also be created
to specification. For details, contact specialsales@abramsbooks.com
or the address below.

ABRAMS The Art of Books
195 Broadway, New York, NY 10007
abramsbooks.com